The Budapest School of Psychoanalysis

The Budapest School of Psychoanalysis brings together a collection of expertly written pieces on the influence of the Budapest (Ferenczi) conception of analytic theory and practice on the evolution of psychoanalysis. It touches on major figures Sándor Ferenczi and Michael Balint, whilst concurrently considering topics such as Ferenczi's clinical diary, the study of trauma, the Confusion of Tongues paradigm, and Balint's perspective on supervision. Further to this, the book highlights Jacques Lacan's teaching of Ferenczi, which brings a fresh perspective to a relatively unknown connection between them.

The book highlights that the Hungarian analysts, influenced by Ferenczi, through their pioneering work developed a psychoanalytic paradigm which became an alternative to the Freudian tradition. That this paradigm has become recognized and admired in its own right underlines the need to clearly outline, as this book does, the historical context and the output of those who are writing and working in the tradition of the Budapest School.

The contributions to this volume demonstrate the widespread and enduring influence of the Budapest School on contemporary psychoanalysis. The contributors are amongst the foremost in Budapest School scholarship and the insights they offer are at once profound as well as insightful.

This book is an important read for those practitioners and students of psychoanalysis who wish for an insight into the early and developing years of the Budapest School of Psychoanalysis and its impact on contemporary clinical practice.

Arnold Wm. Rachman is a licensed psychologist, trained psychoanalyst, Member of the Board of Directors at the Sandor Ferenczi Center, The New School For Social Research, NYC, and Honorary Member at the Sandor Ferenczi Society, Budapest, Hungary. Donor, The Elizabeth Severn Papers, The Library Of Congress, Washington, D.C.

PSYCHOANALYTIC INQUIRY BOOK SERIES

JOSEPH D. LICHTENBERG
Series Editor

Like its counterpart, *Psychoanalytic Inquiry: A Topical Journal for Mental Health Professionals*, the Psychoanalytic Inquiry Book Series presents a diversity of subjects within a diversity of approaches to those subjects. Under the editorship of Joseph Lichtenberg, in collaboration with Melvin Bornstein and the editorial board of *Psychoanalytic Inquiry*, the volumes in this series strike a balance between research, theory, and clinical application. We are honored to have published the works of various innovators in psychoanalysis, such as Frank Lachmann, James Fosshage, Robert Stolorow, Donna Orange, Louis Sander, Léon Wurmser, James Grotstein, Joseph Jones, Doris Brothers, Fredric Busch, and Joseph Lichtenberg, among others.

The series includes books and monographs on mainline psychoanalytic topics, such as sexuality, narcissism, trauma, homosexuality, jealousy, envy, and varied aspects of analytic process and technique. In our efforts to broaden the field of analytic interest, the series has incorporated and embraced innovative discoveries in infant research, self psychology, intersubjectivity, motivational systems, affects as process, responses to cancer, borderline states, contextualism, postmodernism, attachment research and theory, medication, and mentalization. As further investigations in psychoanalysis come to fruition, we seek to present them in readable, easily comprehensible writing.

After 25 years, the core vision of this series remains the investigation, analysis and discussion of developments on the cutting edge of the psychoanalytic field, inspired by a boundless spirit of inquiry.

Vol. 50
The Budapest School of Psychoanalysis:
The Origin of a Two-Person Psychology and Emphatic Perspective
Arnold Wm. Rachman

Vol. 51
Treating Dissociative and Personality Disorders:
A Motivational Systems Approach to Theory and Treatment
Antonella Ivaldi (ed.)

Out of Print titles in the PI Series

Vol. 11
Cancer Stories: Creativity and Self-Repair
Esther Dreifuss-Kattan

Vol. 15
Understanding Therapeutic Action:
Psychodynamic Concepts of Cure
Lawrence E. Lifson (ed.)

The Budapest School of Psychoanalysis

The Origin of a Two-Person Psychology and Emphatic Perspective

Edited by Arnold Wm. Rachman

Routledge
Taylor & Francis Group
LONDON AND NEW YORK

First published 2016
by Routledge
2 Park Square, Milton Park, Abingdon, Oxon OX14 4RN

and by Routledge
605 Third Avenue, New York, NY 10017

Routledge is an imprint of the Taylor & Francis Group, an informa business

British Library Cataloguing in Publication Data
A catalogue record for this book is available from the British Library

Library of Congress Cataloguing in Publication Data
Names: Rachman, Arnold Wm., editor.
Title: The Budapest school of psychoanalysis : the origin of a two-person psychology and emphatic perspective / edited by Arnold Rachman.
Description: Abingdon, Oxon; New York, NY : Routledge, 2016. |
Series: Psychoanalytic inquiry book series |
Includes bibliographical references and index.
Identifiers: LCCN 2015046767| ISBN 9781138195202 (hardback) |
ISBN 9781138195219 (pbk.)
Subjects: LCSH: Psychoanalysis–History. | Psychoanalysis–Hungary–Budapest– History. | Ferenczi, Sâandor, 1873–1933.
Classification: LCC RC503 .B83 2016 | DDC 616.89/17–dc23
LC record available at http://lccn.loc.gov/2015046767

ISBN: 978-1-138-19520-2 (hbk)
ISBN: 978-1-138-19521-9 (pbk)

Typeset in Times New Roman
by Out of House Publishing

The Budapest School of Psychoanalysis

The Origin of a Two-Person Psychology and Emphatic Perspective

Edited by Arnold Wm. Rachman

Routledge
Taylor & Francis Group
LONDON AND NEW YORK

First published 2016
by Routledge
2 Park Square, Milton Park, Abingdon, Oxon OX14 4RN

and by Routledge
605 Third Avenue, New York, NY 10017

Routledge is an imprint of the Taylor & Francis Group, an informa business

British Library Cataloguing in Publication Data
A catalogue record for this book is available from the British Library

Library of Congress Cataloguing in Publication Data
Names: Rachman, Arnold Wm., editor.
Title: The Budapest school of psychoanalysis : the origin of a two-person psychology and emphatic perspective / edited by Arnold Rachman.
Description: Abingdon, Oxon; New York, NY : Routledge, 2016. |
Series: Psychoanalytic inquiry book series |
Includes bibliographical references and index.
Identifiers: LCCN 2015046767| ISBN 9781138195202 (hardback) |
ISBN 9781138195219 (pbk.)
Subjects: LCSH: Psychoanalysis–History. | Psychoanalysis–Hungary–Budapest– History. | Ferenczi, Sâandor, 1873–1933.
Classification: LCC RC503 .B83 2016 | DDC 616.89/17–dc23
LC record available at http://lccn.loc.gov/2015046767

ISBN: 978-1-138-19520-2 (hbk)
ISBN: 978-1-138-19521-9 (pbk)

Typeset in Times New Roman
by Out of House Publishing

The Budapest School of Psychoanalysis

The Origin of a Two-Person Psychology and Emphatic Perspective

Edited by Arnold Wm. Rachman

Routledge
Taylor & Francis Group
LONDON AND NEW YORK

First published 2016
by Routledge
2 Park Square, Milton Park, Abingdon, Oxon OX14 4RN

and by Routledge
605 Third Avenue, New York, NY 10017

Routledge is an imprint of the Taylor & Francis Group, an informa business

British Library Cataloguing in Publication Data
A catalogue record for this book is available from the British Library

Library of Congress Cataloguing in Publication Data
Names: Rachman, Arnold Wm., editor.
Title: The Budapest school of psychoanalysis : the origin of a two-person psychology and emphatic perspective / edited by Arnold Rachman.
Description: Abingdon, Oxon; New York, NY : Routledge, 2016. |
Series: Psychoanalytic inquiry book series |
Includes bibliographical references and index.
Identifiers: LCCN 2015046767| ISBN 9781138195202 (hardback) |
ISBN 9781138195219 (pbk.)
Subjects: LCSH: Psychoanalysis–History. | Psychoanalysis–Hungary–Budapest– History. | Ferenczi, Sâandor, 1873–1933.
Classification: LCC RC503 .B83 2016 | DDC 616.89/17–dc23
LC record available at http://lccn.loc.gov/2015046767

ISBN: 978-1-138-19520-2 (hbk)
ISBN: 978-1-138-19521-9 (pbk)

Typeset in Times New Roman
by Out of House Publishing

To my grandchildren, Gabriela Sara Rachman and Matthew Adam Rachman, who provide an emotional undercurrent of joy, love and embrace that gives motivation and meaning to my life.

Contents

Prologue

Arnold Wm. Rachman

I can first trace my interest and discovery of Ferenczi and the Budapest School back to my undergraduate education at the intellectually and politically liberal University of Buffalo in the late 1950s. At Buffalo, my intellectual awakening and interest in psychology occurred. Marvin Farber, a student of Edmund Husserl, the founder of phenomenology, taught me about the meaning of logic and the scientific method and phenomenology for understanding human behavior. The psychologists Aron Herskovitz and Olive Lester affirmed my capacity to be a psychologist. Here, the foundation was formed for a liberal intellectual perspective, not based on dogma but on an independent evidence and experience-based perspective.

In my doctoral work at the University of Chicago in the early 1960s in the Committee on Human Development and the Department of Clinical Psychology, I was fortunate to be taught the value of a interdisciplinary perspective to human behavior by Robert Havinghurst and Bernice Neugarten. In the Department of Clinical Psychology, I had contact with Samuel Beck, William Henry, and Heinz Kohut. Training in the Counseling and Psychotherapy Research Center, founded by Carl Rogers, provided the idea of nonmedical professionals capable of being psychotherapists and psychoanalysts and helped me gain an identity as an psychotherapist. It also provided an appreciation for applying phenomenology to understanding human behavior and developing an active, responsive, and empathic attitude for clinician interaction. I greatly benefited from the teaching, supervision, personal interchanges, and empathic atmosphere provided by Jack Butler, Rosalyn Cartwright, Eugene Gedlin, Laura Rice, John Shlien, and Fred Zimring.

Initially, postgraduate training at the Postgrad Psychoanalytic Institute was very difficult for me, because the emphasis was on silence, interpresentation, and minimal clinical responsiveness. It was this struggle to learn psychoanalysis and integrate it with Humanistic Psychology, Psychotherapy, and Phenomenology that fueled my journey toward finding Ferenczi and the Budapest School.

In this struggle, I found several analysts at the Postgrad Institute, which allowed my dissident approach to flourish, while providing intellectual and emotional support from the late Ben Fielding, Asya Kadis Ted Reiss, and Alexander Wolf, and others. My personal analysis with Betty Feldman became a historical connection to Sándor Ferenczi. I became a fifth-generation analysand of Ferenczi in the following way: Betty Feldman was an analysand of Lewis Wolberg, who was analyzed by Clara Thompson, who was analyzed by Ferenczi.

Forty years have passed since I discovered the works of the founder of the Budapest School, Sándor Ferenczi, in the library of the Postgraduate Institute, in New York City. Ironically, my intellectual and clinical struggle with psychoanalysis was able to be successfully resolved in the same institute that initiated this struggle. In my attempt to reconcile my Humanistic and Phenomenological perspective with psychoanalysis, I found an article on activity in psychoanalytic therapy that referred to Sándor Ferenczi, a name I had never heard mentioned in all my previous education and training. Ferenczi's ideas in the article on analytic activity, provided a moment of enlightenment and reconciliation. I quickly sought and read Ferenczi's *Collected Papers*. As I read his work, I immediately experienced Ferenczi's ideas and methods as the bridge between Humanistic Psychology and Psychotherapy and psychoanalysis. His work provided me with an intellectual, emotional, and interpersonal roadmap for a career dedicated to the history of psychoanalysis, especially, the contributions of the Budapest School.

Since discovering Ferenczi, three colleagues and friends have been instrumental in affirming my interest in, and providing enlightenment about, Ferenczi. The late Esther Menaker was a model for a creative and respectful dissident. She shared her personal journey of going from analysis with Anna Freud to embracing the ideas of an original analytic dissident, Otto Rank, to finding an intellectual home in the

Self Psychology perspective. She generously responded to me, after having been introduced by my colleagues and friends Joyce Nathan and Robert Prince. We met on a regular basis for years, with her inviting me into her home, serving me dinner and affirming my dissidence in a warm and empathic atmosphere.

The late Paul Roazen opened the door to a revisionist view of psychoanalysis and helped me to appreciate an alternate perspective to analytic orthodoxy. In Ferenczi terms, he helped me, "to find my own voice" as an analytic dissident. I am appreciative of his pioneering examination of the history of psychoanalysis in the relationships, politics, and rivalries in the field. He helped me understand that there was an alternative to analytic dogma. He also focused on Ferenczi, Goddeck, Jung, Rank, and others, as significant contributors to psychoanalysis.

Jeffrey Mouseaieff Masson has been a beacon of light in the darkness of the suppression of Ferenczi. Unfortunately, Masson has been ostracized from mainstream psychoanalysis because he is considered to have been disrespectful in his criticisms of Freud. But, Masson's work can also be seen as a courageous, eye-opening, and pioneering attempt to educate psychoanalysis to the suppression of Ferenczi.

I am grateful to colleagues in the Relational Track at New York University's Postdoctoral Program in Psychotherapy and Psychoanalysis, such as Lewis Aron and Adrienne Harris, and in the Sándor Ferenczi Center at the New School for Social Research, such as Jeremy Safran, for their shared belief in and support of Ferenczi and the Budapest School.

Through the years, a variety of colleagues and friends in the United States and Europe have provided support, affirmation, and insight. In the United States, they are Beatrice Beebe, Jill Choder-Goodman, Henry Kellerman, Suzanne Klett, Harold Kooden, Robert Marshall, Paul Mattick, Harriet and Wolf Pappenheim, Eva Papiasvili, Joseph Reppen, and Nellie Thompson. In Hungary, they are Judith Dupont, André Haynal, the late Gregory Hidas, and Judit Mészáros. In Italy, they are Carlo Bonomi, Franco Borgogno, and Gianni Guasto.

Introduction

Joseph Lichtenberg

The Budapest School? Everyone who studies the history of psychoanalysis knows of the Vienna Circle, its inclusions and expulsions. And the Zürich Center, with Jung and Bleuler, and its research on association. And then came the Berlin School with Abraham and Alexander and a host of others, including Americans – with its formalizing of institutes and training. Of course, in Budapest there was Ferenczi – but a School? Really?

Really yes! This wonderful book, with its diverse, innovative chapters, explains and confirms the Budapest School and its contribution. If a school means followers, Ferenczi certainly had those, but that alone will not make the case. The persuasive argument presented to the reader is based on the *influence* of the Budapest (Ferenczi) conception of analytic theory and practice. As stated by several authors in this volume, if you trained at one of the U.S. classical institutes under the hegemony of ego psychology (as I did), you would have little knowledge of that influence. Sometimes the influence is easy to trace, like with the Balints in the Middle Group in England. Sometimes it is difficult to tell if there is influence or simply similarity of vision, as in American relationists and self psychologists. Sometimes the influence comes as a surprise (at least to me) in the chapters on psychoanalysis in France that identify Lacan and Joyce McDougall. Each author builds his or her narrative around one or more of the influences, and André Haynal gives a thorough, clear portrayal of the historical sequence. I will give my understanding of these influences, to assist the readers in identifying them as they are taken through each author's interesting narrative.

1. A conception of a field of interactions based on openness and honesty
2. A shift from the exclusive focus on the oedipal triangle to include the mother-infant dyad
3. The recognition of sexual abuse and trauma in infancy
4. A major focus on the analyst's feelings, intentions, reactions, and experiences – countertransference
5. Entering the analysand's perspective especially as he/she experiences the analyst
6. A deeper exploration of regressive states
7. (Possibly most important) a taste for experimentation in therapeutic approach and supervision

A further theme that permeates the book is Ferenczi's relationship with his grand vizier, Sigmund Freud. Many chapters give wonderful vignettes that cast the two intellectual giants in both parallel and strongly oppositional postures. Many authors here place the relationship of the ambivalent father and the never-getting-enough favorite son in the cultural swirl of psychoanalytic politics and rivalries (Ernest Jones) and the unsettled issues of homo/heterosexuality and anti-semitism.

Each reader, like an analyst reacting to a new analysand, will bring to his or her responsiveness conscious and unconscious impressions based on his or her lived experiences. I bring to my reading no specific knowledge of the Budapest *School* traced through Balint and others – even Lacan(?) – but I do bring a strong sense of the influence of the Ferenczi approach to analytic theory and practice passed on to me by my principal mentor, Lewis Hill. When I was a resident and then Clinical Director of the Shepard and Enoch Pratt Hospital, Lewis was the Director of Education. He had gone to Budapest for several months of analysis with Ferenczi and then continued with Clara Thompson.

Lewis joked that he came back from Budapest thinking he had learned Hungarian phrases only to discover they were Yiddish. Lewis and I systematically met weekly with every patient for brief "conversations" – that is, interactions conducted in a spirit of openness and honesty. This freedom to use our (Lewis and mine) intuition in a direct, often penetrating way differed greatly from the training

I received at my institute to be neutral, abstinent, and anonymous. In that training, countertransference was the bad stuff I brought in which interfered with my strict focus on the patient's intrapsychic conflicts. What a contrast! Looking back I can identify many of the principles of approach I have advocated as the product of my Ferenczi-from-Lewis and my reading: a spirit of inquiry, openness to experimentation, an appreciation of dyadic intersubjectivity and early life intrafamily traumas, the joint working with model scenes, and the therapeutic occurrences and value of "disciplined spontaneous engagements." But, I confess I have never as fully appreciated my indebtedness to the Budapest School as I do now. I suggest many others who read the unique studies in this book may come to the same realization.

Chapter 1

The Ferenczi House as a space for identity formation[1]

Judit Mészáros

Through an international effort in 2011 – a year before the International Ferenczi Conference in Budapest in 2012 – the Ferenczi Society and the International Ferenczi Foundation purchased the apartment that had served as Ferenczi's office in what had once been his villa.

Many of those who attended the Budapest conference also visited the Ferenczi House at the time, but there are certainly those here in Toronto who will see these few images and gain a better insight into the House and what it means to us.

What is the Ferenczi House? What does it represent? Why did the professional community that makes up the Ferenczi Network feel that it was important to have this place? And why did it put so much effort over so many years into acquiring part of the villa where Ferenczi spent his last years?

Indeed, what did the Lisznyai Street villa mean to Ferenczi?

Ferenczi was happy to have become the owner of a sunlit garden and villa for the first time in his life. The place stimulated him. This is where he completed his most widely cited publication – the one that represented a paradigm shift in trauma theory – "Confusion of Tongues between Adults and the Child" (Ferenczi [1932] 1980), which has also inspired many of your papers at this conference. It was also within the walls of this house that Ferenczi wrote the last chapters of his correspondence with Freud, Groddeck, and Jones as well as the notes and results for the *Clinical Diary* (Ferenczi [1932] 1988).

> we have bought a villa, consisting of three floors with a garden, over the Ofner hill and will be moving in towards the end of this month. So we have become homeowners at the same time as you. Another apartment on the first floor will be let. It was a good buy (for approximately 70,000 Marks) but the necessary alterations will be rather expensive (around 30,000!). I look forward to getting fresh air and sun, which I greatly missed here.
>
> (Ferenczi to Groddeck, Budapest, June 15, 1930; Fortune 2002)

Ferenczi hired an architect for the rebuilding design, which would involve all three storeys. The documention can be found in the house. The Ferenczis moved into the first storey. The speed of such a project at the time becomes clear from the date on the design. In all likelihood, the architect showed the plans to Ferenczi at the end of May and Ferenczi signed them in late June. Afterwards, Ferenczi wrote an enthusiastic and jovial letter to Freud.

> Dear Professor, … We are already packing; the new house, almost spic-and-span, awaits us. The move will take place on July 3 or 4. The new address will read: I. Lisznyai utca 11 … In the meantime, I am working diligently: seven-eight-nine hours a day; the finer mechanism of "psychic trauma" and its relation to psychosis are also shaping up into a very impressive picture, at least for me. Perhaps I will make something of it during October vacation. (We want to stay in Budapest all summer.) Many kind regards and best wishes. Yours, Ferenczi.
>
> (Ferenczi to Freud, Budapest, June 29, 1930; Freud and Ferenczi 2000)

> The move is over. I inhabit the ground floor premises of a pretty villa (the second floor is empty – the cares of a homeowner!). The purchase, the setting things in order and the unavoidable new acquisitions have devoured quite a large part of my assets; the regular expenditures will also increase in the new household, so that I have to work very diligently in order to bring in only enough to meet expenses. But I'm not worried about that for the

> time being, and what comes later will somehow get straightened out. – The nicest thing about the villa is the fact that, for being situated in a capital city, it has a very spacious garden with much grass and some big old trees. Unfortunately, the quiet is often disrupted by gramophone and radio loudspeakers in the neighbourhood, but my study is hermetically sealed.
>
> (Ferenczi to Freud, Budapest, July 20, 1930; Freud and Ferenczi 2000)

Finally he sent the message about the new house to Jones:

> "Perhaps you have already heard," he tells Jones, "that I have bought a home in the same sort of location as yours, near the city, yet in the country. However, our garden does not yet have the beautiful, smooth English lawn that 400 years of culture have produced in yours. Once again, my warmest greetings to you."
>
> (Ferenczi to Jones, January 4, 1931; Ferenczi and Jones 2013)

The *Diary* uniquely documents Ferenczi's observations and experiments in his effort to understand what was taking place during therapy in both the patient and the analyst and to draw conclusions from the phenomena they experienced.

It was there in the House that Ferenczi saw his American patients, among them some of the key figures in Ferenczi's empirical studies, which he conducted to better understand the interpersonal and intrapsychic processes during analysis. Among them were Elizabeth Severn, Isette de Forest, and Clara Thompson (Brennan 2011; Fortune 1993; Rachman 2015), with Thompson becoming one of the founders of the William Alanson White Institute in New York, which would carry on Ferenczi's way of thinking in the United States.

Ferenczi's drive to know more and develop useful techniques in the healing process led Ferenczi to his empirical studies with mutual analysis, thus drawing attention to a process which we take entirely for granted today and leading to strict requirements for training analysis and a new approach to trauma. And there is no doubt that for Ferenczi those years he spent in the house gave him a more independent/liberated life, both from a personal and professional point of view.

What does the House mean for today's generation? What does the House represent?

To borrow an apt description by Pierre Nora, the House is an example of "*lieux de mémoire* [sites of memory] where memory crystallizes" (Nora 1989, p. 4) and where "[m]emory takes root in the concrete, in spaces, gestures, images, and objects" (ibid., p. 9). As something happening in the present – as something experienced among individuals and groups – memory is a sign of a lived attachment. It is precisely through memory that a sense of continuity grows, the link between past and present. In the words of Pierre Nora, it is the *milieux de mémoire*, the environments of memory, that fill the spaces of the *lieux de mémoire*, the sites of memory. In this spirit, the very function of museums and archives is one of "anchoring memory" (ibid., p. 9), and as such they will have a role in forming identity and shaping intellectual history. According to Nora, "The passage from memory to history has required every social group [including every professional community] to redefine its identity through the revitalization of its own history" (ibid., p. 15).

Undoubtedly, like a missing link in the history of psychoanalysis, the Ferenczi House has now been integrated into the wide-ranging history of science and into that of human relations both then and now. The House is naturally not merely about Ferenczi, but also about the Budapest School that he formed, a school that came about in much the same way as children grow up around a liberal-minded father, one who is accommodating, attentive, and considerate of others: where everyone can do what he or she needs to do based on his or her talents, without any force, and as an equal partner to the founder of the school. They learned from each other, they developed common perspectives, and it was this shared basic approach that characterized the members of the Budapest School. It served as a source after their forced exile, as well – just consider from Margaret Mahler, through Sándor Radó, Franz Alexander, Michael and Alice Balint, and René Spitz to David Rapaport (Mészáros 2014). Many of the Budapest analysts also visited the House, including Michael Balint and Alice Balint, Vilma Kovács, István Hollós, and Lajos Lévy (the charismatic GP to both Ferenczi and the Freud family) as well as writers and artists. Among them, Oscar Nemon and two of our contemporaries also went to the House a number of times as children through their family relations: Judith Dupont and a nephew of Ferenczi's wife, Gizella, Balázs/Blaise Pásztory.

Jones, who was always Ferenczi's rival, sent red rose plants to the house from London, which became the centerpiece of the garden. At the same time, after Ferenczi's death, Jones's poisoned thorns paralyzed Ferenczi's reception for decades (Bonomi 1999; Mészáros 2003). The last entry in Ferenczi's *Clinical Diary*, on October 2, 1932, expresses this precisely as well:

> (I have just received a few personally friendly lines from *Jones*. He has sent roses …) Can not deny that I was pleasantly touched even by this. I did indeed also feel abandoned by colleagues … who are all too afraid of Freud to behave objectively or even sympathetically toward me, in the case of a dispute between Freud and me. A more restrained circulation of letters between Freud, Jones and Eitingon has certainly been going on for a long time now. I am treated like a sick person who must be spared.
>
> (*Clinical Diary*, October 2, 1932, pp. 212–213)

Colleagues may think of this as well as many other things when they visit the Ferenczi House. The spirit of the House recalls the emotions tied to the stories. And beyond the emotions, everything that Ferenczi represents and the decisive influence this had and continues to have on the theoretical development of psychoanalysis and therapy itself. For our generation of psychoanalysts, this "representation" took material form when we purchased what had once been Ferenczi's office so that we could develop an International Ferenczi Center there. It metaphorically expresses everything that Ferenczi and his students stood for; it was now assigned a lot number in the world, just as the Freud Museums in Vienna and London both had been.

The Archives

The Archives of the Ferenczi House constituted the soul of the House, the legacy of the members of the Budapest School, even from the perspective of what is MISSING from the House, of WHAT IS NOT there, but certainly also from the perspective of WHAT IS there and WHAT IS GROWING. Emigration tore the Budapest School apart: those who emigrated and those who remained and survived not only the Holocaust and the dark days of Nazism, but also, later – for psychoanalysis, too – the chill years of Stalinist dictatorship.

The Archives contain the legacy (the correspondence, photographs, publications, and manuscripts) of those from the first and second generations of analysts who remained in Hungary, such as Imre Hermann, István Hollós, Lilly Hajdu, Tibor Rajka, and István Székács-Schönberger. After the death of Ferenczi, three of them – Hollós, Hermannn, Hajdu – also became presidents of the Hungarian Psychoanalytical Society, which had been founded by Ferenczi and was dissolved in 1949. Informative period documents can also be found here that make reference to the persecution of psychoanalysis and to the underground years of its practitioners surrounded by the political and social tensions of the day.

Part of the legacy originates from an émigré psychoanalyst Edith Ludowyk-Gyömrői, who, amid the two waves of emigration, first settled in Vienna and then Berlin, was later forced to flee Budapest again to Ceylon (Sri Lanka), and finally settled in London. Her legacy – her correspondence, works of art (fabrics she had woven), manuscripts, and some of the books dedicated to her – was returned from London to the Ferenczi House.

Ferenczi's legacy met the opposite fate. Judith Dupont first offered to donate it to the Ferenczi House, provided that it be established, but then changed her mind and granted the documents in her possession to the Freud Museum in London a few years ago. The material in the Balint Archives in Geneva was returned by André Haynal to the place where Balint had worked after his years of emigration: the Archives of the British Psychoanalytical Society.

In this regard, the Ferenczi Archives represent a clear impression of the dichotomy brought about by emigration. The exile that was brought on by the anti-Semitism and Nazism of the twentieth century divided contemporary analyst communities – and here I am thinking not only of the Budapest analysts, but also all of the other European analyst communities, including primarily the societies in Berlin and Vienna and the youngest and last one to form before the war in Prague.

The European analyst communities fell into one of two groups: those who emigrated and those who did not. The later fate of these two groups stood in stark contrast to one another. However, there is still one common denominator: losses on both sides. Those who left struggled with the major challenges and difficulties of émigré existence (the loss of mother tongue, homeland, and previous culture and relationships, in addition to the hardships of resettling). Still, they were able to enjoy the chance offered by the freedom of democracy, and they were able to establish a life for themselves based on the knowledge they had acquired, which was accompanied by the solidarity and supportive power offered by their professional communities.

Those who remained in their homeland and survived the Holocaust and their own country's Nazism had to face personal losses: the painful mourning of family members, friends, and colleagues who had perished. And, with an incredible suddenness within three years, they were burdened with a fate brought about by another dictatorship. Stalinism even snatched their very livelihood from them: psychoanalysis. Those who left lost their past, and those who remained grieved for their losses as they mourned their future as well.

In addition to focusing on individual life paths, the documents in the Ferenczi Archives draw one's attention to challenges once posed by the political situation. These are exceptional period documents which call to mind memories from contemporaries and represent sources for research that can be placed in a historical context for today's generation and for those of the future.

I also have to mention that we have received copies of the original handwritten correspondence between Ferenczi and Groddeck from Baden-Baden. Arnold Rachman – during the Ferenczi Congress, Faces of Trauma, in Budapest in 2012 – offered to donate a copy of the Severn Papers to the archives at the International Ferenczi Center. He donated the original copies to the Manuscript Division of the Library of Congress, where an Elizabeth Severn Section of the Freud

Archives has been established.[2] It would also be beneficial for future generations to be able to access copies in the House of other materials from Ferenczi, his pupils, and Balint already donated to other Archives.

In the past few years, the International Ferenczi Center has been enriched by donations of books which have taken the long path of emigration and return. This is how we received first editions of Ferenczi's books owned by András József (alias Adolf Fisch), the father of our analyst colleague Kati Morrison, who kindly returned them from Canada, as well as the complete legacy of István Székács-Schönberger – a contemporary of Robert Bak's. One of these is among those who emigrated (Bak), while the other (Székács-Schönberger) is among those who, although he would have liked to emigrate, was denied a visa – and in the system of Stalinist dictatorship in Hungary, like András József noted above, he languished in prison on trumped-up charges.

We see it as a priority to make the documents of the Ferenczi Archives available in digitized form as soon as possible. This year, in cooperation with the Budapest City Archives, we will launch the digitization of over 25,000 pages of material.

The function of validation in the *genius loci* (the spirit of the place) – education in the Ferenczi House

For today's generations, however, the Ferenczi House also represents a space for academic exchange. Thus, from the perspectives of the past, present, and future, the spirit of the House is not an unchanged entity. It is shaped by those who have established it, who use it, and who visit it.

The content of the educational activities conducted in the Ferenczi House is validated by the *genius loci*, or the spirit of the place. In this case, it could be said that the student is enriched by the natural features of the *lieu de mémoire*, thus creating a continuity between the work of the key figure in this intellectual heritage and the student's own lived experience. Many visit the House precisely for that reason and deepen their knowledge during the lectures there with this added emotional element. For example, the American students in the summer school at the Institute for the International Education of

Students Abroad in Vienna return year after year to hear lectures on Ferenczi in the Ferenczi House and then take in all the familiar sites in Budapest that are associated with the history of psychoanalysis in Hungary.

Since the last Budapest conference, there have been colleagues from abroad who have visited the House and held lectures or to whom we have offered lectures and seminars. Among these, for example, have been: Emily A. Kuriloff from the William Alanson White Institute; Professor Anat Berko from the Interdisciplinary Center in Herzliya, Israel; and Robert Kramer, a visiting professor from Washington, DC at the Corvinus University in Budapest.

We have given lectures to Norwegian peers, to colleagues from Istambul, and to fellow professionals in Lemberg (or Lviv, in Ukraine). In the past few years, the House has welcomed a great many visitors. In addition to those already noted, we have received guests from Paris, Nice, and London, including Dawn Kemp, the newly appointed head of London's Freud Museum.

Celebrating together – having a future together – the red rose as a symbol

And, for one afternoon in 2013, on the hundredth birthday of the Hungarian Psychoanalytical Society founded by Ferenczi and the twenty-fifth anniversary of the Ferenczi Society, the Ferenczi House tied the past to the present through a special collective experience. What else could have captured the desire for historical continuity better than the red rose plant that the current generation of analysts put into the ground on behalf of both societies eighty years later in the very spot where Ferenczi had once enjoyed his roses?

Conclusion

The Ferenczi villa was once Ferenczi's home. The Ferenczi House was brought to life by the current generation of the Ferenczi Network in order to create a site of "memory captured by history" as a point of identity (Nora, cited in K. Horváth 1999).

> Based on the concept of the *lieu de mémoire*, "we are not the heirs of a past that once was, with its cultural traditions passed

on ready-made; … rather, as participants in the present in a continuous interaction, we take possession of 'the past' and we *shape* it in accordance with a particular political, cultural, and esthetic consensus."

(Horváth 1999)

It is possible to say that the Ferenczi House, as a *lieu de mémoire*, is "the ultimate [embodiment] of the memorial consciousness" (Nora 1989, p. 12), a site for the formation of identity, which has been created by the will/intention of the community in a process of transformation and renewal and whose efforts build and maintain it.

And, in the future, the Ferenczi House will become what the community of the Ferenczi Network makes of it, in keeping with its activities, its interests, and its intentions.

Notes

1 Read at the opening of the 14th International Ferenczi Conference: Heritage of a Psychoanalytic Mind, Toronto, May 7–10, 2015.

2 In 2016, a Severn Section of the Ferenczi Archives will be established with the donation of the Severn Papers, which includes the following: *The Letters of Margaret Severn* to her mother, Elizabeth, from the 1920s to 1940s; Margaret Severn's autobiography, *Spotlight*; unpublished photographs of Ferenczi and Severn; copies of Severn's three published, out-of-print books; materials concerning Severn's early clinical practice; and Severn's unpublished papers and books.

References

Bonomi, C. (1999). Flight into sanity: Jones's allegation of Ferenczi's mental deterioration reconsidered. *International Journal of Psychoanalysis*, 80: 507–542.

Brennan, B.W. (2011). On Ferenczi: A response – from elasticity to the Confusion of Tongues and the technical dimensions of Ferenczi's approach. *Psychoanalytic Perspectives*, 8: 1–21.

Ferenczi, S. (1980). Confusion of Tongues between adults and the child. In M. Balint (ed.), *Final Contributions to the Problems and Methods of Psycho-Analysis*. London: Mares Reprints, pp. 156–167.

Ferenczi, S. (1988). *The Clinical Diary*, ed. J. Dupont. Cambridge, MA: Harvard University Press.

Ferenczi, S., & Jones, E. (2013). *Sándor Ferenczi – Ernest Jones: Letters 1911–1933*, eds. F. Eros, J. Szekacs-Weisz, & K. Robinson. London: Karnac Books.

Fortune, C. (1993). The case of "R.N.": Sándor Ferenczi's radical experiment in psychoanalysis. In L. Aron & A. Harris (eds.), *The Legacy of Sándor Ferenczi*. Hillsdale, NJ: Analytic Press.

Fortune, C. (2002). *The Sándor Ferenczi–George Groddeck Correspondence*. London: Open Gate Press.

Freud, S., & Ferenczi, S. (2000). *Correspondence, vol. 3, 1920–1933*, eds. E. Brabant, E. Falzeder, & P. Giampieri-Deutsch, trans. P. Hoffer, with an introduction by Judith Dupont. Cambridge, MA: Harvard University Press.

Horváth, K. (1999). Az eltűnt emlékezet nyomában. [In search of lost memory.] *Aetas*, 3. sz. – EPA, accessed from http://www.aetas.hu/1999_3/99-3-9.htm

Mészáros, J. (2003). Could Balint have done more for Ferenczi? *American Journal of Psychoanalysis*, 63(3): 239–255.

Mészáros, J. (2014). *Ferenczi and Beyond: Exile of the Budapest School and Solidarity in the Psychoanalyic Movement during the Nazi Years*. London: Karnac Books.

Nora, P. (1989). Between memory and history: Les lieux de mémoire. *Representation*, 26 (Special Issue, *Memory and Counter-Memory*), 26: 7–24.

Rachman, A.W. (2015) Elizabeth Severn: Sándor Ferenczi's analysand and collaborator in the study and treatment of trauma. In Harris, A., & Kuchuck, S. (eds.) *The Legacy of Sándor Ferenczi, vol. 2, From Ghost to Ancestor*. London: Routledge.

Chapter 2

A multifaceted legacy

Sándor Ferenczi's *Clinical Diary*

Judith Dupont

Translated by Michael Larivière

"Be realistic, ask for the impossible!" This slogan of the students of May 1968 suits Sándor Ferenczi perfectly. Confronted with the reality of the needs and sufferings of some of his patients, he tried meeting them on their own ground, getting lost in the fog with them and bringing them back out with him. It was for him a painful encounter with the bounds of possibility.

Sándor Ferenczi left us an imposing body of work. Articles promoting his ideas and intuitions, a wealth of correspondence enabling us to know the man behind the scholar and, finally, a diary.

This last piece of writing, his *Clinical Diary* of 1932 (1985), has a very special place in his work, as well as in psychoanalytic literature in general. It is a most unusual piece of work, from which psychoanalysts today can draw lessons on many levels. To be more precise, it isn't only about lessons; one could speak of education in the broader sense of the term, much like the one parents give their children, in words as well as in deeds, consciously as well as unconsciously. This *Clinical Diary* is the detailed review, step by step, of Ferenczi's journey towards the impossible. He was able to venture forth upon this perilous journey for as long as he felt supported by Freud, if not in his experiments, at least as a man. After this support was withdrawn, the journey ended with death. Is one justified in establishing such a connection, I don't know. Michael Balint, student and close friend of Ferenczi's, puts forward the hypothesis.

The *Clinical Diary* presents a number of enlightening ideas, based upon an experience and an experimentation scrupulously reported, along with their successes, their mistakes, and their failures. But it also shows how Ferenczi understands the very practice of psychoanalysis, as well as how he envisages the position of the psychoanalyst. He sketches out what he considers to be the kind of mental functioning required for the practice of psychoanalysis. In describing with rare, perhaps unequalled honesty what he does, thinks, and feels, he reveals the practical details of his own commitment. One is left with the impression that he is trying to do away with all forms of censorship, and that he is on the verge of achieving his ends. This at least seems to be his aim.

Only one form of censorship is exercised, with regard to the possible future readers of the *Diary*. This is definitely intended, conscious, and acknowledged. Indeed, this *Diary* was obviously intended for publication (according to Michael Balint), typed, dictated to a secretary, with the exception of a few passages that concern Ferenczi's deep feelings towards Freud. Those passages give evidence of a very painful relationship at the time of the writing of the *Diary*. They are not dictated to a secretary but written in longhand on all kinds of papers, and it is quite likely that Ferenczi didn't envisage, or at least hesitated, to publish them.

If Ferenczi himself strived to do away with any kind of censorship during the writing of this *Diary* (1932), such wasn't the case with his successors in charge of handling his legacy. That piece of history, which goes from the writing of this document to its publication, perfectly illustrates the difficulty the psychoanalytic community had in following Ferenczi in this lifting of censorship. Amongst the heirs, the one who was most faithful to the Ferenczian spirit was Michael Balint, his literary executor (after having been his analysand, his student, his collaborator, and his friend): he was determined to publish that *Diary*, but was quite aware of the explosive effects it would have in the psychoanalytic community, which at the time considered Ferenczi to be a mentally ill person with delusional ideas. Balint wanted to publish the Diary at the same time as the Freud–Ferenczi correspondence, thinking that these two very personal texts shed light on one another and would hence be made both more intelligible and acceptable to the analytic community. Balint didn't have time to carry out his project, as he died in 1970. But he still had time to translate the *Diary* into English.

Afterwards, at the request of Gizella Ferenczi's two daughters, Elma and Magda, Ferenczi's literary representation was passed down to me.

This decision, taken during the year 1967, was approved by Michael Balint. I therefore took up that post at the end of 1970, after Balint's death. However, Enid Balint, Michael's widow, felt that she should take care herself of the *Clinical Diary*, as well as of the Freud–Ferenczi correspondence, as she thought she knew better than me what Michael Balint's intentions were with regard to them. I accepted this partial – but important – infringement of my responsibilities as executor, for there were many other things that needed doing to promote Ferenczi's underestimated work. I only had access to these two documents when it became obvious to both Enid and I that I could not carry out my duties as literary executor if I didn't have at my disposal all the writings of the author I was to represent.

After having read the *Diary*, I was utterly convinced that it should be published. Enid Balint was quite reticent. The legend propagated by Ernest Jones, according to which Ferenczi was suffering from paranoid psychosis, was still widespread and believed in the psychoanalytic community, and Enid was afraid that the *Clinical Diary* might confirm this conviction. It was therefore decided that the text would be submitted to the arbitration of two colleagues of excellent reputation, Alexander and Margarete Mitscherlich.[1] Both, having read it, considered it unpublishable. Nevertheless, the translation group of the *Coq-Héron* journal – who had just translated the fourth volume of the complete works of Ferenczi (1982), as well as his correspondence with Groddeck (1992, 1996, 2000) – decided to translate the *Diary* into French as well, in its complete version, and afterwards to see what should be done with it. This difficult translation took a long time, a time during which the psychoanalytic community changed considerably. Ferenczi's complete works were now available, translated into many languages, and new generations of analysts, less impressed by Jones's authority, had read and appreciated them. The time now seemed appropriate to publish the *Clinical Diary*, even without the Freud–Ferenczi correspondence (1982), the publication of which was still being met with reticence from Anna Freud. An understandable reticence, as all her family's intimacy was therein exposed.

So the *Diary* was published in French by Payot, much before the German original, in 1985. Instead of the scandal feared by many, it was received with respect and admiration. No one had yet dared expose themself to the extent Ferenczi had in this unparalleled text, and no one has been able to reproduce the feat since. Is this surprising?

The tremendous legacy passed down with this *Clinical Diary* can be classified under three headings: the ideas and intuitions elaborating on what he had already started on in his published articles; the technical experiments, the last one notably, the most audacious, mutual analysis; and finally the account of a dangerous exposition of his own emotions in what he calls the "furnace of transference", a transference that works both ways, transference and countertransference, the two components of which the analyst must pay attention to.

Ideas and intuitions

For many years, Ferenczi had been occupied with the issue of trauma. His attention was first caught by the traumas endured by soldiers during World War I; the importance of early traumas then became more clearly obvious to him in the course of his clinical work during the 1920s. His last articles – notably the most important and most controversial "Confusion of Tongues Between Child and Adults" – deal with this issue, and there are many observations on the matter in the *Diary*. His theoretical conclusions are based upon the clinical observation of the last patients he treated during the year 1932, first and foremost Elisabeth Severn (R.N.) and Clara Thompson (Dm).

This clinical work convinced him that any analysis taken sufficiently far will touch upon the "hysterical traumatic foundations of the illness".

There then gradually appear the observations and clinical experiences on the basis of which Ferenczi developed his views on the splittings, the processes of division, of fragmentation that take place after a trauma. The hypocrisy, the lies that lead the traumatized person to doubt his own senses play an important role. That is how even perfectly good-intentioned parents can throw their child into great despair by denying the existence of what the child can see with his own eyes, or by maintaining the existence of things he can clearly see don't exist. Social hypocrisy traumatizes the mentally ill; and the professional hypocrisy of the analyst, should he suggest through word or attitude feelings he doesn't have, renews the patient's trauma. The honesty, the sincerity of the analyst towards his patient is not, for Ferenczi, a "technique", but a basic principle of psychoanalysis. A mistake is certainly less harmful, less puzzling than a lie, on condition, of course, that it is acknowledged.

One of the consequences of this duty to establish a sincere relationship is the necessity to accept hearing and analysing all things negative the patient can direct towards his analyst, without immediately getting rid of them by interpreting them for the patient as an effect of his transference. This, by the way, is a reproach he will make to Freud – not having analysed the negative transference during the three episodes of the mini-cure he did with him. Freud denied this in his well-known article "Analysis terminable, analysis interminable", stating that nothing of the kind had taken place during that analysis. However, to a careful reader of the two men's correspondence these negative demonstrations seem obvious from the very onset of their relationship, for example, when the clash occurred in Palermo during one of their first holidays together.

Any kind of rigid adhesion to theory or to a standardized behaviour will paralyse the patient. At the beginning of his *Diary*, Ferenczi talks about "professional hypocrisy", the effects of which are as traumatizing as those of social or family hypocrisy.

Throughout the *Diary*, Ferenczi makes it plain for all to see the attention he pays to the interaction or, to perhaps be more precise, the cooperation between the physical and the mental. His intuitions about this are no doubt what drew him towards Groddeck, finally leading him to call upon this German physician whose clinical work was based upon the certainty of such a cooperation.

The traumas with the heaviest consequences are those suffered unconsciously, says Ferenczi, unconscious either because they had taken place at an extremely early age, or for other reasons, for example, because they had been suffered while the person was under the influence of drugs. In order to have access to such traumas, one must find a way of letting them come alive again, for the first time consciously.

Ferenczi also introduced the notion of "terrorism of suffering". The other, notably the child in relation with a parent, becomes the servant and nurse of the suffering one, letting himself be assailed and overwhelmed by this foreign personality that will insidiously take over part of his own.

A note dated 10 March 1932 seems particularly important and interesting with regard to the evolution of psychoanalysis since its beginning. Ferenczi realizes that a process initially conceived of as purely intellectual – understanding the origins of one's malaise by clearing away the obstacles to this comprehension – must gradually take into account all the feelings that come into play in the course of the analytical work. And he then further realizes that, in certain states of regression, to which he refers here as "deep relaxation", the intellect is totally inoperative, and words or reasoning without effect. It is in this respect that Balint later on considerably deepened our understanding. In this same note Ferenczi defends – albeit timidly – the legitimacy of his wish to "cure", which often brought reproach on him, his detractors calling this "furor sanandi".

The note of 5 April 1932 tackles a problem from which stem serious and harmful consequences: that of hatred, which Ferenczi describes as "projection, in truth psychopathic". He understands it as a successful attempt to relieve oneself of a suffering by shifting it onto the person seen as responsible.

It can then be attributed to an entire family, or an entire nation. Our century, as well as the previous one, knows this well. Ferenczi pleads for the acknowledgement of suffering, followed by the grieving of what had gone wrong. For grief can facilitate a positive outcome.

It is impossible here to do justice to the wealth of ideas and intuitions offered to us in this *Clinical Diary*. With each new reading, others are discovered. And they are always either preceded or accompanied by the development leading to their conception. All theoretical formulations follow from a clinical experience that deeply implicates Ferenczi's very being, and this is an integral part of the emotional aspect of the legacy contained in the *Clinical Diary*.

Technique

Ferenczi was always fascinated by the problems of analytical technique. He believed that it wasn't for analysis to select the patients who will benefit from it as it is, but that it was for the analyst to adapt the analytical method and its techniques to each person who asks for his help. It is for him to invent a way for each of his analysands.

Throughout his analytical career Ferenczi kept adding technical experiences: active technique, technique of indulgence and flexibility, and finally the mutual analysis experience meticulously described in the *Clinical Diary*. That experience was never adopted as a technique. Ferenczi soon realized it had many inconveniences, that it even presented insuperable obstacles, not to mention how difficult the situation it created was for himself. However, we are not talking here about a mistake, but rather about an actual impossibility. This experience was an effort to respond to a very real situation mentioned earlier, where the analysand is in a state of distress and disorientation. And being in such a state endows him with a hypersensitivity – but not with an actual knowledge – with regard to the emotional state of his analyst. And he needs for the reality of what he feels to be confirmed, even if it is a complex, or even hostile, feeling. Not denying what his sensitivity tells him in such moments seems vital if we are to avoid that the trauma due to the hypocrisy at the origin of the illness be renewed. The analysis of the analyst by the analysand (in this case R.N., who was a psychotherapist herself) strives to give the analysand access to those essential markers. This inadequate experience therefore makes sense. It was an impossible answer to a problem that nevertheless required one. It was in this respect that Michael Balint unquestionably made headway.

Over and beyond this major attempt at mutual analysis, innumerable observations focus on the technical aspect of analysis: Ferenczi touches upon the limitations and/or limits of floating attention, which is exactly what is needed in situations where the end of the thread that leads to the essential issues is hidden in a hank which at first seems inextricable, but that seems inadequate when the patient approaches the most sensitive areas of his inner world. The problems that come with regression are dealt with at length: Ferenczi is in favour of neither impeding nor shortening this phase. He believes it is necessary to let the patient regress, even to encourage this regression, a state that enables him to accede to those parts of his story that had hitherto remained unreachable. But the situation sometimes gets bogged down and ends with a breakup in disappointment and despair. So it was Balint who pushed ahead with the research, and this during Ferenczi's lifetime, which led Ferenczi to say, in a note written in Luchon in 1932, that "Balint picked things up where I had got stumped." Balint later went on to distinguish between benign and malignant regression. In order to avoid the malignant form, which leads to an endless spiral of demands and disappointments, he recommends that the analyst grant his regressed patient some gratifications, but not just any gratifications: only those that could, he says, correspond to preliminary pleasure. The last piece of work published by Balint, *Le Défaut fondamental* (*The Basic Fault*, 2003), sums up the whole of his work by bringing to the fore his relation to the research tackled by Ferenczi. A chapter entirely dedicated to the Freud–Ferenczi relationship and its painful outcome buckles down to expose the bedrock of their quarrel and its effects on the psychoanalytic community as well as on the evolution of psychoanalysis.

Another issue, theoretical as much as technical, also very much preoccupied Ferenczi: that of the ending of analysis. I am not talking here about treatments interrupted by either one or the other of the protagonists, but of those treatments considered by both to have reached their end. How does one decide that a treatment has reached its term? Defining theoretical criteria is relatively easy. Pinpointing them in the course of an analysis is clearly less easy. Can one say that all endings are identical? Can we assume that the end comes when all problems have been solved? One thinks of that excellent film *The Snake Pit*, in which a long and difficult therapy ends with this comment by the therapist: "There will undoubtedly still be moments of obscurity, but you now know where to look to find the switch."[2]

Emotional involvement

The very fact that this *Diary* exists is in itself a legacy. Perhaps that is even the most important legacy it bequeaths us. It displays an effort at sincerity, an abnegation verging on sacrifice, for the benefit of the analytical experience ventured with each of his patients, that made Ferenczi the doctor of patients considered incurable, whom colleagues would send him from all over.

Is this an example to be followed? This calls for careful thinking. Some believe that this effort to abandon all self-defence contributed towards bringing Ferenczi to his death. Now, one of the analyst's important duties is to stay alive in spite of all the transferential attacks he may be subjected to, whether they come from analysands or from colleagues. One may wonder if the readiness with which the analytic community believed the allegations made by Jones – according to which Ferenczi was mentally ill, and which denied any value to his last works – wasn't the expression of a need to recoil before the extreme exigency of the Ferenczian attitude. Surely it wasn't, as Jones pretended, paranoid delusion, but it was nevertheless a limitless involvement. Ferenczi strived to make up for this excess with an equally limitless sincerity. He was willing to acknowledge before his patient his negative feelings towards him, notably on the sexual level, so that neither one of them would lose touch with reality. According to his own testimony, Ferenczi always carried his experiences "to the absurd", even if it later meant backtracking and judging more aptly how far not to go. But if this way of behaving is neither recommended, nor even possible, for everyone, it nevertheless teaches us something essential – namely, not to fear anything if we have good reason to believe it might help make progress in the treatment. No order coming from a recognized and respected authority should impede us from thinking on our own and taking full responsibility for what we do.

The *Clinical Diary* also teaches us this precious lesson: that we never imitate anyone, be it Ferenczi himself. But this independence leaves every analyst "exposed", without any exterior protection. It wasn't without reason that Ferenczi never founded a "school", with the explicit wish to pass down what he thought and did. It was left up to the younger colleagues to draw from all this whatever could be of use to them.

The very strict training, involving a precise programme, advocated by certain institutions, justifies the strictness of this supervision by the need to protect patients against the incompetent and the charlatans. Respectable, but illusory project. The charlatans are, by definition, uncontrollable. As for those who did follow a training programme and who didn't discover in the course of that training that they were not cut out for the analytical profession, they are seldom incompetent. And, if by chance they were, then it would be that their incompetence was detected neither by themselves nor by the people in charge of their training. What is more common is that an analyst will approach certain situations inadequately, or that he will show blindness or weakness in the face of his own impulses or urges. What kind of training would it be that would claim to do away with human fragility? The best way to assure patients of a maximum of security still seems to be to encourage future analysts to think for themselves, to act according to their own conviction and to take full responsibility for what will ensue, even if they are very impressed with this or that theoretical construction or with the wisdom of this or that prestigious colleague. Total adhesion to what comes from others, whatever the value or interest, will only place the analyst on shifting sands if it isn't processed through the filter of the adept's personality. Any unexpected incident will encourage him to look to other people's work rather than to himself. Ferenczi, subjugated by Freud's genius, never gave up his right to freedom of thought and feeling.

It therefore seems to me that what an analyst can do best is to act according to his better conviction and to deal with the consequences of what he does. All this, naturally, after having trained with his experienced colleagues, read the available writings and, most importantly, after his own analysis. It is during what is called supervision, which I feel would be more aptly called clinical discussion, that the trainee analyst can acquire a broader vision of the various ways of approaching a clinical situation. On the way to independence and courage to take one's responsibilities, few amongst us will be able to go as far as Ferenczi did. But exploring one's limits and taking them into account is also part of the analytic apprenticeship. I prefer speaking of learning rather than teaching. For I am convinced that psychoanalysis can't be taught – but some are able to learn it. Each in his own way and at his own pace, drawing from here and there what suits him.

All this is part of the precious legacy that Ferenczi bequeaths us, notably through his *Clinical Diary*. We all know how rare it is to hear someone reveal what he actually said and did during an analytic session. First, it is very difficult, as one can realize during those "clinical discussions". Even the most meticulous narratives can't give a complete account of the gestures, the facial expressions, the surrounding noises, the thoughts and the fleeting impressions, and all the other elements that make up the atmosphere of a therapeutic encounter. But the deeper the narrative goes, the more exposed we are, and the greater is the risk of being hurt. Ferenczi experienced this at length.

It is we, today, who reap all the benefits from this, more than eighty years after his death.

Notes

1 Alexander Mischerlich (20 September 1908, Munich–26 June 1982, Frankfurt) was a German psychoanalyst notably interested in psychosomatics. He left a wealth of works, one of the better known of which is *Society Without the Father (Auf den Wegzur vaterboden Gesellschaft. Ideen zur Sozialpsychologie*, 1963). Having left Germany during the Nazi years, he studied Medicine in Zürich. One of his works deals with German medicine during Nazism: *Medizin ohne Menschlichkeit (Medicine Without Humanity)*. He was married, his third time, to Margarete Mitscherlich (17 July 1917, Grästen–12 June 2012, Frankfurt), a German psychoanalyst. The Mitscherlichs jointly published, in 1967, *The Inability to Mourn: Principles of Collective Behaviour*, which dealt with the repression of the German people's guilt after the Nazi years. This work was actually quite badly received.

2 *The Snake Pit* is an American film directed by Anatole Litvak, with Olivia de Havilland, Mark Steves, Robert Cunningham, etc. It came out in 1948, and was adapted from a novel by Mary Jane Ward, a writer who had spent several years in a psychiatric hospital. It was one of the first films where a psychoanalyst was seen working in a psychiatric hospital.

Bibliography

Balint, M. (2003). *Le Défaut fondamental*. Paris: Petite Bibliothèque Payot.

Balint, M. (2010). *Les Voies de la régression*. Paris: Petite Bibliothèque Payot.

Dupont, J. (2004). La formation analytique est-elle une utopie? *Le Coq-Héron*, 178, Toulouse: Erès.

Ferenczi, S. (1985). *Le Journal clinique*. Paris: Payot.

Ferenczi, S. (1982). *Oeuvres complètes*, vol. 4. Paris: Payot.

Freud, S., & Ferenczi, S. (1982, 1992, 1996, 2000). *Correspondence Freud–Ferenczi*, 3 vols. Paris: Calman-Lévy.

Freud, S., & Groddeck, G. (1982). *Correspondence Freud–Groddeck*. Paris: Payot.

Chapter 3

Ferenczi

Lacan's missed rendez-vous?

Yves Lugrin

Translated by Michael Larivière

In the past ten years – in other words, more than 30 years since Lacan's death – many analysts who claim to follow Lacan's teaching have come out of this denial. Some keep to a "Ferenczi after Lacan", i.e. to the discovery of an analyst whose intuitions, innovations and impasses are only emphasized and thrown into relief thanks to Lacan's advances. Others, to the contrary, are surprised to discover with Ferenczi an author who makes it possible to come out of the "imprisonment in our French circle", i.e. to come out of a far too univocal relationship to Lacan. Finally, others again, reading Ferenczi for themselves, discover a strange congruity between Lacan's last advances and the analyst he had for so long seemed to ignore, if not to despise. Might these various readings of Ferenczi today bear the hitherto-unseen traces of what had been Lacan's initial approach of Ferenczi?

At the end of our development, as we shall see, a paradoxical observation will seem necessary. Indeed, might it be that Lacan who, in 1953, claimed that his teaching was congruent with Ferenczi's "spiritual heritage", in actual fact remained more faithful than it seemed to this aim which he obviously had not maintained? Might the distance at which he had for a very long time and unfairly kept Ferenczi have been his unconventional way of remaining faithful to a "spiritual lineage" he intended to rediscover by himself, in his own fashion and outside any influence? Might his steering clear of Ferenczi have been his way of claiming this heritage? Is that what we see in some of his followers, as if the evidence of that lineage once claimed by him could only now, after his death, be acknowledged by them?

A partial, relative and straightaway ambiguous relationship?

Two temporal – historical – factors characterize Jacques Lacan's (1901–81) paradoxical relationship both to the person and to the work of Sándor Ferenczi (1873–1933).

First point: this relationship took a new and peculiar turn in the early 1950s. At that time, Lacan was about to impose himself as the major contemporary figure in French psychoanalysis, and this even before he had begun to lift the thick veil of silence that had since his death hung over Ferenczi's unequalled stature in the history of psychoanalysis. With Lacan, reference will unexpectedly be made to Ferenczi's merits, something that will be quite an event, as France was no exception when it came to ignoring Ferenczi's name. As was pointed out by Alain de Mijolla (2010), "there was in France no known allusion, either in the correspondences or in the reports of the Paris Psychoanalytic Society, to Ferenczi's death on May 22 (1933), and this in spite of the fact that it had occurred shortly after he had spent some time in France, something that had also strangely gone unnoticed by his colleagues."

Second point: the surprising extolling of Ferenczi's virtues by Lacan preceded the remarkable work of translation and circulation of all of Ferenczi's writings accomplished in France by Judith Dupont, which began in 1962 with the publication of *Thalassa, Psychoanalysis of the Sexual Origins*, followed by volumes 1, 2 and 3 of the *Complete Works*, in 1968, 1970 and 1974, respectively. Lacan never had access, in French, either to the fourth volume of the *Complete Works* published in 1982, i.e. one year after his death, or to the *Clinical Diary* published in 1985, nor to the three volumes of the Freud–Ferenczi correspondence published in 1992, 1996 and 2000. So we must bear this in mind: Lacan was paradoxically full of praise for Ferenczi, even though he only had a very partial knowledge of the results of the last theoretical-practical advances of the analyst considered by Freud, in 1923, to be the most eminent analyst, as well as the best-advised tutor for the younger talents of the so-called pioneer generation. So, this begs the question: what other prior knowledge could Lacan possibly have had of the man on whom he heaped praise for his exemplary qualities? If at the start of his long analytical career he didn't have access to Ferenczi's work in French, it is more than likely that he read several articles that had previously been published in German or in English, *Introjection and Transference* (1909) amongst others, the first important Ferenczian paper. Even if it is difficult to know exactly the extent of Lacan's prior knowledge of Ferenczi, the fact remains: it was, as I said, in the early 1950s that this prior knowledge took a particular turn. Indeed, if he probably very early on read *The Elasticity of the Psychoanalytic Technique*, published in 1928 in German, it was only in 1955 that he declared this article to be "luminous" (a term he will use twice when speaking of Balint). Why this delay, if not because Lacan only took note of the importance of Ferenczi's work thanks to a decisive encounter that took place at that point in his life, namely with Michael Balint, Ferenczi's pupil and friend, the finest expert on the whole of the work of the man whose literary heir he became. Lacan, in our opinion, intuited what the "spirit" of psychoanalysis was for Ferenczi in the light of what he read in his heir, Monsieur Balint. A relative reading, therefore.

Immediately after the war, when new life was brought to things analytical, Lacan had access to the recent work done in England by Ferenczi's friend and closest collaborator Balint, who had emigrated there in 1938. A member of the British Psychoanalytic Society, he was also in charge of the literary heritage of the man from Budapest, a responsibility he was later to pass on to Judith Dupont in Paris. In the early 1940s, Balint took an active part in the Controversial Discussions that opposed Anna-Freudian and Kleinian analysts. Joining the Middle Group of Independents, he strived to pursue the dialogue that would make it possible to avoid a split in the British Society. In so doing, and keeping in line with the Ferenczi of *The Development of Psychoanalysis* and of the *Clinical Diary*, he very soon came to question the old modalities of the training analysis. Indeed, throughout his work, Ferenczi was the first, if not the only one, to question the very principle of a "training" analysis, as opposed to a "therapeutic" analysis. This difficult question, which was a cause of great unrest in Great Britain, was soon to become a burning and divisive issue in Paris as well. If Balint was for Lacan an intermediate, it was for the Ferenczi of the "second fundamental rule" (1928) that of the analyst's analysis understood as needing to be brought to a "termination" – in other words, challenging analysis as it was understood at the Berlin Institute in 1920.

With this Lacan/Balint/Ferenczi triad, we are brought back to that point in time where the history of psychoanalysis swings over from a "before" to an "after": after Freud's death, and after World War II. With these three, we immediately find ourselves in a minefield, where the analytical and the political compound with one another following the modalities of training implemented by this or that analytic circle. But there is more. Indeed, in the encounter between Lacan and Balint that takes place in Ferenczi's shadow, the capital of psychoanalysis changes place, moving, over roughly ten years, from London, where controversies between Anna Freud and Melanie Klein were brewing, to Paris, where a new twist will be given to the issues of the training of analysts, of the termination of analysis, and of its transmission after Freud. Let us formulate a hypothesis: Lacan found in Balint a remarkable interlocutor, "one of the better representatives among analysts of the Ferenczian school of authenticity" (1966); he found someone who could introduce Ferenczi to the French, but without talking about his work as candidly as he perhaps could have done. Thus, in 1967, when he introduced a totally new procedure for the designation of analysts, it was Balint whose name Lacan quoted, not Ferenczi's.

By multiplying references to Balint, might it be that Lacan, without realizing, was surreptitiously minimizing Ferenczi's importance? Wasn't he being rather woolly? One can certainly think as much considering what he publicly stated on 2 June 1954 during his seminar. As he was about to focus on a particular idea which, he insisted, "we owe to Balint", he rightly pointed out that it stemmed from a "very particular tradition", namely the Hungarian tradition – but, he goes on to add, Hungarian "in so far as it happened to be, *by chance*, dominated by Ferenczi's personality". So we must ask: what misreading, or what obscure prejudice, moves Lacan to say that the central role played by Ferenczi, a role that is today acknowledged as such by the historians of psychoanalysis, was *incidental?* How could he possibly treat Ferenczi so disparagingly? "We will certainly broach the subject of the relationship between Ferenczi and Freud through many an anecdotal facet. It is all quite amusing" (1975), Doesn't this thoughtlessness border on contempt or cynicism? The question deserves to be asked. In 1964,

Lacan, who had just founded his own school, devoted his seminar to "the four fundamental concepts" of psychoanalysis. As he discussed the first of those concepts, that of repetition, he took up again, in his own way, the issue of trauma, but – surprise, surprise! – without once making reference to Ferenczi's earlier explorations. And when he did indeed mention Ferenczi ... it was only to entertain his audience and make them laugh. Thus, during the session of 29 April 1964, just after having talked about phantom pregnancy, Lacan mentioned another symptom related to the implication of the analyst in the course of the treatment: "One shouldn't only consider what the analyst intends to do with his patient. One should also consider what the analyst intends for his patient to do with him. Abraham, so to speak, wanted to be an accomplished mother." Now, we know this is a reproach that Freud made to Ferenczi himself. In the same vein, Lacan forged ahead: "I could also have fun by adding comments in the margins of Ferenczi's theory, drawing from a famous song of Georgius' – *I Am an Unmarried Father* (Je suis un fils-père)" (1973). A cabaret artist, music-hall character, Georgius amused and had fun evoking the sad fate of a poor girl sexually abused by a man who disappeared after making her pregnant. Are we to think that Ferenczi was made pregnant by Freud and was then abandoned? Was that the amusement advertised by Lacan ten years earlier? We need to ask again: how could Lacan underestimate, or how could he so consistently pretend not to know, both the stakes and the history, which were neither incidental nor anecdotal, and which were certainly not amusing, of Ferenczi's relationship with Freud? (Lugrin 2012).

In 1964, was he erring with arrogant carelessness, or was he duped by his own early prejudice, clearly expressed in his very first seminar? On 2 June 1954, he indeed declared that "we could call a halt to Ferenczi's personal influence around 1930. Thereafter, it was his pupils' influence that manifested itself" (1975). With this conclusion, as inaugural as it was premature, Lacan forged ahead with his prejudice: the Ferenczi chapter was closed before it was read in its entirety, and the bid was thenceforth his pupils'. And he repeated this in a paper dated July 1958, speaking of "that hot bed, the Hungarian school, the firebrands of which are now dispersed, and are soon to turn into ashes." Ferenczi was thus buried before having spoken his last word.

Was it this partial, relative and ambivalent relationship to Ferenczi that entitled Lacan to be so heedless with regard even to the title of the "luminous paper", talking about "the elasticity of psychoanalysis" instead of "the elasticity of the psychoanalytic technique"? What did this slip, or this forcing of Ferenczi's thinking owe to the reasoning that led Lacan to call upon Balint: "Starting from where we now stand, going back in time as of Balint, we shall try to see what the notion of active psychoanalysis means for Ferenczi, which he is credited for having introduced." Lacan couldn't have been more clear, using Balint in order to draw attention to a paper dating from 1928, and from there to come back to the Ferenczi of the years 1918–24, i.e. to the Ferenczi advocating the active technique. So we must ask: in so doing, was Lacan saying that he had little regard for the work and the experimentations done by Ferenczi after 1928, with his techniques of neocatharsis and relaxation? This innovation was considered appropriate for the analysis of the return of the trauma in the transference, of its incidence in the discourse of the child who, through regression, expresses himself in the adult. Did this deliberate instrumentation of Ferenczi by Lacan force him into a contradictory partiality as he acknowledged Ferenczi as "the most discerning author of the first generation with regard to the assessment of what is required of the analyst, notably *a propos* of the termination of the treatment – while at the same time turning a blind eye to his last effort at conceiving of analysis 'with a termination', taking precisely trauma into consideration?"

An eminently partial relationship

Lacan's partial, relative and ambivalent relationship to Ferenczi sheds light, I believe, on its fundamentally biased dimension – the praise being as excessive as the criticism that comes with it is too rapid. Lacan seems to conjure up a made-to-measure Ferenczi, cut out to suit his purpose. Ignoring the development as well as the coherence of Ferenczi's research, he seems to "cleave" him in two parts, a luminous one and another one, fundamentally obscure and mistaken. He stresses the relevance of Ferenczi's intuitions as a sensible clinician, only to immediately denounce what he does with them, lacking an adequate theory. Ferenczi is thus the object of the same praise, as well as of the same dismissal, that Balint initially had to put up with, Lacan taking once again aim at the master through the pupil, whose writings he knew better.

The extolling of Ferenczi's virtues was at its height mid-July 1953, as Lacan closed the letter he wrote to Balint with the following words: "Until soon, dear friend. Please know that I always put the greatest emphasis on Ferenczi's spiritual lineage in my teaching". In 1966, Lacan seemed to maintain the praise, repeating that he held Ferenczi to be "the most authentic examiner of his responsibilities as therapist, as well as the most scrupulous scrutator of concepts".

Even if it was limited to what Lacan could and indeed did wish to know about Ferenczi, it remains to be seen whether this praise stemmed from respect for his work, or if it was the product of some obscure identification with what he knew about his fate in the analytical community. Might it be that through the flattering picture he painted of Ferenczi-the-analyst, Lacan was actually talking about himself and what he anticipated with regard to his own destiny? Indeed, he couldn't not know that in the end Freud no longer trusted Ferenczi and that he (Ferenczi) had to endure what he (Lacan) was experiencing in Paris. Some of his colleagues questioned not only the orientation that his teaching was taking, but even more so his choice of doing sessions that varied in duration, intent that they were on getting his name taken off the list of training analysts.

The use of one particular word attests to the importance of this probable and more or less conscious identification with Ferenczi: "school". Lacan indeed stressed the merits of what he called "Ferenczi's school of authenticity" (1966). Belatedly acclaiming Ferenczi as the leader of a school is surprising for two reasons. First, we know of his awkward position with regard to leadership and power games; we need only to remember his refusal, in 1932, to accept the presidency of the IPA, which Freud, even if not without ambivalence, thought should be his. And, second, we also know that Lacan would, in 1964, found not an Institute but a prestigious School, the Freudian School of Paris. What is most surprising in all of this is that Ferenczi was the very first to conceive of a school that would take on a new mission: it would be up to this superstructure to encourage the acknowledgement of experienced analysts capable of contributing to the task of elaborating a doctrine (which at the time he felt was in need of more thought) with regard to training analysis. This mission, which would be twofold, would therefore be added on to the task, as was the case in Berlin, already undertaken by the various analytical societies. It would see to the training of analysts, and it would defend their professional activity.

Ferenczi dreamed of a Freudian school that would train "masters" whose task it would be to give structure and expression to the very spirit of psychoanalysis, as well as to pass it on, and this by virtue of both their passion for and experience of analysis – and not because they would have been given mandate to do so by some institution. So, in 1930 Ferenczi had this intuition of a School of Psychoanalysis surprisingly similar to the one Lacan would found in 1964, whose ambition would become even more radical with the "proposal of the *Passe*" in autumn 1967.

Here, then, is what Ferenczi writes in the post-scriptum of his letter to Freud dated 17 January: "I pay tribute to the results presented by the Berlin Institute, which could serve as model for all of us. In fact, the idea came to me of a supplement at the organizational level: the creation of several new modes of training". At an initial level, "popularization (University, extension)" would be "part of the programme of the Association". At a second level, "the greater medical and pedagogical public's clamorous request for special abridged courses" would be answered. At the higher level, there would be "the analytical Faculty (training of practicing analysts), which could perhaps follow the Berlin Institute model". Nothing really new in this differentiation of levels of interest for analysis. What was most surprising, then, was the last level – absolutely unheard of – that Ferenczi suggested: "The affiliation to a School of Masters" (both terms to be understood as the ancient Greeks did), "(Guild), (academy) would require as a precondition a personal analysis, even if this was to take several years, which entails knowledge and complete mastery of one's personality; in other words, what I refer to as termination of analysis". Did Ferenczi take full measure of the radically subversive aspect of his suggestion as – before Lacan – he proposed to predicate becoming an analyst not on an institutionalized training, but on a radicalization of the analytical cure? I don't think so. On 29 August 1932, the eve of his last visit to Freud, two days before the Wiesbaden Conference, he seems to think that what he is about to put forward in "Confusion of Tongues Between Adults and the Child" will be easily accepted: "I feel unfettered by any wish to found a School; I shall first address myself to the colleagues of the 'older generation' with proposals for discussion, hoping that I will be understood". He was greatly mistaken, for not only would he not be heard by his colleagues, but Freud himself would disapprove of this piece of work and, even worse, would not take the hand that he extended in farewell. So, at the end of his journey Ferenczi dreamed of a School where those who would become masters were not the disciplined pupils but those who would have carried their analysis to its end, i.e. who would have reached that last phase, the obscure part of which, as his *Clinical Diary* demonstrates, never ceased to torment him. Very much tormented in the same way, Lacan knew quite early on that he wouldn't escape his fate as Founder. After two splits, first in 1953, then in 1963, he founded his School in 1964 and then went on, three years later, to propose a totally new institutional procedure for the selection of analysts, very much in accordance with Ferenczi's own suggestion. This procedure, known as "*la passe*", would cause scandal inside his own School, much in the same way that *The Development of Psychoanalysis* had in 1924 – or, to a lesser degree, "The Confusion of Tongues Between Adults and the Child" in 1932.

If in those distant times Lacan seemed to be identifying more with the figure of Ferenczi than to be taking interest in his analytical options and intuitions, if they were both destined for a certain marginality, or even to distance themselves from the IPA, there was nevertheless a limit to the resemblance between the two men. Over and beyond the difference in time and analytical context, over and beyond the fact that Lacan started on his trajectory at the exact point where Ferenczi had left off, there was also the incidence of the difference in style and personality between the two men. Ferenczi never could overcome his emotional dependence on Freud and free himself from the transferential after-effects of his relation to the father figure he represented, Freud never having done anything to help him in that way. Instigator of the symbolic function of the Name-of-the-Father, Lacan never needed such a dependency and he predicated the founding of his School on the solitary nature of the act he claimed responsibility for. Such a step, such a crossing of the line, was unthinkable for Ferenczi who, if he did gain a following, never really envisaged founding a School, least of all a Ferenczian School. Against the background of this possible identification of Lacan with Ferenczi, bringing Ferenczi to the forefront always meant immediately and progressively distancing himself from him, soon formulating a succession of strong reservations. A few examples will suffice.

First example. A few days after having claimed to be following Ferenczi's spiritual lineage, Lacan wrote his founding *Rome Discourse* (Discours de Rome, 1966c), in which Ferenczi is the first author to be quoted, in a footnote. In that paper appears the first reference to *Confusion of Tongues Between the Adults and the Child*, but it is an almost negligible reference, as Lacan uses Ferenczi's phrase "confusion of tongues" mainly to ridicule the mess pervading amongst the higher executives of the analytical movement. (It should be noted here that the promise that had been made to Ferenczi in 1932 of a publication in English of his testament was not honoured. We will have to wait for Balint to do it in 1949 – and without much success at that – in an American journal. It is that version that Lacan quotes.) Furthermore, when he lays stress on the "confusion of generations" (1966) and its traumatic consequences, the author of *The Unwelcome Child and his Death Instinct* is not quoted. Lacan's paper thus makes no other mention of the Wiesbaden Conference that broke the magical thread linking Freud and Ferenczi. In so doing, does he fail to understand or does he choose to ignore the interest that Ferenczi also takes, perhaps more so than Freud, in "the field of language and speech in psychoanalysis", and this even if he doesn't have the linguistic tools at his disposal? Many of Ferenczi's writings attest to this.

This apparent negligence toward Ferenczi's contributions is all the more surprising as, in addition, Lacan, in passing by, quotes authors of lesser importance such as C.I. Obendorf, or Jules H. Massermann, whose *Language, Behaviour and Dynamic Psychiatry* he makes reference to (1966). Does the fact that these authors' papers are, as was Ferenczi's, quoted in their English versions enable us to guess what it was that led Lacan to be remiss about Ferenczi? Might Lacan's lack of interest in the history of psychoanalysis, as well as in "analytical genealogy" (something that would have led him to take a real interest in Ferenczi) be the consequence, as it were, of his passion for analytical current affairs, which were the grounds on which he intended to lead his battle? Hence his desire to fight with American analysts, to fight what they had done to psychoanalysis, as well as the stronghold that was theirs in the IPA. Hence, again, the attention paid in his "Roman" paper not only to C.I. Obendorf or Jules H. Massermann, but also (and for a long time afterwards) to E. Kriss, R. Fliess or the British E. Glover. Another anglophone, the friend Balint, is also delivered a first blistering critique in the same paper.

Second example. Eleven years after his *Rome Discourse*, during the re-foundation seminar that he held under the aegis of his new School, Lacan re-examined the issue of trauma in the light of "his" category of the "real", once again without the slightest allusion to Ferenczi. He devoted the first three lessons to the fundamental concept of "repetition", again without mentioning that Ferenczi had been the first, with Rank, and later on on his own, to stretch to such lengths the attempt to renew the idea of what to expect from analysis, taking into consideration the notions of repetition and trauma as they were introduced in *Beyond the Pleasure Principle.* Yet what was at stake analytically was of major importance, Ferenczi's analytic trajectory establishing a link between Freud and Lacan.

We must remember that Freud first related trauma to its sexual dimension – the intractable flood of urges – to then, in *Inhibition, Symptoms and Anxiety* (1926), lay stress on the importance of its infantile prototype, i.e. the primitive distress (*Hilflosigkeit*) experienced by the child when he finds himself helpless in the face of ordinary adversity (*Not des Lebens*). Afterwards, Ferenczi gave priority to that second Freudian approach to trauma, taking hold of it and turning it around, relating the fundamental trauma to the early distress of the child who, in the "earnestness of his entry into Otherness" has the cruel experience of the unreliability of the parental word, which sooner or later he realizes is to a certain degree incoherent, untruthful, deaf or, worse, dismissive. Hence my surprise at seeing that Lacan, whose teaching had begun with an emphasis on the symbolic, made no reference in his own approach of trauma to Ferenczi's constant effort at understanding its "linguistic" dimension. This being said, with this final step forward Ferenczi remains Freudian: relating the traumatic aspect of the experience to the "unwelcoming of the child", or to the "confusion of tongues between the adults and the child", is in no way a desexualization of the Freudian theory. For him, the confusion of tongues is inseparable from a confusion in conducts and acts, where the sexual "contaminates" the very language that governs the evolution of the child towards becoming a sexual and, so to speak, embodied subject – hence its devastating traumatic impact. Isn't it always the case when the adult's pleasure (*jouissance*), as well as, reciprocally, the child's pleasure, prematurely "drives" (as in "sexual drive") the parent–child dialogue instead of felicitously eroticizing it? Therefore, in 1964 how could Lacan avoid making any significant reference to Ferenczi, from whom he had twice borrowed (in 1953) the term "confusion", in a way claiming it as his own? Did he not at that time talk about the ravages of the "confusion of generations" described in the Bible as the "abomination of the Word"? Wasn't that exactly what Ferenczi, more than anyone else, shed light on when he expounded on the presence of the precociously traumatized child, a child that precedes the little "polymorphous-perverse" that the Oedipal child is? Relentlessly, even in his latest technical experimentations, Ferenczi searched for the traumatized child hiding behind the misdeals inherent to the resolution of Oedipal conflicts, a child who could still be heard in the adult on the couch and who deserved a hospitable treatment. So, why did Lacan – in 1953 as in 1964 – give a wide berth to these explorations rather than submit them to a frontal criticism? Why did he restrict himself to that indirect, rather hasty criticism of Ferenczi by way of Balint, discrediting him even before serving him with a summons?

1953. As we saw, Lacan refused to engage in dialogue with Ferenczi, choosing to sidestep him in his *Rome Discourse.* In his first seminar, he considers him to be outdated, giving his preference to the pupil, Balint, several papers of whom he read with his followers.

1955. An exception that proves the rule? Over Easter, Lacan wrote *Variations on the Standard Cure*, a paper whose title is very similar to that of Ferenczi's "luminous" article, *The Elasticity of the Analytical Technique.* Like nowhere else, he clearly explains what is that "Ferenczian spiritual lineage" he claims to be a representative of. In that paper, meant to defend his own technical innovations, Lacan, who is threatened with "excommunication" by the IPA, uses Ferenczi, for once clearly quoted and commented on. In order to criticize the unsatisfactory notion of "countertransference" understood as "communication between the unconscious of the analyst and that of the analysand", he very rightly calls upon Ferenczi, who, with Freud, asserted that the "connivance" (*Einfühlung*) between analyst and analysand "belongs to the preconscious". Much in the same way, he acknowledges that the second fundamental rule of analysis, that of a true analysis of the analyst, was formulated by Ferenczi in 1928 and by no one else. He thus draws the precise list of directives that, according to the champion of elasticity of technique, should provide guidance to the analyst in his conduct of treatment, and makes them completely his own: "in each of these directives, does the Ego not make way for the subject-point of interpretation? And so they come into force only thanks to the analyst's own analysis, and particularly thanks to his analysis having been carried to its end" (1955). Yes, Lacan here revealed himself to be so Ferenczian that we are led to search elsewhere for the criticism we know always went along with the praise. First indication: a few pages later, Lacan sharply criticizes those who believe in a "strong Ego" and who predicate the termination of analysis on the "identification to the analyst". Surprisingly, he finds proof of the dominium of such an aberration that prefers the Imaginary to the Symbolic in "the analyst best trained in Ferenczi's school of authenticity" – Balint himself. In a footnote, he refers to Balint's two recent publications, *On the Termination of Analysis* (1949) and *On Love and Hate* (1951). Lacan restricts himself to what Balint says about "the phenomena characteristic of the cases he considers to be terminated: whether he describes this narcissistic ardor that devours the individual ... , or this radiation, as he bids goodbye, of an indescribable emotion, to which he goes as far as saying that the analyst contributes". In spite of his Ferenczian training, Balint therefore would seem not to avoid the mistake made by the champions of Ego-Psychology. Might the pupil be guilty of a sin inherited from his mentor? Second indication: amongst the directives for an adequate conduct of treatment suggested by Ferenczi, Lacan refers to the "unforbearing kindness" and adds the following footnote: "Ferenczi couldn't imagine that it might one day be used as a hoarding", i.e. what he, Lacan, was himself ready to use it as.

1958. During an important International Conference held in Royaumont at the initiative of the French Psychoanalytical Society (FPS) still awaiting recognition by the IPA, Lacan presented a paper on *The Direction of the Treatment and the Principles of its Power.* The stakes were high, as he knew that all those who had left the old Paris Society of Psychoanalysis would not blindly follow him, so he had to resolutely legitimize his position as leader. After a first chapter devoted to the issue of interpretation and what certain authors he reviled had done with it, Lacan broached the question of transference, straightaway underscoring "how limited the aspects on which the debates concentrate are, and especially how the usual use of the term in analysis remains quite questionable and improper: reducing it either to the succession or to the sum total of the positive and negative feelings the patient feels towards his analyst" (1966).

He aims to clear the "persistent obscurities" and to "[bring] a bit of orderliness" in the biases of the various approaches of the problem. In order to do this, he distinguishes and comments on three of these fallacious "particular aspects of theory". He first declaims against the "genetism" of colleagues who favour the "analysis of defenses", first and foremost Anna Freud. He then goes on to criticize those who in their practice keep to the "object relation axis", such as Abraham. He can't subscribe to the notion of a "transition from the pregenital to the genital" form of the object: "And what does this absurd hymn to genital harmony have to do with reality?" (1966). He then tackles the third side of "the pyramid, be it heretic" and finds it – with the analyst who introduced "the notion of intersubjective introjection, which is our third mistake, that of unfortunately positioning ourselves in a dual relationship", and therefore an imaginary one. It is of course Ferenczi who is here criticized for being partial to what Lacan ironically refers to as "theoretical sauces", the kind of which Balint had offered with his notion of "terminal narcissistic transe". A few pages later, Lacan refers to *Introjection and Transference*, Ferenczi's first important paper, and says ironically: "Doesn't this author reach an extremist position in stating that the termination of treatment can only be reached with the doctor telling the patient that he himself finds it painful being abandoned?" (1966). Irony then borders on cynicism: "Must one pay this comical price of seeing the individual's 'failure at Being' [*manque à être*] recognized as the core of the analytical experience?" (1966). Why this toning up in Lacan between the years 1955 and 1958? We should perhaps remember that, as early as 1953, forgetting how tragic his fate had been as an analyst, he spoke of Ferenczi as an amusing author – at whom one could laugh. But there was more at stake behind all this: there were the political issues.

After 1958, "political" issues come into the analytical debate, further complicating Lacan's relationship to Ferenczi. The French Psychoanalytic Society (FPS), founded in 1953 with the breaking up of the Paris Psychoanalytic Society, was at that time in turmoil over institutional issues. Some distinguished analysts were anxious to see their Society recognized by the IPA and were therefore ready to accept its requirements, namely Lacan's radiation from the list of its training analysts. Others, faithful to his teaching, refused to see him deprived of pupils, forbidden to teach and reduced to silence. In October 1963, one of the FPS's negotiators with the IPA, Wladimir Granoff, obtained of a certain number of colleagues that they endorse Lacan's radiation. The second schism then became effective and two new analytical Institutes were founded shortly thereafter. In May 1964, the Psychoanalytical Association of France (PAF) was created and recognized by the IPA. In time, Lacan founded his Freudian School of Paris (FSP), an institution that not only would never be recognized by the IPA but, furthermore, no longer wanted that recognition. We must remember two names here: that of Wladimir Granoff, who became an important member of the PAF, and that of his friend François Perrier, who for a time was an important figure in Lacan's School. These two men, as we shall soon see, would later interfere in Lacan's relations with Ferenczi. I have already recalled how things stood in that respect before those painful events took place. But what about afterwards? How did Lacan treat Ferenczi then?

1964. We have already seen how Lacan treated Ferenczi during that year's seminar, not quoting the works of his last years on the analytical treatment of trauma, and reducing his so-called conception of transference to a "father–son" fantasy, only worthy of the cabaret artist Georgius' derisive treatment.

1966. Lacan included in his *Writings* (*Écrits*) a paper written that same year, *On the Subject Who is Finally in Question*, in which he contrasts his concept of "divided subject" with the notion of a strong ego, an imaginary instance. Because of its place in the book, it was in this article that Ferenczi's name came up for the first time, exactly at the point where Lacan comes back and to declaim against them, to the "obvious mistakes that are circulated in the conceptualization promoted in the official circles", i.e. among those who fall for the "mirage that is not even discussed: that of the wholeness of the subject, a radical mirage that is for him equivalent to an unthinkable effacement of castration". But, Lacan goes on to say, even the best of analysts can go off the rails and, for want of a rigorous theorization, make such mistakes. It was the case with Ernest Jones, he says, and even more so with Ferenczi.

I should now like to complete the quotation I gave only partially: "This is the origin of the theoretical extravagance ... of which the most authentic interrogator of his own responsibility as therapist, as well as the most rigorous examiner of concepts can be guilty" (1966). Lacan is here alluding to "Ferenczi and his frenzied biological imaginings about amphimixis" (1966).

What we have here is a perfect illustration of what Lacan does with Ferenczi: calling upon him on the one hand, rejecting him on the other. He praises the responsible analyst and acknowledges the importance of his reflection on the practice of analysis, on the termination of treatment and on the training of analysts. He refers to him as a brother in analysis (as one would speak of a brother in arms), only to immediately declaim against his failures and the inadequacies in his theoretical work. Perhaps Lacan will have presented this "fabricated" image of Ferenczi to his pupils without realizing that many of them would come to the conclusion that he was an author to be avoided, or to be visited only out of a taste for amusing anecdotes. In my opinion, this is how, as early as 1958, references both to Ferenczi's work and to the incontrovertible role he played disappeared.

Here, now, is where Lacan stood in relation to Ferenczi when he became Director of a School that was to know immense success. Let's just say that Lacan used Ferenczi to fabricate for himself a very useful bugbear. In order to legitimize his subversive institutional positions, he extolled the unexceptionable qualities of the great therapist that Ferenczi was and denounced the impasses of his theoretical work in order to justify his own theoretical developments, even if it meant jauntily leaving him behind or on the sidelines. But how could one not see how Lacan used artful devices to reach his goals? Thus, when he extols the virtues of "the most authentic of examiners of his responsibility as therapist", Lacan – as he acknowledges it – clearly refers to the Ferenczi of 1928–30, whereas when he aims to denounce the theoretician's shortcomings, he gives greater importance to *Transference and Introjection*, a 1909 paper. In the same way, to inform against his would-be "delusion", he limits himself to *Thalassa ...*, a piece of work begun in 1915 and published in 1923 – a book Freud thought was promising.

Why this constant avoidance of the very last Ferenczian developments on trauma, about which Lacan was probably more or less informed? Why relate Ferenczi's very last reflections on analytical treatment to his very first theoretical essay? Did Lacan shamefully think, as Jones soon would, that Ferenczi's last works were those of a paranoid man soon to be demented, and that it would be better to forget them in order not to tarnish his memory? I don't think so, for something else indeed sustained Lacan's unfair severity – namely, the political and institutional stakes taken into consideration in his examination of analysis, intent as he was on revising its fundamental concepts and thus returning to the spirit of Freud's work.

Ferenczi called on to the Parisian analytical stage in the years 1953–1963

We have so far examined the Lacan–Ferenczi relationship as it fanned out and was dramatized in the years 1953–8. Before we examine what came after – the calling of Ferenczi into the impassioned context of the debates and conflicts that were then taking place within the FPS – we must first briefly recall what determined the elaboration of that context. The already complex relationship between, first Lacan, then his pupils to Ferenczi, was rendered all the more complicated because of the intermingling of the analytical and the political.

1932–53: an irresistible ascent

At the very beginning of the 1950s, to which we have so far devoted our attention, Lacan is just over 50 years old and has had a long and brilliant career, first as a psychiatrist, then as an analyst. Even without realizing it, his trajectory during that early period already was reminiscent of that of Ferenczi.

The Year 1932 was important for the two men separated by one generation. Ferenczi saw Biermer's anaemia progress, Freud's confidence wane, the political horizon darken. In September of that year, at the very time his last important talk in Wiesbaden was undervalued and rejected, the young Lacan had his medical studies viva in Paris, *Paranoid Psychosis in its Relations to the Personality.* The young doctor sent this piece of work to Freud, who, without commenting, acknowledged receipt. In the beginning, Freud the neurologist was a researcher at heart; he was neither a practising physician like Ferenczi, nor a psychiatrist like Lacan. He neither had the former's interest for the ill body, nor the latter's for psychosis. However complex it may have been, his field of research was that of psychoneurotic distress more than that of those difficult cases on the outer edges of the psychosomatic (Ferenczi) and psychotic (Lacan) registers. At the end of 1934, Lacan became a member of the Paris Psychoanalytical Society (PPS), where, in 1936, he introduced his notion of the "mirror stage". One year later, he published an important paper that dealt with a subject familiar to Ferenczi: *Family Complexes in the Formation of the Individual.* At the end of 1938, he was elected Permanent Member of the PPS – and put an end to his analysis!

In May 1939, the PPS ceased its activities for the duration of World War II.

In September 1946, Lacan presented his *Remarks on Psychic Causality* at the Bonneval Conference, and two years later became a member of the PPS's Teaching Commission. Immediately after the war, as his influence grew stronger in the PPS, he was referred numerous candidates for training analyses and supervisions, given that he was himself, like Ferenczi, seen as a "developer of young talents". Over and beyond his daily practice and his work of research, he got involved in the politics of transmission of psychoanalysis and of training of analysts.

As had been the case for Ferenczi, this intermingling of the analytical and the political would prove to be a cruel experience, confronting Lacan with many ordeals. Then again, even if without knowing, he was about to experience – admittedly in a different way – what Ferenczi had had to endure, and with courage, when he protested against the fanaticism of interpretation in the classical treatment, as well as against the medicalization of analysis, or the absence of a carefully thought-out conception of the termination of analysis. We know the price he had to pay: that of a total collapse.

In 1949, Lacan contributed to the writing of the *Regulations and Doctrine* of the aforementioned Teaching Commission. At the end of 1951, he gave a first talk on the sensitive issue of the duration of sessions. With the prior setting of a termination of treatment, Freud and then Ferenczi and Rank tried to take into account the logical function of time with an aim towards stimulating the dynamics of the treatment. Years later, Lacan aimed to do something of the same nature, this time with regard to the duration of each session, trying to encourage its dialectical movement. This unusual technique conflicted with many of his colleagues' position, as Ferenczi had caused offence to some of his colleagues with his technical innovations – active technique, neo-catharsis, then his extreme experimentations with mutual analysis. At the same time, a conflict arose in the PPS over a particularly sensitive issue: that of lay analysis. The leader of the PPS, Sacha Nacht, maintained that only physicians should practise analysis. Then again we know that Ferenczi, relatively isolated, was in his time the most ardent supporter of Freud's position in favour of allowing non-physicians to train as analysts.

It was in that stressful context that, in June 1952, affiliated to the PPS the Institute of Psychoanalysis was founded, a training institute run by Nacht and those who shared his views, and opposed to lay analysis.

The conflict between "the masters" and "the liberals" could not be avoided. We must remember here that the training Institute founded in Berlin in 1920 replaced a first Institute that had been envisaged in Budapest where (with Ferenczi) psychoanalysis was conceived of in a very different spirit.

At the end of 1952, their dismissal having been demanded by Daniel Lagache, Nacht and his group resigned and Lacan was appointed Director of the Institute. The future of psychoanalysis in France was at stake; the breakup was inevitable. In January of that year, Lacan managed to have the amendments that he proposed to the statutes of the Institute accepted and became President of a PPS in crisis. Again, how could we not remember the drama that the affairs of the presidency of the IPA had brought on during Ferenczi's last years? In June, many analysts who were recalcitrant towards those power games resigned from the PPS and founded the FPS, where Lacan was quickly to become the outstanding figure. On 8 July he gave a talk before his new colleagues, introducing his famous ternary: *the Symbolic, the Imaginary, the Real.* On the 26th, the President of the IPA objected to the affiliation of those who had resigned from the PPS, i.e. those members of the FPS who had probably not envisaged such an outcome or such a sanction. At that time, Lacan still wanted to remain a member of the IPA. As if galvanized by this traumatic situation, in August, he wrote *Function and Field of Speech and Language in Psychoanalysis*, and on 18 November he inaugurated at Sainte-Anne Hospital the famous seminar he was to hold until his death. Those are the years with which this paper began.

We already know that on 14 July Lacan wrote to Balint, informing him that he underscored in his teaching "Ferenczi's spiritual lineage". But there was more: in that same letter, he reminds Balint of the "political" situation in the Parisian analytical milieu and talks about a disappointment that, one might imagine, was perhaps reminiscent of the ambivalent relationship (a mixture of friendship and reproach?) that was developing with his friend Balint and, indirectly, with Balint's mentor, Ferenczi. He acknowledges that the support he thought he had found with him (Balint) hadn't held its promise: "I had pinned great hope on your paper [*Psychoanalytical Training*] in the attempt I made to found on the notion of principles a conflict without solution between the students and the leaders of the new Institute. This attempt failed, as had all the others I had previously made." Was he saying this in the hope of getting Balint's support, or was he diplomatically telling him that his institutional theses may have been acceptable in England, but not in France, probably because they lacked satisfactory appreciation of the "notion of principles" – in other words, a more rigorous theoretical approach to what psychoanalysis is? Would Balint, who did not help Lacan in his institutional battle, now support him in the teaching he was about to start with? Yes, oddly, Balint would help him, but in a negative way, as Lacan would take advantage of the impasses created at the clinical level by the theoretical weaknesses he noted in the fine clinician his friend was. As I said earlier, criticisms came out thick and fast as of the end of the Seminar on *Freud's Technical Writings*.

1954 – Ferenczi got at through Balint

On 31 March, Lacan asked one of his most brilliant pupils, Serge Leclaire, to comment on "the difficult text on the introduction to narcissism", which enabled him to clarify the distinction he made between the symbolic and the imaginary. He drew attention to the imaginary and narcissistic dimension of love and denounced the illusory character of the notions of genital maturity and genital love. After this presentation and the questions it raised, Lacan started speaking again and, for the good of his thesis, called upon the man from the Middle Group: "Take any article, for example the last one I read for you, from our dear Michael Balint ... He asks what the termination of treatment might consist of." Very skilfully, Lacan straightaway linked together the question of love (therefore, that of transference and its fate) and the question of the termination of analysis (therefore, that of the training of the analyst). Balint was therefore a special interlocutor, and for two reasons. Preceded in 1947 by his presentation *On the Psychoanalytic Training System*, his recent book *Primary Love and Psychoanalytic Technique* (1952) touched on the core of Lacan's preoccupations and came just at the right moment. Even if he didn't underestimate the originality of Balint's work, Lacan's appeal to him was nevertheless ambivalent, as he seemed to credit him with having raised a fundamental question without ever mentioning that only the leader of the Budapest School, Ferenczi, had tackled it long before Freud would pick it up again and respond in *Analysis Terminable and Interminable*. In the same way, Lacan commented on Balint's thesis contesting the prevalence given to primary narcissism, without paying any attention to the way in which Ferenczi had strongly underscored the need of the child, during the first phase of his development, to love and be loved. And wasn't he, Ferenczi, the first to have proclaimed in many ways: "No special training analysis!"? So, might the conversation he engaged in with Balint have ensued from a refusal to stand up to Ferenczi?

On 26 May, 2 and 9 June, the three work sessions devoted to the announced commentary on Balint's texts were grouped under the heading *Michael Balint's Impasses in the Publication of the Seminar*. Without dwelling on it, let's just say here that Lacan noted that with Balint "one gets the feeling that the concepts do indeed say something about the experience" (1975) but that they miss their aim, for "he totally lacks the conceptual framework required to understand the intersubjective relationship" (1975). The sensible practitioner, Balint loses his way because he lacks the apposite theory that Lacan was introducing with his ternary Real, Imaginary, Symbolic. The assessment is severe: "Failure of theory that corresponds to this deviation of technique" (1975).

To open this chapter of his Seminar, Lacan asked one of his best pupils, Wladimir Granoff, to speak in his place. At that particular time, he didn't know that this analyst would a few years later come between him and Balint, as well as and (more profoundly still) between him and Ferenczi. Just before the summer of 1954, Lacan still wasn't there: "I have entrusted Granoff, whom I know to be one of the people most interested in the journey I am trying to lead you on, with the task of communicating to us today what he will have learned reading Balint's book *Primary Love and Psychoanalytic Technique.*"

At that moment Lacan didn't yet realize that he was giving Granoff the opportunity to read Balint closely enough as to be touched by him in such a way that he would decide to go into supervision with him. He didn't know either that his colleague would definitively come back to Ferenczi, irremediably marked as he was in his very being as analyst: "I am far from being the only one to have stumbled over Ferenczi and never to have recovered" (1958). Hence the fight that would be his to do Ferenczi justice, to lift the black veil that had been thrown over his work since his death (a task Balint had himself just undertaken in London), and above all to spare him the consequences of this misreading that Lacan seemed to be proposing.

Ferenczi revisisted, reanimated and wounded

In 1958, five years after the 1953–4 Seminar, a voice was heard that denounced the fate Lacan had in store for Ferenczi – those last few years, a fate that had very little to do with the proclaimed respect for the spiritual lineage. That voice was Granoff's. The voice of the man who, along with others, would dissociate himself from the Lacanian adventure that was in full expansion and contributed to the rift in the analytical movement that provoked the second splitting in 1963. Initially, Granoff was not a pupil of Lacan's: he was one of his peers, with whom he had in older days supported the revolt of the candidates in training at the PPS. A polyglot, Granoff had a passion for the history of psychoanalysis, as well as for the history of analytical genealogies. He read Ferenczi in a way that was totally different from the way in which Lacan read him, i.e. without really taking him into consideration. The conflict, again, was inevitable.

In 1958, Granoff, whose knowledge of Ferenczi had become still more profound, presented a rather sensational paper before the members of the FPS, the title of which spoke for itself: *Ferenczi, False Problem and Real Misunderstanding.* The paper did justice to Ferenczi, not only in offering a reading different from that of Lacan's but also in restoring him to the place he deserved in the history of psychoanalysis, a place the analytical community, to the exception of only a few of its members, had always denied him. That same year, Lacan outlined his ideas concerning *The Direction of Treatment and the Principles of its Power* where, as we have already seen, he was particularly critical of Ferenczi. Contrary to Lacan, who "instrumentalizes" Ferenczi, who manoeuvres him as he pleases to serve his purpose and eclipses him behind Balint, Granoff presents Ferenczi as "the central figure of psychoanalysis" (1958) He says: "if Freud invented psychoanalysis, Ferenczi *practised* psychoanalysis" (1958). With this paper Granoff distances himself from Lacan, whose name is not mentioned once. Moreover, the "real misunderstanding" he underlines indeed points at Lacan's personal relationship to Ferenczi. In inviting each analyst to make up her or his own mind about Ferenczi, Granoff was in actual fact encouraging his colleagues to not blindly adhere to the somewhat univocal portrait Lacan drew of him. Hence he stated that "when it comes to Ferenczi, every analyst is well enough placed to form his own opinion. It will be new. For it would seem that there is none. Yet the figure can't be ignored" (1958). With such a statement, wasn't Granoff reproaching Lacan to have run away from the debate, thus missing his rendez-vous with Ferenczi? The rest of his statement certainly pointed in that direction, denouncing the way in which Ferenczi is got rid of at very little cost; he was targeting Lacan: "We get rid of him by expressing the admiration owed to great men when it comes to their work as a whole, sprinkling as it were a few drops of holy water, but in a somber, reproachful manner, yet with indulgence for the man and his last years" (1958). We should note that both Lacan's and Granoff's papers were published in 1961, in the same edition of *La Psychanalyse*, the short-lived FPS journal in which – surprise, surprise –the French version of "Confusion of Tongues Between Adults and the Child" was also published. Recently translated by Balint, the Wiesbaden paper was translated into French by Granoff's wife. Long deprived of a proper circulation in the anglophone public, would this Ferenczian paper find in France, with and in spite of Lacan, the audience it had previously been denied? Yes and no.

In 1958, and with Ferenczi, Granoff both identified and analytically explained his admiration for the richness of Lacan's theoretical reflection, as well as expressed his reservations towards his way of practising analysis. These reservations would grow stronger, in the end leading to a breakup even though Granoff never ceased to have respect, be it a critical respect, for Lacan's oeuvre. This first step was followed by a second one, a last step which, in my opinion, announced the imminent and cruel separation that was to take place between the two men. In 1963–4, Lacan devoted his Seminar to *Anxiety*, pushing forth with his theorization of the object cause of desire, the so-called "object *a*", as well as with his theorization of the "lack", a theory of which he would later say that it was his major, perhaps his only, contribution to psychoanalysis. Faithful to his Symbolic, Imaginary, Real ternary, he distinguished Castration (symbolic lack) from Frustration (imaginary lack) and Privation (real lack). During the 30 January 1963 Seminar session, he pursued with his examination of that function of the lack as made manifest in transference. As he began to examine the notion of "privation", he turned to the work of Margaret Little published in 1956, "*R" – the Analyst's Total Response to his Patient's Needs.* He added that he would also turn to the works of Thomas Szasz (*On the Theory of Psychoanalytic Treatment*) and Barbara Low (*The Psychological Compensations of the Analyst*).

As we can see, Lacan turns to authors who were mostly preoccupied with countertransference, i.e. with the analyst's positioning in his use of transference. There again, Ferenczi was the one who, throughout his oeuvre, from beginning to end, expatiated on this issue, embracing it in its full force and breadth. Even if he intended to approach it from a new angle, Lacan also considered this issue to be fundamental. What was at stake in his eyes was indeed radical, as he thought that the possibility of terminating an analysis was predicated upon the positioning of the analyst towards his analysand's transference, i.e. of truly terminating it in a way such that the unsurpassable buttress that Freud saw in the castration complex when it came to men, or the *Penisneid* (penis envy) when it came to women, could be reassessed.

At the end of his talk Lacan informed his audience that he would be absent for the February holidays, but that he still wanted the Seminar to be maintained, even if without him, and gave the names of the two speakers he had chosen to speak "in his stead", two eminent analysts I have already talked about: W. Granoff and F. Perrier. Did Granoff see in this offer of a prestigious platform more than a mark of his esteem and trust? Did he see a challenge, a demand that he clearly state his personal positions, which Lacan knew in part were critical of his own? One could think so, given the way he held forth. Two indications of this will suffice. On 20 February, in Lacan's absence, Granoff disregarded the orders that had been given him: if, as agreed, he commented on the works of Margaret Little and Barbara Low, he did so introducing a third woman in the debate, an author Lacan hadn't yet talked about in his Seminar – Lucia Tower, whose 1955 talk on countertransference had just been published. Moreover, Granoff made reference in his speech to his own famous talk, *Ferenczi: False Problem or Real Misunderstanding?* He obviously took advantage of this opportunity to speak "in Lacan's stead" to put the issue of anxiety in analytical practice and conduct of treatment on the agenda. Like a true Ferenczian, Granoff, in a more radical way than Lacan, conceived of treatment as being essentially therapeutic, taking into consideration the "traumatized" child's "real" presence in the adult on the couch. And that is why his own approach of anxiety by means of taking countertransference into account couldn't really find its place in the train of the theoretical revisions Lacan deemed necessary in order to tackle the problem. This explains the fact that, on 30 January 1963, he didn't follow Lacan on the way he was trying to pave, and that he instead backtracked, reminding his audience of Ferenczi: "in the last pages of a paper on Ferenczi, I talked precisely of nothing but the wish, or the will to be cured – borrowing it from Ferenczi who, in a certain way, was after all, via Melanie Klein, Maragaret Little's spiritual father".

This "masterly" stance was in line with a series of other disagreements with Lacan concerning his reading of Ferenczi and Balint, as well as concerning his way of practising analysis. That history is also one of political issues, as Granoff was at the time the foremost figure in the trio and was negotiating the recognition of the FPS by the IPA. Indeed, a few months after that speech, in October, Granoff obtained from his colleagues who were members of the "Commission of Studies of the FPS" that they vote for Lacan's exclusion. Lacan would see this as an unforgivable betrayal, speaking of the excommunication he was condemned to.

In 1958 as in 1963, obviously without having asked for anything, in France Ferenczi became the unacknowledged emblem of a doctrinal debate all the more impossible, as in those times of fratricidal discord the intermingling of the analytical and the political kept nourishing an atmosphere of confusion. Could it then be that Lacan, who in 1953 claimed to follow Ferenczi's example, felt betrayed by him in 1958, as he saw him providing ammunition for the "enemy", i.e. for those colleagues who, little by little, ceased adhering both to his theoretical options and his institutional positions? If Lacan initially presented himself as, in a certain way, a "Ferenczian", was it now Ferenczi who seemed to be "anti-Lacanian"? Was Ferenczi thus made the victim of the fantasies that accompanied his postmortem mobilization? One would think so, reading the following anecdote reported by Granoff in a paper from 1953. Having asked Lacan what he thought should be done with Ferenczi, he was given this cruel and scornful response: "Do a czi, or don't do anything at all" (1993).

In the dismantling of the name, in the play on the phoneme "czi" (ksi, ix, x), was it the name of the analyst that Ferenczi was that was ridiculed, or was it Granoff? And who was being got at? The man who for the first time authentically introduced Ferenczi in France, or the FPS colleague who, responding to an order issued by the Inquiry Commission mandated by the IPA, would obtain from several of his colleagues that they sign the request for Lacan's radiation? If Lacan was obviously thinking of the one who betrayed him, it was still Ferenczi's work that the curse "not to do anything with it" was secretly alluding to. Indeed, Lacan first, then most Lacanians, would for a long time forget him. At the end of 1963 the breakup between those who followed Lacan and those who took their distance from him was complete, this new split giving birth in 1964 to two new analytical institutions. The FPA (French Psychoanalytical Association), of which Granoff was a member, was soon to be recognized by the IPA. This would not be the case for the second institution, Lacan's new School, the FSP (Freudian School of Paris), where Leclaire and Perrier would follow Lacan. Here it should be noted that Granoff, Perrier and Leclaire formed the

"Troika", the small group Lacan had mandated to negotiate with the commission called upon to decide on the recognition of the PPS by the IPA.

The insistent return of Ferenczi on the Lacanian stage

Surprisingly, ten years after the "do a czi, or don't do anything at all" response to Granoff, it was to the faithful Perrier that the same response was given. During a session of his seminar *On Love* (24 March 1971), Perrier talked about the double language of love and called upon Ferenczi, recounting the following anecdote: "Ferenczi or do nothing – responded Lacan when I tried broaching the problem of the theory of treatment in the FSP" (1971). He was probably referring to something Lacan had said during the years 1967–8, therefore in an atmosphere that was at that time extremely tense because of the impassioned debates that were generated by the disagreements over Lacan's wish to institute the procedure known as the "Passe". In 1969, these disagreements led to a third split, which in turn gave birth to a new institution known as the FLPO (French Language Psychoanalytic Organization), later to be known as the Quatrième Groupe (Fourth Group). Perrier was one of its eminent figures.

The rampant malaise that would in the end cause a breakup in the FSP hinged on this proposal for an unusual procedure aiming for the recognition and nomination of the School Analysts, an appellation, or title, that would replace the worn-out term of "training" analyst. For, according to Lacan, no analysis can be declared to be of the "training" kind before the fact, its outcome, like that of any analysis, always being uncertain. Lacan's idea was that the analysis would reveal itself to have been a "training" one only after it had been done. The function of the "training analyst" therefore had no more sense, and the appellation became obsolete. Whoever wished to go through with the "Passe" and be named School Analyst (in French, *Analyste de l'École*, or *AE)*, would need to tell two *"passeurs"* what he believed had made an analyst of her or him, and these two *"passeurs"* would in turn report the candidate's exposé to a jury, known as the *jury d'agrément*. After long, frenzied debates this somewhat revolutionary proposal with regard to the established analytical order wasn't approved by all of Lacan's oldest fellow analysts, many of whom were psychiatrists with a long experience of psychosis. It should be noted here that from the day he founded his School, Lacan no longer held his Seminar at the Hôpital Sainte-Anne but at the École Normale Supérieure before a new audience made up essentially of brilliant intellectuals, not experienced clinicians. In 1969, some of those experienced clinicians definitively parted with Lacan, one of the most famous of which was Perrier.

For him (Perrier), indeed, there was no real ending to analysis: for the person who becomes an analyst the analysis goes on forever – with his daily practice, with the supervision sooner or later made necessary by the transference endured in the chair, with the participation in the work of this or that group of analysts. The question of "remaining an analyst" seemed more important to him than that of "becoming an analyst". Behind this difference in views hid a more profound divergence, which had to do with the relationship between theory and practice. That was the question that Freud raised and put to his colleagues in 1922. Rank and Ferenczi were the only ones to respond. As Ferenczi had done vis-à-vis Freud, so did Perrier vis-à-vis Lacan, arguing against the precedence he gave to theory over experience acquired over long years of practice. For Lacan, that exigency of theoretical rigour, which many put down as exaggerated intellectualization, was there from the very beginning of his Seminar – for example, in the debate he had with Balint the Ferenczian. Let us remember the way in which he had approached him, criticizing his theory but not his experience as a practitioner of analysis: "we must analyse the theoretician analyst in order to identify certain contemporary theoretical, as well as technical tendencies" (1966).

Did Perrier become for Lacan "Freud's Ferenczi", maintaining as the author of the *Clinical Diary* had done, that "the analyst is neither an archaeologist of knowledge, nor a logician", but a linguistic being capable of "staying on the edge of the well"?

Did this posthumous mobilization of Ferenczi on the Parisian stage in what was at stake between Lacan and his followers in 1953, in 1958 and then in 1967, serve his cause, or not? And what became of him later on in the Lacanian sphere at a time when the publication of his work, initiated as early as 1962 by Judith Dupont and her group of translators, was accelerated? When and how would Lacan's pupils turn the direct access to the incontrovertible richness of Ferenczi's work to good account? As early as 1958, and even more so after the events of the years 1967–9, there was, as I said, a long eclipse, Ferenczi no longer being part of Lacan's preoccupations and references.

It should be noted, however, that there was one fortunate exception: in volume 9 of the *Revue Analytica* (1978), dedicated to the *Studies on the Transmission of Psychoanalysis*, two important members of the FSP, Diane Chauvelot and Philippe Julien, devoted to Ferenczi's place in the history of psychoanalysis, as well as to his work. The tone is respectful, the critical debate rigorous, the ensemble indeed making one want to read both Freud and Ferenczi "with Lacan". At that time, the problems related to the institution of the "Passe" led Lacan to say that it had failed, bringing on a new, growing malaise in his School.

In 1980, Lacan disbanded his School. The following year, he died. The members of his School rebounded in various groups, each with different appellations. Lacan's son-in-law came on to the stage, took charge of his literary heritage and founded a strong group which claimed to represent the Lacanian orthodoxy, something other post-Lacanians groups would either contest or nuance.

Ferenczi – with Lacan's first heirs?

In the winter of 1985–6, after the disbanding of the FSP, and therefore after Lacan's death, a group of analysts from the young FSP devoted half of issue 35 of the *Revue du champ freudien Ornicar?* to a severely critical presentation of Ferenczi, his mistakes, his impasses and his symptoms. The titles of the articles speak for themselves: "Ferenczi's Para-praxis", "The Ferenczi Case", "Ferenczi Judged by Freud and Lacan". Whatever their obvious interest may be, these papers, which I don't have the time to comment on here, faithfully keep with the condemnation of Ferenczi proffered in older days by Lacan. In fact, mightn't they bear the traces of that reading of Ferenczi by Lacan, the chicanery of which I am trying to make obvious? Those militant papers, alas, don't arouse in the least the wish to know Ferenczi. To the contrary, they lead to giving him a wide berth in order to set about dealing with Lacan as quickly as possible. Coincidentally, that same year the *Clinical Diary* was at long last published, translated by Judith Dupont and a small group of translators, among which we find Pierre

Sabourin, who wrote the Postface. A psychiatrist and psychoanalyst, member of the Fourth Group, Sabourin published in that same year (1985) *Ferenczi, Paladin and Secret Grand Vizier.* This was the first book in France devoted to the work and analytical life of Ferenczi. But it was another twenty years before – from various sources – a new interest for Ferenczi was confirmed amongst analysts coming from the Lacanian sphere of influence.

Conclusion: Ferenczi in the post-Lacanian region today?

In May 2006, several "Lacanians" belonging to different groups got together at the French Institute in Budapest for a conference devoted to Ferenczi. The only thing all those colleagues, open and faithful to Lacan's teaching, had in common was that they no longer belonged to the "orthodox" Lacanian current of thought represented by the *École de la Cause Freudienne.* All of them, anyway, expressed their astonishment, as if they were discovering Ferenczi. Two examples will suffice. One colleague, Catherine Millot (2006), who, after Lacan, took close interest in mystical experiences, showed great surprise at the resemblance between those experiences and the traumatic experiences described by Ferenczi in his *Clinical Diary.* Another, Jean-Jacques Gorog, said the following: "I chose to follow Ferenczi in one of his most controversial productions, mutual analysis, only to find there, to my great surprise, a remarkably sophisticated understanding of psychosis. Lacan would certainly have mentioned it, had he known of it" (2009).

At the same time as that Budapest Conference, the interest shown for Ferenczi expressed itself in yet another post-Lacanian circle, the Freudian Psychoanalytic Society (FPS), a group that from its very beginning had taken note of the failure of the "Passe", much in the same way that Ferenczi had in his time acknowledged that mutual analysis was but a lesser evil. During an important university conference, Patrick Guyomard (FPS) presented a soundly argued paper on the Ferenczi–Lacan relationship (2006). In addition to organizing a Ferenczi Day, his publishing house – Éditions Campagne Première – has since published four books devoted to the work and figure of Ferenczi: those of Pierre Sabourin (2011), Helene Oppenheim-Gluckman (2010), Yves Lugrin (2012) and Jose Jimenez Aello (2013).

Recently, Mustapha Safouan, one of Lacan's earliest colleagues and one of the best scholars of Lacan's teaching, published a book (2013) in which he underscores, with force, the resemblance between Lacan and Ferenczi, both of whom he sees as dissidents from the IPA. He develops a fundamental theoretical argument which enables him to maintain that, throughout his oeuvre, Lacan further explores the fields of enquiry earlier discovered by Ferenczi himself. What conclusions can we draw from this renewed interest for Ferenczi's merits? If this was to be confirmed, a question would remain: why did it come so late? And how should we understand the double ambiguity of the following statement: "There is a lot to wager on stating that Lacan was a good reader of Ferenczi, Freud's analysand, at least as good a reader as he was of Freud himself " (Safouan 2013)? What uncertainty, or what doubt, imposes to talk of a wager? And, more fundamentally, what might we miss in seeing Ferenczi as Freud's analysand?

So, between Ferenczi and Lacan, between Lacan's heirs and the man from Budapest, today is there a true reciprocity or merely circumstantial interest? Only the future will tell what will come of this new reading of Ferenczi by those who, without realizing it, were long held in relative ignorance of his work. As far as I am concerned, I sense in the proliferation that could result from this rendezvous with Ferenczi the chance for the very survival of psychoanalysis. This, on the condition that the interpretations offered by these "new" readers of Ferenczi are not inhibited by what the remaining consequences of what Ferenczi was, for Lacan, a missed rendezvous.

References

Gorog, J.-J. (2001). La Conception de la cure analytique selon Ferenczi: Un exemple controverse, vanalyse mutuelle. In *Ferenczi après Lacan*. Paris: Hermann.

Granoff, W. (2001). *Lacan, Ferenczi et Freud*. Paris: Gallimard.

Guyomard, P. (2007). *Ferenczi et Lacan, la confusion des langues. La sexualité infantile de la psychanalyse*. Paris: PUF.

Jimenez Avello, J. (2013). *L'Ile des rêves de Sándor Ferenczi. Rien que la pulsion de vie*. Paris: Éditions Campagne Première.

Lacan, J. (1966). *Écrits*. Paris: Seuil.

Lacan, J. (1975). *Les Écrits techniques de Freud*. Paris: Seuil.

Lacan, J. (1973). *Les Quatre Concepts fondamentaux de la psychanalyse*. Paris: Seuil.

Lacan, J. (XXXX). in *La scission de 1953*, supplement au n° 7 de *Ornicar?*

Lugrin, Y. (2012). *Impardonnable Ferenczi. Malaise dans la transmission*. Paris: Éditions Campagne Première.

Mijolla de, A. (2010). *Freud et la France 1885–1945*, Paris: PUF.

Millot, C. (2009). La mystique ferenczienne. In *Ferenczi après Lacan*, ed. J.-J. Gorog. Paris: HermanN.

Oppenheim-Gluckman, H. (2010). *Lire Sándor Ferenczi, un disciple turbulent*. Paris: Éditions Campagne Première.

Perrier, F. (1978). *La Chaussée d'Antin*. Paris: Christian Bourgois.

Sabourin, P. (1985). *Ferenczi, paladin et grand vizir*. Paris: Éditions Universitaires.

Sabourin, P. (2011). *Sándor Ferenczi, un pionnier de la clinique*. Paris: Éditions Campagne Première.

Safouan, M. (2013). *La Psychanalyse, science, thérapie – et cause*. Paris: Thierry Marchaise.

Chapter 4

From Lacan to Ferenczi

Michael Larivière

We have all heard the shrill debates that have accompanied the development of psychoanalysis since its beginning. Indeed, the controversies raging around its major ideas never seem to wane. And so there is an understandable reluctance on the part of psychoanalysts to speak simply and freely about what they actually do in the secrecy of their consultation rooms, about what kind of pleasure they derive from their work, or about how they came to choose this very particular way of life.

What I hope to do in the pages that follow is to tell the story of how I first came to psychoanalysis in its Lacanian version, and how I then moved away from that version after having become more familiar with other analysts' legacies, all of whom, whether French, British, or American, had been profoundly influenced by Ferenczi's work. That I should choose to tell a story means that what I don't want to do is to embark on a theoretical discussion of what it might mean to choose such a way of life. All I wish to do is to recount what it was that made sense to me and brought me where I am today, first and foremost by setting it against what didn't make sense to me. But why want to tell such a story? I am not quite sure – and perhaps it will be in the telling itself that I will come to discover the more or less hidden reasons for wanting to tell it. For the moment, let me just say this: it is certainly in part because I often (not always, of course) find theoretical discussions to be elaborately unrewarding; and it certainly is *not* because I feel psychoanalysis needs to be defended, nor is it because I would need, as one of its would-be representatives, to defend my corner: psychoanalysis never was for me a cause to defend. Freud bashing neither interests nor worries me; I even find its snobbery (for it does have a snobbery) rather touching.

So, again, why want to tell such a story? Perhaps to see more clearly what makes this way of life worth having. This is something that is virtually never talked about in psychoanalytic literature: what kinds of pleasure do analysts derive from doing what they do and living as they live? What is it exactly that they enjoy? Simply put: why do they do this? What does it earn them, what are they interested in getting from it? These (and many others) are questions about which, as we know, conjecture is rife but about which very little is said. Might it be that these are questions that play on analysts' deepest resistances? Perhaps – but it is not for me to say about others, it is for others to say about themselves. And anyway, resistance (in and out of analysis) never comes to the ball as Resistance. It comes dressed as something else: Prudence, Wariness, High Standards, Necessary Discretion, even Common Sense. For analysts, one should never forget, are read by their analysands, and so they tend to refrain from revealing too much about themselves for fear it might compromise the work people do with them. But the truth of the matter is that all analysts, and this not surprisingly, have a novel in them. After all, they spend much of their time listening to stories and then talking and writing about them. But the problem is, in my view, that instead of writing prose narrations about the stories their patients tell them, what they feel they have to do is to produce theoretical essays they hope will make psychoanalytical sense of them. In other words, instead of allowing themselves to write the novel they have in them, analysts write memoirs. Well, to each his own. I happen to think that they should write with less artifice, or with artifice of a different kind – but perhaps this is just pampered intolerance on my part. At any rate, I will not, as I said, offer here yet another theoretical discussion. Nothing abstract. I will try and tell a story. But before I start telling that story, I need to preface it with two precautionary remarks: one, I believe that one of the most important lessons psychoanalysis teaches us is that we should always question the very possibility and value of biographical truth, i.e., the credibility of any discernible continuity or pattern in a given life. And two, it is my contention that we rarely know what we are doing as we are doing it – for example, when telling our story.

And so: where to begin? Where to begin with oneself? Where, in other words, do I begin?

This is the question every analysand who couldn't avoid becoming an analyst never stops asking: where do analysts come from? One way of answering that question is by saying something about the cultural and institutional context in which one's training and practice took – and, if it is the case, is still taking – place. So, let's see.

I have to begin by saying that if I can (and perhaps must) do this, it is because my father is dead. It's not that he is missing: it's that he is out of the way. As for my mother, she is demented (ill with Alzheimer's), so she is out of the way as well. And I always knew that I would have to revisit my story once I would be sure that they would be once and for all, as it were, securely out of earshot. It may even be that one can only truly revisit one's story when one's parents are gone – one way or another. How is it for you, dear reader? It isn't about setting the record straight, I don't think; it's more about wanting to protect them, thus sparing oneself the guilt of hurting them with the telling of the fiction we consider to be the Truth.

Martin Amis is right: "We live in the age of mass loquacity. We are all writing it or at any rate talking it: the memoir, the apologia, the c.v., the *cri de* [sic] *coeur*" (2001, 6).

Might it be that we only ever live to have a story to tell? Or that we know we are alive only if we tell the story of the experience that was ours? I don't know. It might even be that the stories we tell only tell of what it is we would have wanted to experience but never quite managed. The stories we tell perhaps always tell of what was missing in the experience we had, hence are always both ironic and sorrowful. Perhaps the stories we tell never actually get to the point, always going *around* the experience we try to recount. Julian Barnes said something along those lines somewhere. At any rate, I am a psychoanalyst, trained to use stories (including my own) for ends they couldn't always foresee. And since the object of psychoanalysis is the place in the unconscious where these stories come from, i.e., the infantile and the sexual, the question of its own unconscious origin should indeed be returned: in what ways are the sexual and the infantile at play in the practice, the theory, the training of analysts (again myself included, of course)? This is a question someone like Sándor Ferenczi wouldn't have shunned. By this I don't mean to say that we should attempt to analyze analysis: not only would this be absurd, it would be trying to make too much sense. And, as Adam Phillips (1996, 87) in my opinion very rightly suggests: "When psychoanalysis makes too much sense, or makes sense of too much, it turns into exactly the symptom it is trying to cure: defensive knowingness."

Furthermore, we need to remember that no one can be one's own analyst (in my opinion, not even Freud), nor can one be the theoretician of one's own analysis (as Lacanians still believe every analyst should be, and this in spite of Lacan's admission that he had been wrong in thinking this might be possible). It is even terribly difficult, it seems to me, when talking about one's analysis, to do so in what singers call a *true voice.* This is not to say that one can't say anything at all, or that what one says should necessarily be regarded as spurious. But talking about one's analysis, as I will be doing here, is always difficult, if only because most times very little is remembered: the atmosphere in the room, the analyst's physicality, his attitude, his voice, the decor, how the couch felt, a few words – almost nothing, considering the hundreds (if not thousands) of hours spent on the couch. So, when talking about one's analysis one should, I believe, make one's own the painter Antoni Tàpies' advice to artists: do not try to explain.

So this is where I shall begin: with the questioning of biographical truth.

One of the things Lacan wrote urgently about is the idea that because we are born into language we are born alienated from ourselves. I agree. And it is because we are at once inescapably semantic, and therefore alienated, that we are vulnerable to all forms of neurosis and madness. Between me and myself, there is as insuperable a gap as there is between myself and others. In other words, I have no more an *immediate* access to myself than I do to anything else. To paraphrase Oscar Wilde, between me and myself, as well as between me and the world, there is a mist of words, always. Or, as George Steiner writes: "The Cartesian *ego sum* finesses an inherent uncertainty. It is a boast rather than a self-evident truth" (2008, 93).

The relations I have to my identity are opaque, stressful, replete with all kinds of ambiguities. Neither my name nor my origins, or my place in my family's history, guarantees real substance or certainty. To the contrary: all of this perplexingly banishes me from myself. Which is why we look up to others – first as children to our parents, later on to all kinds of tutelary figures – in the hope of finding reassurance as to who we are, might be, or could become. The Jewish master, Freud, referred to this as the *Ichspaltung*, the division, cleavage, split in/of the self. And perhaps it had to be a Jew who exposed this essential alienation, for, as again Steiner writes, "More, perhaps, than any other ethnic, social or indeed mythological type, the Jew can be a stranger to himself or herself. His famed wandering is the allegorical-empirical representation of a search, of an incessant peregrination inward. He or she is alien to himself, to herself, before being alien to others" (2008, 93).

At any rate, the tools I was unexpectedly given (for I was born into an almost illiterate family) to cope with this essential unhousedness and try and answer for myself were the tools of literacy: I was allowed, encouraged even, to enroll in what was then known as Classical Studies. And, to my great surprise, I found a home in the exile these studies provided. A home without domestication. As was revealed to me the delight in what Charles Péguy called *la terrifiante responsabilité de lire* (the terrifying responsibility of reading), I felt I was given a measureless privilege. This is where I have since been coming from; this is where, to this day, I feel I was at last *humanly* born. For it was then and there, in that discourse of our answerability to what is written, that I got the first inkling of what an early companion of Lacan's once referred to as the *poetic price* of living, i.e., the very simple, brutal fact that our inescapably linguistic existence promises, in the radical sense of the term, a forever *restless* existence.

First it was literature, then philosophy.

For years I sat in the shade of their monuments, acquiring a very private, very intense language. A language incomprehensible to those who pretended to have nurtured me. Nothing gave me greater joy than keeping out of things, alone with a book. The joy of separation. Silent ecstasies.

Of course, those years didn't bring me only joy; they were difficult years. Coming from that almost illiterate family, how was I to embrace the unbounded charge of cultural, intellectual, literary, scientific riches I was suddenly met with? The rules of their usage were incomprehensible; each attempt at making those riches mine was a leap in the dark – and for good reason: as I was later to understand, it was the very rules of reality that had been altered. Insoluble possibilities (Kierkegaard spoke of the *wounds* of possibilities) had been forced onto me. I became obsessed – and "intellectual obsession", as Steiner writes, "is a cancer of aloneness."

But a day came when I realized that I had merely been trying to get a foothold on absence. That I had spent years looking for a counterweight to evils older than myself, the existence of which I had never even suspected. Childhood revealed itself for what it was: a heritage of incurable wounds. Hence my life very soon derived from the books I read. Books were my decoys. They enabled me to escape the family community, the gangs children formed; at a later age they enabled me to escape even the most elementary aggregations, even the friendly, even the loving.

Years passed.

And one morning, a Philosophy professor arrived in class carrying two books. "Read this," he said as he put them down on my desk, "it's for you." This was 1967. The books were Jacques Derrida's *L'Écriture et la différence* (*Writing and Difference*) and Jacques Lacan's *Écrits* (*Writings*), both of which having just recently been published. The tragic twins of psychoanalysis, as I would later come to refer to them.

I read both books – and that was it. I felt enthused, galvanized, inspired, enlivened. Both (but Derrida's book more so than Lacan's, I must say) touched on the raw. I was reminded of Kafka's judgment: no book that doesn't hit you like an ax, that doesn't crack the frozen sea inside you is worth reading. And that is exactly what they did: they broke something in me. It was the writing itself, the way each used language, that had as vivid and disturbing an impact on me as did the theoretical contents of the books. Both would map the terrain of almost all my future work. I had discovered models of consciousness that put language at its center and made patent the detergent emptiness of all marketplace psychological (or would-be psychoanalytical) parlance. Derrida and Lacan restored a vital genius of innovation and truth to our reading of many classics, one of which is of particular interest to us: Freud. Something immensely destructive had happened to Freudian studies (perhaps especially in the United States); Derrida and Lacan re-enlivened them. They forced in us a conversion in our ways of questioning. They brought in the question of the very possibility of any verifiable "final sense." "Meaning"was shown to be a play of interpretative possibilities. No text, no theory, no author (themselves included, of course) could any longer aspire to the privilege of Truth. They told of an epilogue in our culture. Each in his own way re-examined the notions of subject and subjectivity, of identification and identity, aiming at deconstructing (although Lacan would not use that word) the fantasies of authority, mastery, and identity. What they both stressed is that identity is the product, or the creation, of language; that identity is, in the Latin sense of the word, *a fiction*. Which is why we all have issues with authenticity. We are all afflicted with authenticity problems – if by authenticity we understand at once the purity and incontestability of provenance, birth, and authority.[1] For we have no choice but to come to terms with the fundamental inability of language to make itself transparent to itself. It isn't, as Steiner often suggests, that language has lost the capacity for truth; it is that language never could but operate, self-doubtingly, on the sharp edge of silence: Hofmannsthal, Kafka, Wittgenstein, Karl Krauss, Canetti, Heidegger, Celan, Mandelstam, to name a few, all speak to and of the impossibility of telling the whole truth and nothing but the truth – something, as I had expanded upon in an earlier paper (Larivière 2006), Lacan would later (but without any mention of these authors) insist upon. And this is how Derrida and Lacan restored to philosophy, literary studies, humanities, and psychoanalysis a lost passion, a lost intellectual challenge. This is why their voices were immediately unmistakable. And this is why they immediately spoke to me. For all these authenticity issues were very much my own – and I now had a language in which to articulate them.

But something else also happened.

That same Philosophy professor advised me to leave for France, where he felt I would have a better chance of finding the kind of cultural, intellectual environment he thought would better suit me. I would soon follow his advice, but during the year prior to my departure, as I had developed a keen interest for psychoanalysis while reading those books, I contacted a training analyst from the International Psychoanalytic Association (IPA). I had naively thought that he should be only too happy to tell me how and why he had chosen this way of life, what it meant for him to be an analyst, etc. Well, he wasn't. What happened instead was that he turned his analytical ear to me and questioned my "need" to put such "indiscreet" questions to him. I didn't understand his defensive attitude. How was I being indiscreet? Was I asking him to reveal something terribly intimate? Were my questions in some way threatening? Was I in some unconscious way trying to steal the forbidden truth? I told him that I truly didn't understand his resistance, that I couldn't see what it was I was touching upon that was so sacrosanct it shouldn't even be approached. This only made matters worse. He told me that I should ask myself whether I wasn't in actual fact there to seek analytical "treatment" (that was the term he used). Amused (as much as annoyed), I asked him to explain what exactly this might entail. When he told me (so many weekly sessions at a price that seemed astronomical to the very young man I was), I asked him why on earth he wanted that much money for the "treatment" he was suggesting I needed. His answer, honest as it was, left me speechless: he needed that money in order to maintain the standard of living he had chosen for himself. "Then go be a movie star!" I wanted to tell him (but didn't). He also asked me what had got me interested in psychoanalysis. When I told him it was Derrida and Lacan, he frowned. "Derrida is not an analyst, and Lacan is a fraud," was his answer. I had heard enough. I knew I could never learn to accept such abysmal stupidity. The man had just proven Lacan right: psychoanalysis might be able to do something for dishonesty, but it couldn't do anything for imbecility. I knew then, if only intuitively, that the analyst, much like the literary critic, is not a man to stay in his own garden: if I may risk a pastiche, chauvinism has already cried havoc in politics; it has no place in psychoanalysis.

All this took place in June 1972. Three months later, I was in Strasbourg. I was about to turn 23.

Two other professors, both friends of Derrida's, finished turning my life around: Philippe Lacoue-Labarthe and Jean-Luc Nancy. Their teaching was unparalleled. One of the things they taught me was that we are read by the books we read; that is why we are answerable to them, much in the same way that we are answerable, as analysts, to the stories we listen to. The words we read, the words we listen to take hold of the place we strive to make ours. I read, I write, and I listen for reasons very similar: because I need to reflect on the place those words occupy in me, on what they do in my stead. What I came to think as I sat in their classes, as I read the works they commented on, was that analysis and reading shared a common goal: to welcome, to accommodate, to make room for, and to carry through one language the foreignness of another. To try and disturb, unsettle each language so that *between* them, in some undefined, undecidable space, there might emerge a new and real freedom of speech. The critic Geoffrey

Hartman wrote somewhere – I quote from memory, I can't remember where he says this (in *A Scholar's Tale* perhaps, or in *A Critic's Journey?*) – that "there is something radically strange in the language of others." I would say: not only in the language of others; there is something radically strange, foreign, in the language one calls one's own. And reading, writing, and analysis should be efforts at trying to confront that strangeness and learn to live with it. But at that particular time, I had been, since childhood, limiting my efforts to reading and writing (and, as for the writing, it had been limited to two things: pastiches and translating). So a day came when I realized that I had spent those years waiting for something I couldn't identify, sitting, as it were, on usurped chairs, gathering the ashes of spent lives. This no longer was enough. I knew the time had come for me to take different risks: it was time for analysis.

So the time had come – but where to go? I was new in town, I knew no one, or of no one, and if truth be told I wasn't even sure I knew exactly what it was I was looking for. The only thing that was relatively clear to me was that most analysts here were Lacanians. So, as I was coming out of class at university one afternoon, a Linguistics professor I very much appreciated passed by me in the corridor; he taught a course on Lacan and Saussure. I stopped him and asked if he might recommend a good analyst. He readily obliged. Now that I had a name, I needed to make arrangements to get the money; this took several months, but I finally managed.

As I didn't have a phone (they were a relatively rare commodity at the time in France), I went directly to his office to make an appointment. It was situated in a quiet, *haut bourgeois* street near the canal. The pale-stone building dated back to the late nineteenth century. The entrance hall was faintly lit; a wide wooden stairway, curving to the right, led to the *piano nobile.* On the door was a small brass plate: *Entrez sans sonner* ("Enter without ringing"). I entered. No sooner had I taken place in the waiting room than a gnome-like figure erupted from a side door, looking cross, an appointment book in hand. "I don't have time!" was how he greeted me. I burst out laughing and told him I was only there to make an appointment. He wouldn't even do that: "Come back in September [this was July] and we shall see," and he promptly disappeared through the same door.

The poor welcome I was given left me feeling rather confused. And disappointed. Why wasn't this man more courteous? I wondered. I remember walking along the canal for a while, in two minds as to whether I would go back in September, or go see someone else. But the prospect of going back to that professor to explain what had happened and ask for someone else's name was, for some reason, disheartening. So I decided to give the man another chance.

When September came around, I went back. This time he was more affable. We talked for about twenty minutes and decided that the analysis could begin. It lasted for a little over five years, three sessions per week. I will come back later to how things went during that first experience.

Shortly after having started the analysis, I also started to assiduously frequent the analytical milieu, and with this frequentation the project of doing this for a living was formed. Of course, I had no idea as to how to go about getting a proper training. So I asked my analyst if he might have any suggestion as to ... where to begin. I did what I was told: I joined groups, workshops, seminars, presented papers, published some of them, etc. This went on for several years.

At first, I was somewhat intimidated by many of the people I met, but I rapidly grew disillusioned. Indeed, what they wrote and said about both their practice and the texts they studied, by comparison with what the philosophers and writers I had the privilege of working with offered, seemed muddled and, I must say, fenced in, short of breath. Also, the mimicry pervading in the milieu made me wary. Why, I wondered, did most of these people need to imitate all of Lacan's mannerisms? Not only did they strive to imitate his amphigoric style of writing, they imitated his delivery, developed the same tics, wore the same type of clothes, smoked the same Culebra cigars. In the end, from wary that I was, I simply grew weary. But what could I do? I felt trapped: I wanted this way of life (or, rather, the way of life I imagined analysts had) and couldn't yet imagine practicing analysis without belonging to their club. So I made an appointment with the Secretary of the *École freudienne de Paris*, the institution founded by Lacan in 1963. I told him I was considering becoming a member (I didn't talk about "applying for membership," which I later realized must have sounded terribly arrogant) but that I needed first to know more about the actual organization of the structure: what were their requirements, how did they go about recognizing someone as one of their own, how were they different from other institutes, etc. In other words, I naively (or arrogantly) thought that in the end I would be the one to decide whether or not I would become a member. He was, I must say, rather irritated. He simply, and rather curtly, told me that I would first have to make myself known *as an analyst* before they would decide whether to accept me as a member or not. In other words, I would first have to start seeing patients, on my own (there are no state laws regulating the practice in France), discuss my work with colleagues in groups, go into supervision if I felt I needed to, present and publish papers – and they would see. And that is exactly what I did – except that I rapidly changed my mind about joining their guild. For I found the deluge of commentary and would-be exegesis they poured out (mostly of Lacan's texts) to be, for the most part, hollow. They just seemed to be trying very hard to prove that they spoke Lacanian fluently (then again, as I was to quickly realize, all analytical institutes are, first and foremost, language schools). Their persuasions and quarrels had a very public role, as each looked upon herself or himself as an arbitrator of Lacanian orthodoxy. I didn't particularly appreciate the dour and rigid guise that orthodoxy assumed. I was disappointed, yes, but above all I was bored. The pattern was one of desperate monotony: interminable discussions as to whether this article or that book was in accord with the school's doxa. As Adam Phillips writes:

> Psychoanalysis ... teaches us that we don't often know what we are saying ... No amount of scientific research will diminish the waywardness of our words: there will always be the clamor of the incongruous ... When psychoanalysts spend too much time with each other, they start believing in psychoanalysis. They begin to talk knowingly, like members of a religious cult. It is as if they have understood something. They forget, in other words, that they are only telling stories about other stories; and that all stories are subject to an unknowable multiplicity of interpretations ... When psychoanalysis is not the means to a personal style, it merely hypnotizes people with a vocabulary.
>
> (1996b, xvi–vxii)

Adam Phillips and I met in London in October 2003, at my request. We talked about many things, one of which was how difficult it sometimes is knowing who to recommend when we are asked for the name of an analyst. How do we choose those to whom we refer people? What are the criteria? Competence (but how exactly do we know?)? Scholarship? Experience? Hearsay? Reputation? Notoriety? Publications? All of these things, surely, play a role – but only to a very limited extent. As for the analyst's affiliation to this or that group or institution, it plays no part at all (except, perhaps, in a negative way). So, how do we choose? I told him that the deciding factor for me was a capacity to care – which I rarely found amongst Lacanians. Masud Khan (who was Phillips' analyst) talked about taking people into "therapeutic care." "Yes," said Phillips, "it's a question of kindness." Now, kindness is not an analytical concept, it is not taught in analytical institutes, it can't be learned – any more than integrity, sensitivity, rigor, or honesty for example. All this to say that we base our choices, in my opinion, on the sole representation that we have of the analyst we trust, whether it be for ourselves or for someone else. The criteria are impossible to determine objectively, and they have very little to do, if anything at all, with anything "analytical." To use a term linguists use when talking about the instinctive way in which one knows what is right or wrong when speaking one's own language, even without knowing the rules of its grammar, it is a matter of *feeling* or *sentiment*. We *sense* (we think we know) who is, and who isn't, an analyst. It isn't even certain we ever know exactly how it was that we came to believe that this or that person indeed qualifies as an analyst, or even precisely what it is we mean by the word.

What I believe is that we recognize as analyst, that we *take to be* analyst, the person to whom and with whom we feel comfortable enough to talk, full stop. In a way, transference is there before the analyst is even met. Someone says that they are an analyst? So be it: it's their business. What remains to be seen is whether or not I want to talk to her or him. There will be time to see during the analysis if the impression was founded. If I am not comfortable enough with that person, then whatever their competence may be, their rigor, honesty, whatever their qualities, it will be useless to insist. In the end, one chooses an analyst much in the same way one chooses a friend or a lover: in total ignorance of the stakes that will only after the fact come to be revealed. And as for the analysts, only those who do not desperately cling to their theories will be able to tolerate not knowing, will let themselves be affected by the very singular experience of truly engaging with someone. For in the transitional space we refer to as the "analytic setting," reference to theory, whether it be by the analyst or the analysand, is always a resistance to what is threatening to take place. And it was their constant reference to theory, their inability to say anything in their own voice, that I found stultifying with the Lacanians. All they were interested in, it seemed to me, was speaking this new language in order to secure their acceptance in the magical circle of their newfound family. If certain members of the community demonstrated admirable intellectual rigor, the vast majority was capable only of a dogmatic rigidity intolerant of any real questioning. This being said, it must be stressed that Lacanians are in no way exceptional in this respect: the whole of the so-called analytic "community" is held together less by a common exposure to the unconscious than by a fascinated allegiance to Great Analysts – Freud, Jung, Klein, Ferenczi, Lacan, etc. – who are seen as leaders or guides. What prevails in all analytic institutions is identification with the Analyst. And this is what Lacan had hoped to change. Psychoanalysis, in his eyes, needed to be, as it were, readjusted to itself, it needed to relinquish the orthopedic function it had come to fulfill after its exile in America. His theory (for want of a better word) was based on a reading, similar to that of Melanie Klein's, of Freud's second topic: the ego (*das Ich*) should in no way be seen as the product or the result of a progressive differentiation from the id (*das Es*), as a representative of reality whose function would be to contain, as well as to maintain the individual's drives. To the contrary: Lacan thought that there is no such thing as an autonomous ego. The ego, he thought, is not the agent of adaptation of the individual to reality: it is an instance, progressively structured through the borrowing of different *imagos*. Lacan, in other words, in re-examining the notion of identification, defining it not in terms of the constitution of any definitive identity but, rather, in terms of a process seen as interminable, aimed at fundamentally deconstructing the fantasies of authority, mastery, and identity. What Lacan stressed, as I said before, was that identity is the product, or the creation, of language: that it is, literally (i.e., in the Latin sense of the word) a *fiction*. And in so doing, it is the analyst himself that he dragged onto a scene where he is no longer the master: it is the analyst's very authority (*auctoritas*) that Lacan called into question. But asking analysts to acknowledge this as both the paradoxical condition of possibility and the self-subversive blind spot of their very being and thinking was asking too much. It was asking them to question their transferential relation to power and knowledge, as well as the uses thereof. How indeed could they have questioned a theory that guaranteed them so many advantages – "therapeutic," perhaps, but more to the point professional and financial? And how could they have reassessed their notion of transference when that particular transference had long been carefully set up, preserved, perpetuated in and by the institution itself? And indeed they didn't.

What they did instead was, they joined his *École* in an act of denial, a denial of almost everything he stood for – politically, theoretically, and even clinically. Indeed, the vast majority of Lacan's followers simply could not take in, could not *read* what he had nevertheless very clearly stated: that it was owing to the distortion of Freud's concepts by the International Psychoanalytic Association (IPA) that psychoanalysis had managed to survive *as a movement*. This, in my opinion, is an absolutely central issue that, to my knowledge, has never been raised by any of Lacan's disciples or readers – and not by chance. For if one is to follow Lacan's interpretation of Freud's decision to found the IPA, then one is forced to ask oneself why Lacan chose to repeat the operation. Why indeed did he choose to engage his troops on a path he himself had declared could only lead to failure? There is an unresolved paradox here: why did Lacan, after having clearly and strongly stated in 1957 that it was owing to the IPA's failure to understand Freud's concepts that psychoanalysis was kept alive, decide six years later to re-engage his disciples on a track he could only know would inevitably lead to the same misunderstanding? Was he hoping against hope? Was he banking on his disciples' better judgment? On their capacity to relate differently to authority? On his own capacity to rescue them from the kind of submission to ideals Freud's disciples had succumbed to? I doubt he was that naive. Lacan, who had read Kant, knew only too well that no institution had ever enabled psychoanalysis to delimit or delineate its own domain (*ditio*), field, territory (*territorium*), or domicile (*domicilium*). He knew only too well that psychoanalysis could not of itself establish its own legitimacy, produce its own concept (as well as the discourse on what that concept would in turn make possible), that it could not introduce itself on its own terms into the field that should contain it. And he knew only too well that no institution could ever preserve the essence of psychoanalysis.

It is this very issue of the legitimacy, or legitimation, of psychoanalysis that Lacan wanted analysts to come to terms with. His reasoning was the following: it was not by chance that the IPA was formed when it was formed – that is, in 1912. Indeed, psychoanalysis at that point in time had come to realize that it needed to expose itself, to open itself up to what largely exceeded the limits of its habitual field of inquiry. That is why Freud had asked Otto Rank and Hans Sachs, through the creation of the journal *Imago*, to encourage, to promote, indeed to instigate, research in the field of what was to be known as *applied psychoanalysis.* This was not anecdotal. Freud, in acknowledging the necessity for psychoanalysis to be aware of what exceeded the limits of its would-be "proper"field of inquiry, was in fact acknowledging the necessity for psychoanalysis to ask itself where exactly its limits lay. In other words, Freud was telling his followers that the time had come for psychoanalysis to *acknowledge the uncertainty of its own identity.* This is something Lacan never ceased to remind us of: psychoanalysis never was and cannot ever hope to be assured of its legitimacy, it will never be safe and sound within the clear and solid limits of its "proper"field. This is not without very real, practical (political as well as clinical) consequences. And that is why the IPA was founded.

Hence, not only is the problem of the institutional grounding of psychoanalysis indissociable from that of its identification, it may even, with hindsight, be understood as the more or less conscious acknowledgment of the necessity, for psychoanalysis itself, of calling its very possibility into question. My point is that, ever since Freud's acceptance of the necessity of entrenching psychoanalysis in an institution whose function would be to provide it with international grounding and recognition, psychoanalysis *knows and doesn't (want to) know* that it must give up the hope of ever being sure of its own conceptual consistency. In other words, Freud, through the institutional grounding of psychoanalysis, aimed at enabling it to, as it were, recover from the realization of the impossibility of inhering, of coming together in the organic or logical unity of one concept.

And yet, in spite of having done all he could to demonstrate, by making manifest how illusory all hopes of everlasting institutional entrenchment are, that Freud's effort at laying the institutional foundations of psychoanalysis was both inimitable and, therefore, impossible to repeat; and further, that the very possibility, the very viability of psychoanalysis is predicated upon the acknowledgment of that double impossibility, Lacan chose to do it all over.

As if he couldn't take responsibility for what he thought, for what he knew. Which begs the question – the only question that matters when it comes to these problems, paradoxes, and contradictions: to what inevitable denial did Freud's decision to give institutional grounding to psychoanalysis lead? What denial can the analytical movement only reiterate in order for the institution – and its members – to keep believing in its own necessity? The answer is obvious: what needs to be "forgotten" (and *is* indeed forgotten) is that, through his discovery of the unconscious, Freud did away with the classical (i.e., philosophical) concept of conscience – and it is precisely that notion of conscience the institution clings to.

And, to get back to what I had started discussing, these were the issues I was most sensitive to. Psychoanalysis (the theory, at least …) told me that my very identity was unclaimable – but it also offered a way of dealing with this loss. It even offered a way of earning one's living (an idiom that deserves to be thought about closely) while dealing with the impossibility of claiming one's identity. A miracle of sorts.

One might ask: is it a failure, choosing such a way? I don't think so – but what, after all, do I know? For I haven't forgotten Lacan's warning: wanting to become an analyst is a symptom. Indeed, this choice, this wish, very often is a wish to hold onto a fantasy that was being compromised by the analytical work itself (unless, of course, one has embarked upon that very particular journey referred to as a "training analysis," i.e., a journey that promises to fulfill the fantasy …). And, as Freud reminds us, the closer one gets to the neurotic kernel, the stronger the resistance and the symptoms grow.

In my opinion, Alice Miller (1981) was right in suggesting that it is always a personal drama that leads one to choose to earn one's living this way. And it is therefore that person's duty to try and keep in touch, as Ferenczi had understood, with both the child and the madness still alive in him or her. It is that person's duty not to shirk the questions that imperil his or her narcissism. And this, as we all know, is a rather tall order. One needs only to frequent (even if only briefly) the milieu to see how terribly right Joyce McDougall was to say that analysts are fragile, narcissistic, neurotic. That they are fascinated by the Analyst. Indeed, the didactics of the unconscious are, essentially, an *ars mimetica:* as a contender to the position of "analyst," one is inevitably referred back to the first analytical "model" – that is, to the "autoanalyst" himself. Which explains why the history of psychoanalysis reads like a perpetual imitation of Sigmund Freud, with all the appropriation and fratricidal rivalry consequences to which we have thenceforth been accustomed. In becoming an analyst, like it or not, acknowledge it or not, one in some way inevitably claims to be representative of the Freudian "doctrine" or "truth" – under whichever guise one chooses to represent it: Freudian, Kleinian, Ferenczian, Lacanian, Modern, Intersubjective, Relational, etc. One, at the very least, involves the memory of Freud, one uses Freud's name. But we must ask: what if Freud himself had claimed to be an analyst by identifying with "himself"? As long as we refuse to pursue our reflection on identification up to the point where the very model itself is seen for the fiction that it is, we will not have effectively departed from the classical notion of conscience. As long as we refuse to acknowledge that Freud's descent – to use a dated word – real or mythical, is still more or less held together only through this sustained mimetic endeavor, we will be resisting what psychoanalysis is about. Why this refusal? Because no analyst is ever quite sure where his competence lies. Or, rather, this is something he knows in theoretical terms. Admittedly, he can sometimes feel that he is indeed in the right place doing what he is doing; that he is doing a proper job; that he knows what he is doing. But there is no escaping the perplexing feeling that he is living on borrowed time: a day will come, surely, when he is found out. What I mean by this is that the analyst is in no better position than anyone else when it comes to claiming his identity. And this isn't any easier for him than it is for anyone else. That is why analysts write, present papers, publish (as well as for all the other narcissistic and mercantile reasons to do so). Being unable to claim their identity may even, for some of us, be more difficult than it is for some of those to whom we offer our services. I would even venture that many become analysts because they were incapable of getting on with, and completing, their analysis. For, as we all know, one of the best ways of resisting something, paradoxical as it may seem, is to not give it up. Hence the need for institutions.

Institutional belonging is a coverup for our unverifiable identity. As are titles. Why else would analysts need to be classified as M.D.s or Ph.D.s? Why isn't it enough to refer to oneself as analyst? This is an issue Freud himself had a difficult time coming to terms with: read his *Selbstdarstellung.* Titles are makeshift identities some analysts need in order to convince themselves (and others, first and foremost their prospective clients) that they are not charlatans. Analysts need institutions to give them letters patent of, if not nobility (let's not exaggerate), at least credibility. As if belonging to an institution were the only way of convincing themselves that what they had committed themselves to was not merely shamanism or romance.

I owe my inability to adhere to such beliefs to my teachers of literature and philosophy. To paraphrase George Steiner, I carry with me a vision of schools of creative reading for psychoanalysis ("school" is far too pretentious a word: a quiet room and a table will do), where we would have to begin at the simplest, and therefore most exacting, level of integrity. Where we would have to wake the numbed muscles of memory, to rediscover in our quite ordinary selves the enormous resources of precise recollection, and the delight that comes of the texts that have secure lodging within us.

What was prevalent in the various groups and seminars I joined (and formed myself) in the *École freudienne de Paris* was vulgarization and loud vacancies of intellect on the one hand, and maddening arcane language trying to hide the near-dyslexia of their reading habits on the other. There were exceptions, of course: some of the analysts who worked there were amongst the most remarkable I have ever met – but those almost all eventually distanced themselves from Lacan's school. Still, I kept with it, for my need to belong was such that I learned all the ropes, spoke the language, and, worse, practiced analysis as I had been taught by my first two analysts, who had both been analysands of one of the guardians of the Lacanian temple, Mustapha Safouan, a brilliant theoretician (but of the fundamentalist kind – at the time at least), a sort of sherif of the Lacanian village.

During each of these analyses, I was left very much on my own; neither one of my analysts hardly spoke a word during the entire length of the time I spent on their couches, not even when I decided to put an end to the work I did with them. But it was only several years later that I was able to take the real and full measure of that solitude, when

I consulted someone who had not been born to the Lacanian fold. This was Joyce McDougall.

The first thing I told her, after having recounted how things had gone with my two previous analysts, was that I needed her to say what she thought as she listened to me, and let me deal with it. I was there, I told her, to run the risk of engaging with someone who would reciprocate. If she felt this was an unacceptable request, she needed only to let me know, and I would go elsewhere. For I had made the same request to my second analyst, who had responded that what I was asking of him was to free-associate – in other words, to play the analysand. Clearly, in his eyes, my request was the expression of a massive resistance. I disagreed but stayed on, thinking he might be right. He wasn't. Anyway, McDougall agreed, so we began. And at last analysis happened.

When I told this story to Adam Phillips, he commented that surely a Lacanian analysis must be a very interesting experience, perhaps even a useful one – on the condition of either having beforehand done an object-relation-oriented analysis, or of having had a good enough mother; otherwise, the experience could only be alienating. Well, having had neither, I couldn't agree more.

My first two analysts did nothing, said nothing to help clarify the obscure desperation in which I was entrapped. I had lived so many years in hiding, with books, in the hope of finding some happiness, of finding at last what childhood had refused me. In vain, of course: no one ever escapes on one's own the culture one's family imposes. That culture then remains the model for all the relationships one later feels forced to form. For one never moves away with impunity from the narrow perimeter to which one's world had long been limited. One can rapidly be overwhelmed by a feeling of tragic helplessness, having to endure oneself much in the same way one sometimes has to endure trying circumstances, to the point of exhaustion. One then finds oneself living out one's story as if it were someone else's, suddenly, inexplicably disjointed. And this is what neither of my two first analysts ever understood, or sensed, far more preoccupied were they with conforming to what they understood as being the analytic dogma of their school – pay no attention to symptoms! – than with engaging with their rather desolate patient. They were, like most Lacanian analysts of that time, mimeticians who aped their idol's language and scarcely ever uttered anything worth listening to.

Someone who, as it was the case for me, has no real bearings, who lives, if you will allow me the neologism, in an identificatory void, in what Bettelheim called an "unthinkable anxiety," who does not know what he is made of, whose name names a stranger; someone, in other words, who is inwardly exiled, will only ever have a chance of repairing if he is not left on his own to revisit his story. Analysis is a space where anxiety should be held so that the unthinkable can have a chance of being thought, and the breach in the existential continuity with others a chance of being repaired. But, again, this can happen only if there is someone there who, like Ferenczi, has remained in touch with the child still very much alive in him.

Epilogue

I hope you will not find it improper of me to end this chapter with a few words about how the work I did with Joyce McDougall restored me, to use Samuel Beckett's words, to the feasible. But before I go into this, let me say a few words about who she was and how she saw psychoanalysis.

She came to London from New Zealand in 1949 – i.e., shortly after the Controversial Discussions which had opposed the Freudians and the Kleinians – to pursue her psychoanalytical training with John Pratt and Donald Woods Winnicott, both belonging to the Middle Group, profoundly influenced by Ferenczi. She made significant contributions to the understanding of perversions – but preferred using the term "neosexualities" (1995) – psychosomatic symptoms, female sexuality, creativity, and addictions. It was her clinical insights as much as her theoretical originality, open-mindedness, and lack of dogmatism that made her unique throughout her sixty-year career and enabled her to create a valuable link connecting the Anglo-Saxon (British and American) and French (Freudian and Lacanian) traditions. She is considered by many in France to be one of Ferenczi's main legatees.

She believed psychoanalysis – the theory and the practice – should offer a space where, having started from an uncompromising and plural erogenous capacity, it becomes possible to question the ways in which we almost inevitably arrive at the narrow sexual alternative we are told is the norm, thenceforth obliged to be a "man" or "woman" in such and such a way. Psychoanalysis, she thought, should offer a space in which it will be possible to tell the story of the ascendancy, of the hold certain *norms of existence* have had on me. These norms of existence compose a sort of grammar of subjectivation: the ways in which I am myself with others. She referred to this as *normopathy* (1992). That is why she agreed with Lacan's definition of the unconscious as the "discourse of the Other," i.e., the very powerful, and forever active, ensemble of my earliest bonds to others, bonds all the more strong and vital as they introduced me to the world. These bonds are heavily charged with affects of all kinds – fear, love, anxiety, anger, hatred, etc. – which contaminate all the mutual holds people have on one another. Mutual, i.e. engaging those involved with one another in a total, if unconscious, reciprocal dependence – which of course doesn't mean that it will necessarily be exercised symmetrically. And this is one reason why "mutuality" in analysis is never exercised without the risk of unwittingly compounding the effacement of the evidences that put a destiny in chains – a risk she was very much aware of. She stressed the fact that these early bonds inevitably give way to misunderstandings; to the fundamental misunderstandings of any existence. It is indeed inevitable that one should find oneself at cross-purposes with those one loves, and it is on such occasions, which are at once dangerous and saving, that are revealed the cracks in the norms of existence we have, again unwittingly, made ours. Those cracks are more or less carefully sealed, usually with lies. It is when they begin to perceive how deadly those warping lies are that people come for analysis. So this begs the question: what is psychoanalysis? How does it work?

Her answer (1991) was that to do analytical work is to let otherness be, to let it happen that the voice of the other is heard and, in so doing, to give voice to whomever, unbeknownst to us, inhabits us: it is to lift the weight of silence, of forgetfulness and ignorance that make for the various kinds of ill-being we call neurosis, psychosis, perversion, etc. How is this done? What should the analyst do?

Her answer was that he should bring into play, by his very presence, i.e. by exposing himself to it, what we refer to as transference. That is his way of trying to give a chance to what I earlier called the "subjectivation" of those who consult him. In order to do this, in order to make it possible for someone to speak in her or in his own name and/or voice, it is of the utmost importance that the analyst allows for the unfurling to take place of the various types of mirrors, alienations, and reclusions in which the singularity of the analysand will now and again disappear. This implies not engaging in a "from you to me" type of relationship: above all, and this is his most difficult task, the analyst must, as it were, *sustain the absence* that will enable the analysand to address the proper interlocutor. In other words, it is important to remember that there are always at least three characters involved in analysis, that the analyst and analysand are never alone together. Analysis never was and never will be a two-body, or two-person, psychology: the structure is ternary, not binary. No analysis is possible if the setting reproduces the maternal, dual model.

And so it was with her that I came to understand that childhood is the fire that language aims to put out. It was with her that I was able to make a mockery of (and see the mockery in) the belief in the necessity of imitative fidelity to exemplary lives. It was with her that I realized that the aesthetic exigency of resemblance never is but a melancholy response to the impossibility of merging with oneself. It was with her that I was able to see that the major illusion in life is the belief in one's "identity." And it was with her that I was able both to forgive and, more importantly if paradoxically, to forget myself.

One of the recurring issues during my work with her was fatherhood.

During the twenty years we had to live with – i.e. endure – one another, my father and I remained timorously installed in a terror as vain as it was exhausting, as ardent as it was secretive. Rage and shame were our arch passions. The spectacle of my father's anxiety distressed me. I knew very early on that I never would be able to bear his shyness, that our relationship would be reduced to fear, to a somber, funereal war, to absence and to idle chatter.

My father's lack of confidence, his self-distrust, his hopelessness, frightened me.

I never could let him know of my despair. I never could break the silence with which (I was told) he had first greeted my birth, and in which he had afterward continued to take refuge.

My father would get up every morning at the same time and on his own. He would immediately light a cigarette, then proceed to the bathroom to get ready for work. Thus began the silence in which he would confine himself for the rest of the day. Once ready, he would return to his wife's bedside, he would kiss her, wish her – without having the slightest notion of what that might resemble – a good day. He would then go down the narrow stairway that led to the garage and take place behind the wheel of his car to drive himself to the office.

I believe that the half-hour of solitude the drive afforded him each morning and evening was, in fact, a journey upstream. That, during that time, he would cease being the son, the husband, the father he had in spite (yes: in *spite)* of himself become, and would return to his secret, thus calling back to life the man he had constantly failed.

That he escaped his age.

I believe those early morning and evening drives were a funereal rite: the rebirth of the man he never could allow himself to be reaffirmed the death of the one he had become. I believe this funereal rite sheltered him from desire.

* * *

My father wore grey suits, or brown, or dark blue. His shirts were invariably white; his ties, which he thought to be daring, were merely gaudy. This dress code, as well as his haircut – clean at the nape and around the ears – had been imposed on him by his own father, and he had kept to it in spite of himself, in spite of the hatred he felt toward what he had been destined for. As a child already I would sometimes ridicule him by daring him to be adventurous and part his hair on the other side. My mean joke always deeply saddened me.

He never could free himself of the obligations that were a common feature of the kind of alienated filiation into which he was born. And, to make matters worse, his wife, my mother, would tell whomever was kind (or perverse) enough to lend an ear that he always was a reticent, and therefore disappointing, lover.

I was born out of that sexual deficiency. I am the fruit of that bitterness. The fruit of inaccessible love. Not surprisingly, the language I was born into was equally deficient. It was poor, unimaginative, spent. A dead language, and deadly. That is how I came to keep out of things, alone with the books thanks to which, little by little, I learned to, as it were, educate my sorrow, thus freeing myself from the terror I had been born into.

And that is the drama (as Alice Miller, as you will remember, calls it) that led me to where I am today. But it was also this drama, those years spent with that reticent father, as my friend Arnold Rachman very cleverly suggested to me, that explains – if not completely, at least to a large extent – how it was that I could later on endure my first two analysts' equally reticent attitudes.

The work with Joyce McDougall (whom I met thanks to the two first French Ferenczian analysts, Wladimir Granoff and Victor Smirnoff) enabled me to find a way of dissociating myself from that devastating past. Of overcoming the influence of archaic narratives that had long subjugated me. No longer am I haunted by the recurrent, obsessive fears inherited from childhood. And a day finally came when I realized that I had become less semantic; less interested in making sense of myself. The loss of this tyrannical interest enabled me to realize that, if nothing will ever make it so that what was wasn't, I no longer experienced this as tragic. A door was opened where none had been.

What triggered all this was a very old memory that had emerged shortly after having started the analysis. I was 10. Every morning during the winter months of that year, I would wake before dawn and go to church to attend the six o'clock Mass. Most days, the church would be empty. I would sit at the back, in a corner near the confessionals, where the light was weakest. I didn't pray; I didn't believe. I went because I was fascinated by the madness of faith, its delusional rituals, the pompous actor in costume who took himself to be his god's vicar, every morning repeating the same gestures and the same Latin words, convinced that what he was saying matched life's grandeur. I would leave at the moment of communion. I would return to the cold night and quickly walk back home, head in my shoulders, hands in my coat pockets, happy and reassured that I didn't belong. And it is much in the same state of mind that, years later, I would attend the High Masses that analysts hold, there again forced to accept that if I was to partake in their secular communion, it would have to be carrying a rather long spoon.

In the end, I turned away and started an itinerant life, working with people (individuals and small groups), in various countries, some affiliated, some not, but most of them indebted to the genius of Ferenczi, where thought has a far better chance of being made at once intimate and festive, a life I am still leading.

And that is where, and how, I keep beginning.

Note

1 I am reminded, as I write this, of something Albert Camus said about his novel *L'Étranger.* Meurseault, the main character, can be seen as someone afflicted with "the madness of authenticity." Someone, in other words, incapable of risking saying anything he wasn't absolutely certain of – first and foremost, his own feelings.

References

Amis, M. (2001). *Experience*. London: Vintage.

Larivière, M. (2006). *Institutional cloning: Mimetism in psychoanalytic training*. In *Power Games*, ed. Richard Raubolt. New York: Other Press, pp. XX–XX.

McDougall, J. (1989). *Theaters of the Body: A psychoanalytic approach to psychosomatic illnesses*. New York: W.W. Norton & Company.

McDougall, J. (1991). *Theaters of the Mind: Illusion and truth on the psychoanalytic stage.* London: Routledge.

McDougall, J. (1992). *Plea for a Measure of Abnormality.* New York: Brunner/Mazel.

McDougall, J. (1995). *The Many Faces of Eros: A psychoanalytic exploration of human sexuality.* New York: W.W. Norton & Company.

Miller, A. (1981). *Du sollst nicht merken*. Frankfurt: Suhrkamp Verlag.

Phillips, A. (1996). *Terrors and Experts*. London: Harvard University Press.

Steiner, G. (2008). *My Unwritten Books*. New York: New Directions Publishing Corporation.

Chapter 5

A "Wise Baby"?[1]

Ferenczi's presence

André Haynal

"The young child is familiar with much knowledge ... that later becomes buried by the force of repression" (Ferenczi, 1923 [257],[2] p. 350); very young children seem amusing to us because they put into words – sometimes a bit awkwardly – what they perceive (still) without repression: adults, for whom the same contents are already repressed, therefore receive their words as a kind of interpretation. The effect may be one of amusing liberation, a sort of " 'aha' experience"; or alternatively, owing to their own repression, they become tense, or even hostile, saying, "How silly!" or "One doesn't *say* things like that", which corresponds to an intention to reinforce their repression and also to encourage the child "not to express him/ herself" or "not to think".

As Ferenczi said of himself in the English text (1932 [308], pp. 271, 274), he had been a "wise baby" all his life. In this respect he was different from his pioneering colleagues and even from his Master, Freud. His clear-sightedness pre-existed his encounter with psychoanalysis, so it is not surprising that the issues that would become central to the work of Ferenczi the analyst *had already emerged* in the pre-psychoanalytic Ferenczi.

By saying that children are "wise", that the baby is wise, Ferenczi was therefore introducing the idea that for them perception, ideation, and the expression of their feelings, their sensations, has not yet been distorted by their defences, by the insincerity and lack of authenticity that will later be imposed on them. In this nucleus we already come across the notion not, as has been mistakenly understood, of a certain "infantile innocence" – it is not a matter of innocence in the "asexual" sense – but of an infantile *authenticity*, to put it in today's terms. This was the programme of Ferenczi the analyst: to achieve sincerity, authenticity, not only in the analysand, but first and foremost in the analyst; as he would write to Freud later on, one should be able to "*tell everyone the truth*, one's father, teacher, neighbor, and even the king" (letter from Ferenczi to Freud dated 5/2/1910; cf. Freud and Ferenczi, 1996, p. 130 [emphasis in the original]) and to succeed in taking care of the *child* in the man, in the human being, for this is the most valuable part of him. If he pointed out that "the idea of the 'wise baby' could only have been found by a 'wise baby'" (Ferenczi, 1932 [308], p. 274), he goes on to present himself as a "wise baby", close to the child, to his desires, and to the sufferings imposed on him by others.

It is interesting in this context to mention the discussion that took place by correspondence as early as 1911 between Ferenczi and Freud – they still barely knew each other – in which Ferenczi suggests that, since young children have no repression, they do not need symbolism to represent the repressed (letter from Ferenczi to Freud, 7/6/1911, cf. Freud and Ferenczi, 1996, p. 290): "[they] need no indirect language" (3/6/1911, ibid., p. 288). In this exchange, we already see him championing the child's authenticity. Furthermore, he was anticipating here the root of the idea that he was subsequently to explain in his "swan song" entitled "Confusion of tongues between adults and the child" (Ferenczi, 1933 [294]) – namely, that it is for this reason that children and adults misunderstand each other ("*missverstehen*", ibid.).

With the "pre-Freudian" Ferenczi we encounter the principal themes that were later to be his preoccupations as an analyst.

1. *Communication* in its most *occult* forms, in the strong sense of the term (Ferenczi, 1899), deep relations in *hypnosis* (Ferenczi 1904b), and the study of communication in *love* (Ferenczi 1901) have their place at a very early stage in this line of thinking and, later on, his preoccupation with the problem of *change*, in psychoanalysis, in particular.[3]

While he was still working as an intern at the Rókus hospital (= St Roch), one of Budapest's oldest hospitals, for a very authoritarian and malignant senior consultant ("a hard-hearted man"; Ferenczi, 1917, p. 430), who had him take care of the prostitutes instead of devoting his time to the study of psychic phenomena within the framework of the neuropsychiatry, he carried out experiments aimed at exploring himself ("in the absence of other observational material, I carried out psychological experiments on myself", ibid.), using a method of "free association" in vogue at the time, "automatic writing", "about which the spiritualists have much to say" (ibid.).[4] So, in this experience of solitude and rejection, he was already doing a kind of self-analysis. It was at this point that he wrote his astonishing article on spiritualism (Ferenczi, 1899), in which the question of unconscious functioning is already present: "What we know today proves beyond any shadow of doubt that there are many unconscious [*öntudatlan*] and semi-conscious elements in psychic functioning" (ibid., p. 478). Furthermore, there are, he says, cleavages or splits in psychic life. He therefore already thought it "probable that most of the phenomena of spiritualism are based on the division of the psychic functions into two or more parts, only one of which is placed at the focus of the convex mirror of consciousness, whereas the others operate autonomously outside consciousness [*öntudat nélkül*]. That perhaps explains how a medium can conduct [his experiments] outside of his consciousness and not intentionally" (*ibid.*).

His conviction that occult phenomena would shed light on aspects of the transference, and that the "*Gedankenübertragung*" (thought-transference) would make it possible to understand the *Übertragung* (transference), would persist to the end; it was a conviction, moreover, that Freud shared. Furthermore, his hypnotic experiments, in particular as regards the deep "rapport", suggested metaphors to him that he would use for studying regressive states in the transference, making it possible to "relive traumatic events in analysis" (Ferenczi, 1931b [296], p. 240), and this right up inclusively until his *Clinical Diary* (1932).

2. Unusual forms of *sexuality*, as in the case of Roza K__ (Ferenczi, 1902), a theme that is already present in his paper "Love in Science" (1901), also attracted his attention, even before he met Freud. In this article which, it is worth recalling, was written three years before the *Three Essays on the Theory of Sexuality* (Freud, 1905a), he asks himself how "*szerelem*", which expresses (by virtue of a linguistic feature specific to the Hungarian language) the term "sexual love" in a single word (in contrast to "*szeretet*", which means simply "love", especially from an affective point of view), "releases immense psychic energies whose destructive

and constructive operation displays the individual and the species at the apex of their capacity to act" (Ferenczi, 1901, p. 190). He stresses "the disadvantageous influence of prejudices for free inquiry", and cites Möbius, the "*franc-tireur*" (in French in the original) of the psychiatry of that period, who says that this chapter of science has yet to be written. Ferenczi declares that, owing to this fact, "even today the only sources of the psychology of love are poetry and the literature of fiction" (ibid., p. 191), that one can learn more from Maupassant and from Heine than from thick volumes of psychology, and he makes links between love and possessiveness, the masochistic love of the "misunderstood" person, jealousy, and those states of love – regressive states, we would say today – that may "threaten the individual with psychosis, with debauchery, criminality, or drunkenness (ibid., p. 192). As can be seen, the pre-psychoanalytic Ferenczi was in truth already psychoanalytic without knowing it. The biography of Roza K__, "a veritable odyssey", is based amongst other things on an autobiography of this person who would today be considered as lesbian, transvestite, or perhaps even transsexual. It has been pointed out that Ferenczi showed, both in this article and in his activity in favour of homosexuals, that he was very sensitive to the need to fight against social repression and to the role of the doctor, and in particular the psychiatrist, in this struggle. In reading the case history itself, one is even more impressed by his capacity for subtle identification with this unhappy woman, and by his attempt to give her account some intelligibility, even at the price of speculation.

3. The unconscious links between the different elements of our imagination, thought and representations, and the idea of *associationism* – already present in his experiments with "automatic writing" – led him to meet Jung who published a study on "word-associations" (Jung, 1906a). With his capacity for enthusiasm for everything that might help him discover the mysteries of the human soul, Ferenczi immediately jumped on this method, bought a stopwatch and made experiments, even in the literary cafés that he often frequented (like the Café Royal on Budapest's main boulevards, near to the old National Theatre, since destroyed by Stalin's mechanical shovels). On 27 May of this same year, 1906, at the Congress of Neurologists and Psychiatrists from southwest

Germany in Baden-Baden, Jung defended Freud's work on Dora (Freud, 1905e) against a virulent attack by Aschaffenburg, and it was at this point that he linked up his research with the ideas of psychoanalysis (Jung, 1906b). He sent a copy of this work to Freud, and the latter's letter of thanks represented the first missive of a long correspondence exchanged between them which was to include more than 350 letters and continued without interruption until 1914. Ferenczi sought to have a personal contact with Jung at the beginning of 1907, and after a visit to Freud in Vienna at the beginning of March 1907 (where he met Freud on the 3rd and took part in a meeting of the Wednesday Society on the 6th), he met Jung, who stopped over in Budapest, where he spent a few days in the company of Dr Fülöp Stein, Ferenczi's colleague, at this time temporarily his friend. Thereafter, moved by his interests for association tests, Ferenczi again made a trip to the Burghölzi psychiatric clinic in Zurich to see Jung. The importance of Burghölzi in the history of psychoanalysis has been underestimated in psychoanalytic historiography: let us not forget that it was the first institution as such that accepted psychoanalysis and provided it with access (as observational material) to a clientele larger than that of private practitioners, in particular to the world of the psychoses; and in 1908 it was thanks to an introduction from Jung that Ferenczi, accompanied once again by Dr Fülöp Stein, met Freud.

4. When Freud invited him, already in the summer of the same year, to give a paper at the Salzburg Congress, Ferenczi spoke about the *child* – the fourth big subject among his scientific preoccupations[5] – evoking new perspectives on the education of children inspired by Freud's discoveries (Ferenczi, 1908 [63]). This line of thinking would be followed up in his contribution on a little Chanticleer (Ferenczi, 1913a [114], a clinical essay which shows Ferenczi the analyst working on several levels in the best traditions of a clinical Sherlock Holmes: discovering the backdrops to the symbolism of the little cock-boy. In his paper of the same year, "Stages in the development of the sense of reality" (Ferenczi, 1913b [111]), he elaborates the child's omnipotence at the beginning of his development and, in more detail, the operations of intojection and projection: Melanie Klein's work was undoubtedly influenced powerfully by Ferenczi's thoughts here and, as we know, she

expressed her gratitude to Ferenczi, adding that "he had a touch of genius" (Grosskurth, 1986, p. 104). In fact, it was Ferenczi who encouraged her to turn her attention to child psychoanalysis and, contrary to certain legends, Ferenczi remained "equidistant", as it were, between Melanie Klein and Anna Freud at the time of their subsequent[6] differences of opinion and tensions – as Michael Balint, the continuator of his work in London, was to do later on, too.

Ferenczi was close to Freud's family and invited Anna several times to Budapest (in 1914 [letter from Ferenczi to Freud dated 18/2/1914; cf. Freud and Ferenczi, 1996], in 1917 and 1918 [Young-Bruel, 1988, p. 79]); we know that Freud even hoped that he would marry his other daughter, Mathilde. Relations with Melanie Klein, on the other hand, became difficult owing to the tensions that had arisen between Ferenczi and Jones since the 1920s (Ferenczi and Jones, 2013). Although Ferenczi never concentrated principally on child analysis, as his predominant professional activity consisted in conducting adult analyses,[7] nevertheless the Wise Baby that he was always remained very close to the child *in the adult*. This is attested by the series of his last writings: "The adaptation of the family to the child" (1928a [281]); "The unwelcome child and his death-instinct" (1929 [287]); "Child analysis in the analysis of adults" (1931a [292]); and, in particular, his last published contribution, "Confusion of tongues between adults and the child" (1933 [294]). This paper, read at the Congress of Wiesbaden in September 1932, was his spiritual testament but it was also the object of reservations on the part of his colleagues, and even of Freud, who wondered if he should or could present these innovative ideas at that moment. His conception of child analysis in the analysis of adults once again created a new opening, as did his last contribution, which sheds new light on the conflictuality between adults and children (Ferenczi, 1931a [292]).

* * *

In 1909, Ferenczi took to the stage of psychoanalysis with his first major original piece of work (Ferenczi, 1909 [67]): one senses that within the current of the great traditions that Freud established, a new voice and a new sensibility had emerged. Ferenczi's "transference", without any shadow of doubt, was not that of Freud's writings; this man, now aged 36, was to introduce unprecedented ideas, especially in his work at the end of the 1920s, which would make him "the father of modern psychoanalysis" (Green, 1990, p. 61).

It is fascinating to see how these themes that emerged so early on in Sándor Ferenczi's work would be pursued throughout his life, throughout the entire period of his creative activity. Just as, in our fantasy life, our elaboration turns around the same basic ideas, this very spontaneous and inventive scientific work seems to boil down to the elaboration of just a few fundamental themes – an elaboration he pursued, notwithstanding different internal and external obstacles, *right to the end*.

In his 1909 contribution, beyond the projective aspects of the transference on to the blank screen of the psychoanalyst's person, already established by Freud, Ferenczi also emphasizes the inclination for introjection, which he conceives of as a sort of "*Sucht*" (of addiction): the subject, and in particular the "neurotic", is moved by a constant desire to receive, to enrich his internal world, to "[take] into the ego as large as possible a part of the outer world, making it the object of unconscious phantasies" (Ferenczi, 1909 [67], p. 47). Here we find the nucleus of the idea of the constitution of an internal object through identification and, with the identification of these two complementary aspects, already the germ of the later notion of "projective identification" that became so important for the school of his student Melanie Klein (Klein, 1946). In the constitution of the transference he stresses the role of *displacement*, in line with the continuity and contiguity of the *associations*, mentioning, for instance, the part played by ridiculously slight physical resemblances, and adding that "a transference established on the ground of such petty analogies strikes us as ridiculous" (Ferenczi, 1909, p. 42). He thus makes a connection with the dream work or with the jokes studied by Freud (1905c) a few years earlier, and also insists on the fact that these introjections are to a large extent unconscious. In this article we can already notice one of the future characteristics of Ferenczi as a mature psychoanalyst: he is not willing to reject all that he has learnt from deep *hypnotic* relations; but he links up these effects with a revival of later parental influences. In the obedience or in the deep *corps-à-corps* between the hypnotist and the hypnotized subject, *as* in deep sessions of psychoanalysis, he rediscovers the relationship with the loving mother and the father representing authority, that is to say, "*the remains of the infantile-erotic loving and fearing of the parents*" (1909, p. 93, emphasis in the original).

The connection between this clarification of his experience, thereby laying down the foundations of his future theory, and the little *clinical gems* published in the following years, is plain to see: the phenomena of the psychoanalytic treatment, notably the "Transitory symptom-constructions during the analysis" (Ferenczi, 1912 [85]) and "To whom does one relate one's dreams?" (Ferenczi, 1913c [105]), are conditioned by the transference and countertransference. A little later he shows an astonishing openness for different sorts of experimentation in the analytic treatment ("Discontinuous analysis", Ferenczi, 1914 [147]).

The elaboration of the problematic issue of the transference took place in the course of the following years in close exchange between his Master, Sigmund Freud and this intuitive, profound, curious, and innovative Wise Baby that Ferenczi increasingly became, albeit at the price of certain very painful ordeals. These involved discovering from experience the immense mobilization that the transference arouses in a hidden way in both protagonists of psychoanalysis. Freud had already been taken aback by the failure of the case of Dora, the publication of which was truly a tale of embarrassment, ambivalence and unexpected incidents until the account of this case was finally made public in 1905 (see Strachey, *SE* 7, pp. 3–5). The following year saw the beginning of the "affair" between the "crown prince" Carl Gustav Jung and Sabina Spielrein, in which Freud found himself involved (Freud and Jung, 1974); Carotenuto and Trombetta, 1980). In 1911, it was Ferenczi who fell in love with one of his patients, Elma Pálos. Suffering, Freud writes, is caused by the mobilization of the analyst's affects: "To be slandered and scorched by the love with which we operate – such are the perils of our trade, which we are certainly not going to abandon on their account. *Navigare necesse est, vivere non necesse.* And another thing: 'In league with the Devil and yet you fear fire?'" (letter from Freud to Jung dated 9/3/1909; cf. Freud and Jung, 1974, pp. 210–211). A few months later he wrote to Jung:

> Such experiences, though painful, are necessary and hard to avoid. Without them we cannot really know life and what we are dealing

> with. I myself have never been taken in quite so badly, but I have come very close to it a number of times and had a *narrow escape.* I believe that only grim necessities weighing on my work, and the fact that I was ten years older than yourself when I came to psychoanalysis, have saved me from similar experiences. But no lasting harm is done. They help us to develop the thick skin we need and to dominate "countertransference", which is after all a permanent problem for us; they teach us to displace our own affects to best advantage. They are a "blessing in disguise."
>
> (ibid., pp. 144–145)

Moreover, it was in this letter that the word "countertransference" was pronounced for the first time and that this concept was born, appearing one year later in a published work (Freud, 1910). These implications of the affective forces that were clearly involved directed the attention of the trio Freud–Jung–Ferenczi, especially during their trip in America to Clark University in 1909, towards the occult, the subject of Jung's thesis, and a longstanding interest of Ferenczi's. It was here that the lines of transference coincided with occult mysteries and both men hoped that the "*Gedankenübertragung*" (transmission of thoughts) might shed light on the transference (*Übertragung*). Ferenczi, moved by his customary enthusiasm, hunted down clairvoyants and pythonesses throughout Europe and Freud participated in these different experiments. They each played mediums in turn and continued to do so for many years to come. Thus, in 1925, Freud observed to Abraham that his daughter Anna had a "telepathic sensibility" (letter from Freud to Abraham dated 9/7/1925; cf. Falzeder, 2002). We should not forget, moreover, that at the famous meeting of the "secret Committee" in the Harz mountains in 1921, he read a memorandum entitled "Psychoanalysis and telepathy" (Freud, 1941) to his inner circle, which would only be published posthumously.[8]

For the moment, there was an exchange of ideas and of exalted feelings on this subject between Freud and Ferenczi and an intention to explore more deeply the impact of the affective forces operating in the transference and in the countertransference. This intention, however, was apparently not followed up, with the result that Freud's project of publishing an "*Allgemeine Methodik der Psychoanalyse*" (*A General Methodology of Psychoanalysis*) never saw the light of day, as was also the case for a systematic work on metapsychology. The only contributions that were published were ones that Freud subsequently said were destined for "beginners" (Blanton, 1971, p. 47) and "essentially negative"[9] (letter from Freud to Ferenczi, dated 4/1/1928; cf. Freud and Ferenczi, 2000, p. 332). As his brilliant intuition had always guided him with the sureness of a sleepwalker, as it were, the renunciation of these two systematic works (metapsychology and technical) was not simply the sign of a failure of synthesis but also a new way of constructing his theory and of advancing his attempts to uncover the deep forces of the human mind. His work thus has the characteristics of a postmodern edifice, going from one island to another, from one insight to another; and its very structure it is well in advance of the scientific ideals of his time.[10]

Ferenczi was always at his side during this epic-making journey: it was no coincidence if his "technical" interests were crowned by the paper he gave at the Congress in Budapest in 1918 (which at the same time was the consecration of Ferenczi's efforts to introduce psychoanalysis to this city, and no doubt its hour of glory). It is worth recalling that on this occasion, with great openness of mind, Freud raised the problem of the need to diversify this technique, saying in particular that it "grew up in the treatment of hysteria ... But the phobias have already made it necessary for us to go beyond our former limits" (Freud, 1919, p. 165).[11] One gets the impression that from this moment onwards Freud expected his pupils to bring him insights in this domain and, as we know, he proposed – it was the only time – a prize for those who would elucidate this field, and particularly the links between technique and theory. Already in 1912, he had implored Ferenczi to take charge of this domain ("I don't want to see technique in Stekel's hands"; letter from Freud to Ferenczi dated 28/1/1912; cf. Freud and Ferenczi, 1992, p. 338), and he was pleased that Ferenczi was collaborating more closely with Rank towards this end ("I have been very happy about the intensification of your intimacy with Rank; it promises good things for the future" (24/8/1922; and to Rank, 8/9/1922: "As you know, your alliance with Ferenczi has all my sympathy").

What happened thereafter is well known; the direct consequence was the radicalization of the concept of the transference in 1926:

> for me and for my analysis it is in advance that I take Rank's suggestion regarding the relation of patient to analyst as the cardinal

> point of the analytic material and regard every dream, every gesture, every parapraxis, every aggravation or improvement in the condition of the patient as above all an expression of transference and resistance.
>
> (Ferenczi, 1926, p. 225)

This was also the period when Sándor Ferenczi, unsatisfied with some aspects of his analysis with Freud and with the persistence of certain inner problems, particularly of a depressive nature, turned towards another analyst/colleague when his depression began to take the form of hypochondriacal symptoms: this colleague was Georg Groddeck, who became a partner with whom he could exchange ideas and even a mutual analysis. It was in this interaction with Rank and Groddeck, and under their influence, that his subsequent contributions would give him his place in the history of ideas in psychoanalysis, a place that is only just beginning to be recognized. This had not been the case previously for two generations of analysts, amongst other things, due to the influence of Freud's biography by Jones, whose treatment of this subject was quite inadequate: to cite Balint, "the aftermath of Jones' Biography was a spate of acrimonious publications" (see Balint, 1969, p. 220).

This place is well deserved, for practically the *entire psychoanalytic community* has since *taken up* the central role of the analysis of the transference, along with the importance, beyond the Oedipal knot, of the mother, and, for many too, of trauma, even though there has been a tendency to forget that historically speaking this is a legacy of the Ferenczi of the 1920s who was then more or less close to Freud. The latter, moreover, had recognized the importance of his contributions on several occasions. Thus Freud says he "greatly appreciates" the work of Ferenczi and Rank "as a corrective to my conception of the role of repetition or of acting out in analysis" (circular letter from Freud to the Committee dated 15/2/1924; Freud, 2002). Ferenczi's researches culminated in a conception of a field of interactions, ultimately that of intersubjectivity (without ever, to the best of my knowledge, using this term), but which scarcely ever become a cheap interactionism – his ardent attachment to the Freudian legacy protects him from this, as well as from the dangers of simplification. He experimented, for instance, with changes in the analyst's role (active therapy and relaxation) during trial phases which were caricatured both in Jones's work as well as in other writings on Ferenczi. He understood the importance of the psychoanalyst's attitude in the analytic treatment and, in breaking with a taboo[12] by taking into consideration his feelings, his inner reactions, he managed to focus his interest on the countertransference, on the analyst's metapsychology, which was merely a logical consequence of this. His taste for experimentation led him even further and, having had some experience of mutual analysis with Georg Groddeck,[13] he even tried out this "mutual analysis" with a few analysands, of which he gives an account in his *Clinical Diary* (Ferenczi, 1932), the final stage of his elaboration. This legacy of a deeper exploration of regressive states, of the repetition of the traumatism within the analytic interaction, and above all of the central role of the *countertransference* – and therefore of the need for a *metapsychology* of the analyst – became the subject of *controversies* between Sándor Ferenczi and Sigmund Freud, particularly after 1927 and up until the former's death (Haynal, 1987; 1991, pp. 201–223; 2002). As Balint points out, these controversies were traumatic for the analytic community and for many years became taboo subjects, shrouded in silence, about which much was left unsaid. So Ferenczi became a figure who was, if not obliterated from the history of psychoanalysis – for example, in certain North American "Psychoanalytic Institutes" where he was not even taught or was completely ignored[14] – at least seen (along with his onetime friend, Rank) as one of those madmen who, according to Jones, both succumbed to psychosis, rather in the manner of a myth or of a Greek drama as a punishment for their so-called revolt, whereas in reality they had simply dared to make an original contribution to the practice of the theory of psychoanalysis.

This second part of the legacy was transplanted by Michael Balint in London, where it initially fell on fertile soil in the English "Middle Group", but also strengthened questionings in the "Kleinian" group: in 1946, Melanie Klein's projective identification took its place within the legacy of Ferenczi – definitely not in Abraham's – along with the work of Rosenfeld and Bion (the latter initiated a contribution to the metapsychology of the analyst's thought processes as outlined in Ferenczi's wishes). In North America, the dominant current, ego-psychology, ignored him superbly: that is hardly surprising, for Ferenczi sensed the danger that could come from an ego-psychology that was too accentuated and unilateral. He wrote: "The critical view that gradually formed in me in the process was that psychoanalysis engages much too one-sidedly ... in ego-psychology" (letter from Ferenczi to Freud dated 25/12/1929; cf. Freud and Ferenczi, 2000, p. 376). The fact that Géza Roheim, in New York, dedicated his monumental *Psychoanalysis and Anthropology* (Roheim, 1968) to the memory of Sándor Ferenczi may have contributed to the fact that until recently he was almost unknown in psychoanalytic circles in the country to which he emigrated, his country of adoption. Franz Alexander in Chicago and Sándor Rado in New York took up again certain aspects of the Ferenczian legacy, in particular through their interest for technique and their taste for innovation. Ferenczi's analysand, Clara Thompson, may be considered as his principal direct continuator on the North American continent owing to her orientation and, more specifically, her articles on the countertransference and the role of the analyst's personality (Thompson, 1956).

In France, Jacques Lacan's work undoubtedly bears the traces of impregnation through his reading of Ferenczi, and in particular the article "Introjection and transference" (Ferenczi, 1909 [67]), which he recognized as "inaugural and as anticipating by many years all the themes later developed on the basis of the second topography" (Lacan, 1958, p. 613 [2006, p. 512]). He also identified the historical aftermath:

> Apart from the Budapest school, whose embers are now dispersed and soon to be mere ashes, only the English, with their cold objectivity, have been able to articulate this gap – to which the neurotic, in wanting to justify his existence, attests – and hence to implicitly distinguish the relation to the Other, in which being finds its status, from the interpersonal relation, with its warmth and lures.
>
> (ibid.)

while recognizing the historical line that leads from Ferenczi to Balint (p. 607).

There can be no doubt that Ferenczi enriched the analytic world of the second part of the last century by the attitude he inaugurated – not without having spent a long time in a state of constant inner struggle – i.e. an attitude of contact with his own experience, and by resituating theory and the construction of hypotheses where it should be: within the context of free reflection on practice. It was no longer a question of introjecting an authority and his "*ipse dixit*" or "*autos efa*",[15] but of laying down a benchmark in an exchange between fathers and peers on the subject of experience and of its formulation. This led to a more fraternal or, if we prefer, "egalitarian" relationship between analyst and analysand, making it possible too to imagine a certain "mutuality" in the extreme, in the form of "mutual analysis", even if Ferenczi was soon bound to recognize the limitations and the exceptional character of such an undertaking.

Some feared that this passage from the father to the brothers might be an anti-Oedipal movement (Grunberger, 1974) or that his insistence on "free inquiry" in the spirit of the *Aufklärung* might endanger the acquisitions of psychoanalysis and contribute ultimately to its banalization. The expansion of this legacy of psychoanalysis in different parts of the world, in different cultures, whether in the British "Middle Group", in the North American interpersonal school, or in certain aspects of Kohut's self-psychology, as well as in French psychoanalysis (with varying degrees of influence in the different schools), shows nonetheless that the grain has taken root. For historical reasons, the reference to this legacy often remains non-explicit; the motives for this lie in certain aspects of the history of the psychoanalytic movement.

* * *

In fact, to understand the history of psychoanalysis, three lines need to be distinguished: a history of the *ideas*, a history of the *people* who had these ideas, and a history of the interactions between these people who constituted what is called the "*psychoanalytic movement*". Each of these lines can be examined independently, even though they are closely interwoven. The "Wise Baby", who anticipated so many Freudian discoveries and who followed his intuitions, entered into personal conflict, over some of them, with Freud, who, legitimately, was concerned to protect his *oeuvre* but reticent about following the explorations of his Grand Vizier[16] (letter from Freud to Ferenczi dated 13/12/1929; cf. Freud and Ferenczi, 2000, p. 374). Although dialogue was never broken off between them, the crisis underwent periods of ebbs and flows and their divergences were never really elucidated before Ferenczi's death: Freud returned to the subject once again in 1937 (Freud, 1937, p. 230). These tensions between Ferenczi and Freud's family were not as important as the other members of the old secret Committee seemed to think, as can be seen from a letter by Anna Freud: "If there is one man that I associate with the development of psychoanalysis and who, for me, is linked inseparably with psychoanalysis itself, it is Ferenczi. My respect and my admiration for his person and his achievements are long-standing" (letter from Anna Freud to Michael Balint dated 23/5/1935, my translation).[17]

In 1910, at the second Congress of Psychoanalysis in Nuremberg, Ferenczi was Freud's instrument for proposing the foundation of the International Psychoanalytic Association. One of the arguments Ferenczi put forward on this occasion was that psychoanalysis, "this pure science … touches so much on the raw the vital foundations of daily life, certain ideals that have grown dear to us, and dogmas of family life, school, and church" (Ferenczi, 1911 [79], p. 299) that an international grouping of analysts is necessary to provide mutual support and also to be able to exchange their experiences (without constantly returning to the discussion of the basic hypotheses). Now, the Wise Baby was not credulous. He says frankly: "I know the excrescences that grow from organized groups, and I am aware that in most political, social, and scientific organizations childish megalomania, vanity, admiration of empty formalities, blind obedience, or personal egoism prevail instead of quiet, honest work in the general interest" (ibid., p. 302). He does not lose hope all the same, and adds:

> The psycho-analytically trained are surely the best adapted to found an association which would combine the greatest possible personal liberty with the advantages of family organization. It would be a family in which the father enjoyed no dogmatic authority, but only that to which he was entitled by reason of his abilities and labours. His pronouncements would not be followed blindly, as if they were divine revelations, but, like everything else, would be subject to thoroughgoing criticism, which he would accept, not with the absurd superiority of the paterfamilias, but with the attention that it deserved.
>
> (ibid., p. 303)

The true history of this Association, and in particular of this secret Committee of the Seven Rings of the elected members around Freud, whose task it was to oversee the "policy" of the Association, has, in a certain sense, as Lacan said, "not been written, nor should it be" (Lacan, 1956, p. 474 [2006, p. 396]). With, perhaps, one reservation aside: we are only just beginning – through the different letters of the internal circle around Freud – to understand how events unfolded. It seems clear today that the circle of those who wore the Rings was set up thanks to the manipulations of Jones, who utilized the tensions surrounding Jung to this end (Paskauskas, 1988); and that gradually, in particular in the 1920s, the Wise Baby was crushed by the political forces of two competing ambitions to organize respectable and organized world centres of psychoanalysis: that of Jones in the Anglo-Saxon world, with a centre in London; and that of Abraham in Berlin.

Access to different correspondences allows us today to realize, better than in the past, that in Freud's entourage, particularly in the secret Committee, there were great tensions between Ferenczi and his onetime ally Rank on the one hand, and Jones and Abraham on the other. This is the *political* history of the Freudian movement and the confrontations between different temperaments: Ferenczi, who was more intuitive and playful; Abraham, who was more conceptual and linked to a more classificatory scientificity; and Jones, who was struggling for the scientific respectability of this same psychoanalytic movement in the Anglo-Saxon world. This resulted in divergent positions on the subject of "lay analysis" (i.e. non-medical), where Freud and Ferenczi found themselves radically on the side of lay analysis, whereas Jones wanted to take more account of the different sensibility of certain American groups. Abraham and Jones were in favour of policies of institutionalizing training and keen on creating important schools, one in Berlin, the other in London. Freud and Ferenczi aligned themselves with those who were more original, more marginal, more unusual, true pioneers without a great desire for organization. Their position was based partly on a certain conservatism and partly on the intention of exploring more thoroughly the instrument of the analytic treatment and its theory, sometimes at the price of painful reversals of which Freud has given us many examples. Ferenczi did not hesitate either to make repeated revisions – trying to strike a balance between his aspirations for authenticity on the one hand and tendencies to take into account institutional considerations on the other.

His retrospective 1928 Madrid paper attests to the latter:

> It is eighteen years since that the International Psychoanalytical Association was founded upon my initiative. It brings together all those who are interested in psychoanalysis and set themselves

> the task of preserving, to the best of their ability, the purity of Freudian psychoanalysis and of developing it as a separate scientific discipline. In founding this Association, I took it as a principle to only admit those who adhered to the fundamental theses of psychoanalysis (today, personal analysis is also one of the conditions for admission). I believed, and I still do, that a fruitful discussion is only possible between those who defend the same line of thinking; those who have taken other basic principles as their starting point would do well to create their own centre of activity. This principle, which we continue to apply today, has earned us the not necessarily flattering term of orthodox analysts, a term to which the sense of reactionary has been unjustly attached.
>
> (Ferenczi, 1928b [306], pp. 242–243, my translation)

But when Freud enjoined him to accept the presidency of the International Psychoanalytical Association a few years later, in 1932, urging him to abandon "the island of dreams which you inhabit with your fantasy children and mix in with the struggle of men" (letter from Freud to Ferenczi dated 5/5/1932; cf. Freud and Ferenczi, 2000, p. 433), Ferenczi chose to stay with the "children of my imagination" – to explore fantasies and not to enter this "struggle of men" whose pathology and vanity were very apparent to him: "I continue my present manner of working for a time" (letter from Ferenczi to Freud dated 19/5/1932; ibid., p. 435). He chose to deepen his understanding of the human soul and its mysteries: the Wise Baby remained faithful to the baby in himself, in his analysands, in each one of us – striving, in a final effort, to get to know them as thoroughly as possible.

Seeking to clarify his position better, he now turned his attention to the problem of orthodoxy (Ferenczi, 1931a [292], p. 126), defining himself as a "restless spirit" and the "*enfant terrible*"[18] of psychoanalysis. After stating that Freud "is certainly orthodox" (ibid., p. 127), he hastened to add: "Let us thank the fates that we have the good fortune to be fellow-workers with this great spirit – this *liberal* spirit as we can claim him to be" (ibid.).

He would only free himself of this ambivalence in the last year of his life, in his *Clinical Diary* (1932), which, after his death – a point confirmed by Balint (1969, pp. 221–222) – aroused Freud's admiration, along with other posthumous writings.

The continuous line represented by Sándor Ferenczi's life and work culminates in the self-affirmation of his conclusion, which, in its form, remains as impressionistic, full of sensibility, and sometimes of contradictions, as its author always was. The Wise Baby would remain faithful to himself until the end. This is also wisdom.

Notes

1 Translated by Andrew Weller.
2 The figures in square brackets, here and throughout this chapter, in reference to Ferenczi's publications, refer to Balint's chronological numerotation of Ferenczi's works as proposed in S. Ferenczi, *Schriften zur Psychoanalyse* (2 vols, Fischer: Frankfurt/Main, 1970–1972).
3 He would write: "It is this confidence that establishes the contrast between the present and the unbearable traumatogenic past, the contrast which is absolutely necessary for the patient in order to enable him to re-experience the past, no longer as hallucinatory reproduction but as an objective memory" (Ferenczi, 1933 [294], p. 160).
4 "It occurred to me that it was already very late; I was tired and somewhat aroused emotionally. All these circumstances favoured the exploration. So I picked up a pencil and, holding it loosely in my hand, I pressed it against a piece of blank paper. I decided to let the pencil move 'on its own', letting it write whatever it wished. Senseless scribbles came first, then letters, words (some of them strange to me) and finally whole sentences. Soon I was having a real dialogue with my pencil – I asked questions and got quite unexpected answers. Being young, first of all I demanded answers to big theoretical problems, but later more practical questions occurred to me. Finally, the pencil suggested the following: 'Write an article on spiritualism for *Gyógyászat*, the editor will be interested' " (Ferenczi, 1917, p. 430).
5 Which had already led him, in 1904, to interest himself in the scientific literature concerning "the development and functioning of the infantile mind" (Ferenczi, 1904b).
6 However, he wished even so to present his experiments and the ideas that arose from them and recognized in one and the same breath the respective merits of Melanie Klein and of Anna Freud, "whose systematic works on this subject are universally known and esteemed" (Ferenczi, 1931a [292], p. 128).
7 "I for my part have had very little to do with children analytically" (Ferenczi, 1931a [292], p. 128).
8 There was also a mystery surrounding his 1922 contribution in *Imago* (Freud, 1922): it ought to have been read before the Vienna Psychoanalytic Society but, for reasons unknown to posterity, Freud declined to do so; however, the text, which was already in press, was published all the same (see, too, Strachey's remarks, *SE* 18, p. 196).
9 "*meine Ratschläge … waren wesentlich negativ*" ("my recommendations … were essentially negative").
10 A terminological remark: in the Vienna of Freud's era, and in his milieu, the word "technical" did not primarily bring to mind technology as it does today, but rather the technique of the arts, that of the pianist or the painter; let us not forget that for Freud, the first Hippocratic aphorism, "*Ho bios brakhus, hê de tekhné makra*" (in Latin, "*ars longa, vita brevis*"), was on everyone's

lips, especially those of medical students; and, in this context, of course, "*technê*" = "art". The technique of psychoanalysis is thus the art of psychoanalysis, in counterpoint to the theory.

11 After announcing in 1912 (Freud, 1912, p. 111) that "this technique is the only one suited to my individuality; I do not venture to deny that a physician quite differently constituted might find himself driven to adopt a different attitude".

12 Though the so-called concept of "neutrality" does not exist in Freud's original writings.

13 Perhaps he would also have liked to have done this with Freud. It is well to remember that then, when Freud fell ill with cancer, Ferenczi offered to analyse him, an offer that touched Freud greatly but which he declined, choosing this time the path of somatic therapies, among others the Steinach-operation that was supposed to be a hormonal therapy (Jones, 1957, pp. 111–112).

14 Tactics of "*Totschweigen*" (the idea comes to me from a personal letter from J. Mahony dated 10/2/1991), "passing over in (deathly) silence": quite clearly, the "political" interests of the movement gained the upper hand, as with other movements (see the "non-persons" in Soviet history).

15 Because it is He who says so.

16 "Prime Minister of the Ottoman Empire" (Larousse, 1958). It's worth remembering that the Ottoman Empire was for centuries the principal enemy of Austria (and still at that time its rival in the Balkans). Could it be that there was some ambivalence on Freud's part in his use of this term?

17 Balint Archives, formerly Geneva, presently BPS, London.

18 In French in the original: a terrible child.

References

Balint, M. (1969). Notes for a preface by M. Balint. In *The Clinical Diary of Sándor Ferenczi*, ed. J. Dupont. Cambridge, MA: Harvard University Press, 1995, pp. 221–222.

Balint, M. (ed.) (1970–1972). *S. Ferenczi Schriften zur Psychoanalyse*, 2 vols. Frankfurt/Main: Fischer.

Blanton, S. (1971). *Diary of My Analysis with Freud*. New York: Hawthorn.

Carrotenuto, A. & Trombetta, C. (1980). *Sabina Spielrein entre Freud et Jung*. Paris: Aubier Montaigne, 1981).

Falzeder, E. (ed.) (2002). *The Complete Correspondence of Sigmund Freud and Karl Abraham*. London: Karnac Books.

Ferenczi, S. (1899). Spritizmus. *Gyógyászat*, 39 (July 23) (30): 477–479.

Ferenczi, S. (1901). A szerelem a tudomànyban. [Love in science.] *Gyógyászat*, 41: 190–192.

Ferenczi, S. (1902). Homosexualitas feminina. *Gyógyászat*, 42 (March 16) (11): 167–168.

Ferenczi, S. (1904a). The development and functioning of the infantile mind, with special consideration for psychic disorders, their prevention, and their treatment. *Gyógyászat*, 44 (December 25) (52): 828.

Ferenczi, S. (1904b). A hypnosis gyogyitoértékéröl. [The healing value of hypnosis.] *Gyógyászat*, 44 (December 25) (52): 820–822.

Ferenczi, S. (1908 [63]). Psycho-analysis and education. In *Final Contributions to the Problems and Methods of Psycho-Analysis*. New York, 1955, pp. 280–290.

Ferenczi, S (1909 [67]). Introjection and transference. In *First Contributions to Psycho-Analysis*. London: Hogarth Press, 1952, pp. 35–93.
Ferenczi, S. (1911 [79]). On the organization of the psychoanalytic movement. In *Final Contributions to the Problems and Methods of Psycho-Analysis*. New York, 1955, pp. 299–307.
Ferenczi, S. (1912 [85]). Transitory symptom-constructions during the analysis. In *First Contributions to Psycho-Analysis*. London: Hogarth Press, 1952, pp. 193–212.
Ferenczi, S. (1913a [114]). A little chanticleer. In *First Contributions to Psycho-Analysis*. London: Hogarth Press, 1952, pp. 240–252.
Ferenczi, S. (1913b [111]). Stages in the development of the sense of reality. In *First Contributions to Psycho-Analysis*. London: Hogarth Press, 1952, pp. 213–239.
Ferenczi, S. (1913c [105]). To whom does one relate one's dreams? In *Further Contributions to the Theory and Technique of Psycho-Analysis*. London: Hogarth Press, 1950, p. 349.
Ferenczi, S. (1914 [147]). Discontinuous analysis. In *Further Contributions to the Theory and Technique of Psycho-Analysis*. London: Hogarth Press, 1950, pp. 233–235.
Ferenczi, S. (1917). My friendship with Miksa Schachter. Trans. Professor Borisz Szegal, Academy of Sciences, Budapest. *British Journal of Psychotherapy* 9 (4): 430.
Ferenczi, S. (1923 [257]). The dream of the "Clever Baby". In *The Selected Papers of Sándor Ferenczi, Vol. 2, Further Contributions to the Theory and Technique of Psycho-Analysis*. London: Hogarth Press, 1950, pp. 349–350.
Ferenczi, S. (1926 [271]). Contra-indications to the "active" psycho-analytical technique. In *Further Contributions to the Theory and Technique of Psycho-Analysis*. London: Hogarth Press, 1950, pp. 217–230.
Ferenczi, S. (1928a [281]). The adaptation of the family to the child. In *Final Contributions to the Problems and Methods of Psycho-Analysis*. New York, 1955, pp. 61–76.
Ferenczi, S. (1928b [306]) Le processus de la formation psychanalytique. *Psychanalyse*, 4. Paris: Payot, 1982, pp. 239–245.
Ferenczi, S. (1929 [287]).The unwelcome child and his death-instinct. In *Final Contributions to the Problems and Methods of Psycho-Analysis*. New York, 1955, pp. 102–107.
Ferenczi, S. (1931a [292]). Child-analysis in the analysis of adults. In *Final Contributions to the Problems and Methods of Psycho-Analysis*. New York, 1955, pp. 126–142.
Ferenczi, S. (1931b [296]). Notes and fragments. In *Final Contributions to the Problems and Methods of Psycho-Analysis*. New York, 1955, pp. 216–279.
Ferenczi, S. (1932). *The Clinical Diary of Sándor Ferenczi*, ed. J. Dupont, trans. M. Balint & N.Z. Jackson. Cambridge, MA: Harvard University Press, 1995.
Ferenczi, S. (1933 [294]). Confusion of tongues between adults and the child. The language of tenderness and of passion. In *Final Contributions to the Problems and Methods of Psycho-Analysis*. New York, 1955, pp. 156–167.
Ferenczi, S., & Jones, E. (2013). *Correspondence 1911–1933*. London: Karnac Books.
Freud, S. (1905a). *Three Essays on the Theory of Sexuality*. *SE* 7: 123–243.
Freud, S. (1905b). Fragment of an analysis of a case of hysteria. *SE* 7, pp. 7–122.
Freud, S. (1905c). Jokes and their relation to the unconscious. *SE* 8, pp. 9–236.
Freud, S. (1910). The future prospects of psycho-analytic therapy. *SE* 11: 139–151.
Freud, S. (1912). Recommendations to physicians practising psycho-analysis. *SE* 12: 111–120.

Freud, S. (1919 [1918]). Lines of advance in psycho-analytic therapy. *SE* 17: 159–168.
Freud, S. (1922). Dreams and telepathy. *SE* 18: 197–220.
Freud, S. (1937). Analysis terminable and interminable. *SE* 23: 216–253.
Freud, S. (1941 [1921]. Psychoanalysis and telepathy. *SE* 18: 177–193.
Freud, S. (2002). Circular letter from Freud to the Committee dated 15/2/1924. In Ernst Falzeder (ed.). *The Complete Correspondence of Sigmund Freud and Karl Abraham 1907–1925*. London: Karnac Books.
Freud, S., & Ferenczi, S. (1992). *The Correspondence of Sigmund Freud and Sándor Ferenczi, Vol. 1, 1908–1914*, ed. E. Falzeder, E. Brabant, & P. Giampieri-Deutsch, trans. P. Hoffer. Cambridge, MA: Harvard University Press.
Freud, S., & Ferenczi, S. (1996). *The Correspondence of Sigmund Freud and Sándor Ferenczi, vol. 2, 1914–1919*, ed. E. Falzeder, E. Brabant, & P. Giampieri-Deutsch, trans. P. Hoffer. Cambridge, MA: Harvard University Press.
Freud, S., & Ferenczi, S. (2000). *The Correspondence of Sigmund Freud and Sándor Ferenczi, vol 3, 1920–1933*, ed. E. Falzeder & E. Brabant, trans. P. Hoffer. Cambridge, MA: Harvard University Press.
Freud, S., & Jung, C.J. (1974). *Freud/Jung Letters*, ed. W. McGuire, trans. R. Hull & R. Mannheim. London: Hogarth Press/Routledge.
Green, A. (1990). Le complexe de castration. *Que sais-je?*, 2531. Paris: PUF.
Grosskurth, P. (1986). *Melanie Klein: Her world and her work*. New York: Knopf.
Grunberger, B. (1974). De la technique active à la confusion de langues. *Revue Française Psychanalyse*, 38: 521–546.
Haynal, A. (1988). *The Technique at Issue: Controversies in Psychoanalysis from Freud and Ferenczi to Michael Balint*. London: Karnac Books.
Haynal, A. (1991). *Psychanalyse et sciences face à face*. Lyon: Césura.
Haynal, A. (2002). *Disappearing and Reviving. Sándor Ferenczi and the history of psychoanalysis*. London: Karnac Books.
Jones, E. (1957). *La Vie et l'oeuvre de Sigmund Freud*, vol. 3. Paris: PUF, 1969.
Jung, C. (1906a). *Studies in Word-Association*. London: Heinemann, 1918.
Jung, C. (1906b). Psychoanalysis and association experiments. *The Collected Works of C.J. Jung*, vol. 2, Bollingen Series. New Jersey: Princeton University Press.
Klein, M. (1946). Notes on some schizoid mechanisms. *International Journal of Psycho-analysis*, 27: 99–110.
Lacan, J. (1958 [2006]). The direction of the treatment and the principles of its power. In *Écrits*, trans. B. Fink. New York: Norton, pp. 489–542.
Paskauskas, R.A. (1988). Freud's break with Jung: the crucial role of Ernest Jones. *Free Associations*, 11: 7–34.
Roheim, G. (1968). *Psychoanalysis and Anthropology*. New York: International Universities Press.
Thompson, C. (1956). The role of the analyst's personality in therapy. *American Journal of Psychotherapy*, 10: 347–359.
Young-Bruel, E. (1988). *Anna Freud: A biography*. New York: Summit Books.

Chapter 6

Freud, Ferenczi, and the case of Schreber

A mutual enactment of homoerotic longings, homophobia, and internalized anti-Semitism[1]

Lewis Aron and Karen Starr

Sigmund Freud and Sándor Ferenczi were close friends and fellow travelers, wandering Jews who traveled and vacationed together regularly for many years. As we demonstrate in our recent book (Aron and Starr, 2013), Freud (1919b) equated the love of a foreign place with the search for origins, the longing for an original home. This particular wandering Jew had to overcome a travel phobia, a fear he would miss his train, as well as his phobia of Rome. Join us, travel with us, all aboard the *Nachträglichkeit* express, for a regressive time travel back a century to the uncanny origins of psychoanalysis.

We have been examining the problematic place of binaries in the history of psychoanalysis, focusing in particular on Freud's "optimally marginal" position at the crossroads of his Jewish racial and German cultural identities. Freud's close friend and colleague, Sándor Ferenczi, shared this divided Jewish Enlightenment identity. Like most of the early analysts, Freud and Ferenczi were from Jewish immigrant families who migrated from Eastern Europe, from the periphery to the center, from the *shtetl* or ghetto to the large cosmopolitan city. They were part of a tradition of migration, acculturation, and assimilation (Erös, 2004). For Freud, Ferenczi, and their middle-class colleagues, medicine, particularly private practice, was one of the free professions that allowed upward mobility independent from institutions that would not accept Jews. Before and during World War I, the Jews of Austria-Hungary were intensely loyal to the State, which allowed them to separate political, cultural, and ethnic aspects of their identity. In Austria, Westernized Jews occupied multiple subject positions, sometimes dissociated self-states, thinking of themselves as German by language and culture or *Bildung*, Austrian by political loyalty, and Jewish by race, ethnicity, or religion. In Hungary, Jews were more fully assimilated into the Magyar nation, a process known as Magyarization. They identified as Hungarian, speaking Hungarian and German along with Yiddish (Rozenblit, 2001). The Freud-Ferenczi correspondence is filled with Yiddish idioms, such as Ferenczi's (1915) describing his own theory that "all libido is based on '*nachas*'" (pleasure) (p. 80). Here we will explore the personal and professional relationship between Freud and Ferenczi, two Jewish Enlightenment men – friends, colleagues, and analytic couple – who traveled with, confided in, and collaborated with one another, and who enacted between them dynamics shaped to a great extent by their characteristic reactions to their anti-Semitic and homophobic cultural surround.

Sándor Ferenczi: progressive Enlightenment Jew

Sándor Ferenczi was born on July 7, 1873, the eighth of eleven children who survived childhood. A twelfth child, his younger sister Vilma, died of diphtheria when Sándor was about 4 years old. We still await an authoritative biography of Ferenczi as well as a coherent and systematic portrait of his historical-political context (Giamppieri and Erös, 1987), but offer the following as a sketch of Ferenczi's background. His father, known as Baruch Frankel until 1879, emigrated from Poland as part of a large migration of Jews from the East seeking to escape anti-Semitism. Born in Krakow, Poland in 1830, Baruch came from the same sociocultural environment as Freud's father. Over the course of a changing political atmosphere, Baruch Frankel gradually became Bernat Ferenczi. At age 18, he participated in the Hungarian insurrection against Austrian domination. Hungary's Jews had been handicapped by discrimination, particularly by the German guilds in Buda and Pest; thus almost all Jews identified with the Magyar national cause in 1848 and thereafter. At this time, Magyar liberals welcomed Jewish assimilation or Magyarization, as many more people were needed to populate large portions of the Hungarian Kingdom (Lukacs, 1988). The rebellion was suppressed until 1867–68, when it led to the constitution of an independent Hungary and emancipation of the Jews. Bernat Frankel was then offered the name Ferenczy with a "y," a sign of nobility in the new Hungary. (Ennoblement was so widespread in Hungary that these titles did not mean much.) Being a liberal democrat, he refused this status symbol, and in 1879, when Sándor was about six, took the name Ferenci, a commoner's name. Gradually, usage added the letter z (see Fortune, 2002).

By 1900, Budapest was a thriving metropolis in which Jews comprised more than 20 percent of the population and about 40 percent of its voters. Thousands more Jews arrived each year. Their influence in finance, commerce, and culture was even greater than indicated by these numbers. Gradually, with their rise in population and prominence, the alliance between Jewish and non-Jewish Hungarians broke down and a new form of modern liberal anti-Semitism began to take hold. The new anti-Semitism was populist and democratic, not religious but racial, and was aimed at assimilated as well as religious Jews, who had acquired power, prosperity, and influence (Lukacs, 1988). This was the Budapest in which Ferenczi lived and worked as an adult. As we will soon see, the years 1918–20 brought the disintegration of the Austro-Hungarian monarchy and the collapse of the socio-political premises of the pre-war era. This is an important historical distinction to keep in mind in comparing Freud and Ferenczi's experiences with anti-Semitism. In Vienna, the liberal political philosophy promising Jews full emancipation and participation in German culture broke down far earlier than in Hungary. Freud had early in his life become disillusioned, increasingly so with the appointment of Karl Lueger in 1897, and especially after World War I. In contrast, the Hungarian political atmosphere was liberal until 1919–20, in spite of growing popular resentment toward Jews. At the time Lueger and the Christian Socialists came to power in Vienna, there was a Jewish mayor in Budapest. Lueger referred to Budapest with the derogatory epithet "Judapest" (Lukacs, 1988, p. 95). Hungarian Jews continued, long after those in Vienna, to seek emancipation and integration into Hungarian society (Sziklai, 2009). By the time Ferenczi faced the loss of his illusion of being a "Hungarian of Jewish faith" (Ferenczi, 1919, p. 365), Freud had already lost his own similar illusions.

Baruch/Bernat became the manager of a bookshop in the center of the city of Miskolc (in northeastern Hungary) that he purchased in 1856 from Michael Heilprin, a Chasidic scholar who returned to his native America. It gradually became a family business, with the family living in the flat above the store. Soon, Bernat added a printing press and then a concert agency, as the Ferenczis were a musical family. By 1880, he was unanimously elected president of the Miskolc chamber of commerce. The Ferenczi house became a gathering place for artists, musicians, and intellectuals and Sándor was raised in a lively, intellectually stimulating, and politically and culturally liberal environment. Sándor was his father's favorite child, accompanying him on excursions to his vineyard on the hills near Miskolc (Kapusi, 2010). Bernat was an upwardly mobile reform Jew who, along with Sándor, attended the synagogue on Kazinczy Street in Miskolc. It is the only synagogue that remains standing in Miskolc today.

Sándor's mother, Rosa Eibenschütz, was born in 1840 in Krakow, but her family soon moved to Vienna. Baruch and Rosa married in 1858, likely in Vienna. Over the years, Rosa was busy raising eleven children; for this reason, she resigned from her prestigious town role as president of the Union of Jewish Women, which she had founded, but whose work required long periods away from home. When Sándor was 15, his father died, and Rosa took over and expanded the business. Very few members of the Ferenczi family survived the deportations of World War II.

Sándor graduated from the Miskolc Calvinist Gymnasium, which would have been the only choice of school for a liberal, enlightened Jewish family. He attended medical school in Vienna, living with his relatives and graduating in 1894, and then left for military service in the Austro-Hungarian army. After his military service, he settled in Budapest, where he began working at the hospice for the poor and the marginal, with prostitutes and society's outcasts. By 1900, he established himself in private practice, as a neurologist at the Elizabeth Hospice, and as a court-appointed forensic neurologist.

Ferenczi maintained a social orientation throughout his medical career and, from the beginning of his involvement with Freud, considered the progressive implications of psychoanalysis. This liberal socialist political leaning was common among the members of Ferenczi's Jewish circle, as they sat and discussed art, science, culture, and politics in the coffee houses of Budapest. After giving a lecture on Freud's *The Psychopathology of Everyday Life* to members of the Galileo Circle on October 30, 1909, Ferenczi wrote to Freud,

> I was happy that I could speak before approximately three hundred young and enthusiastic medical students, who listened to my (or, that is to say, your) words with bated breath … The medical

> students surrounded me and wanted me to promise them, at any price, to tell them more about these things ... Budapest seems, after all, not to be such an absolutely bad place. The audience was naturally composed of nine tenth Jews!
>
> (Ferenczi, 1909b, pp. 91–92)

As early as 1910, Ferenczi wrote to Freud,

> I would like to recommend to you another point for consideration (in case you haven't come upon it yourself). That is the *sociological* significance of our analyses in the sense that in our analyses we investigate the *real* conditions in the various levels of society, cleansed of all hypocrisy and conventionalism, just as they are mirrored in the individual.
>
> (Ferenczi, 1910a, p. 153)

Ferenczi illustrated this sociological significance with several of his analytic cases, including as examples his analysis of a typesetter described as suffering the "terrorism" of oppressed labor conditions; the analysis of the owner of a print shop who was circumventing union rules to swindle his workers; the "inner hollowness" that analysis uncovered in a young countess and members of her social class; and the sexual masochism that kept a young maid working at lower than necessary wages. As early as 1911, Ferenczi spoke of alcoholism as a symptom of a social neurosis that could only be cured by analyzing its social causation (Nyíri Kristóf, cited in Sziklai, 2009). Ferenczi advocated for the rights of homosexuals and transvestites and wrote about his work with prostitutes and criminals, calling for healthier social conditions and better treatment of the disadvantaged (Gaztambide, 2011). Ferenczi was the Budapest representative of the sexologist Magnus Hirschfeld's International Humanitarian Committee for the Defense of Homosexuals, founded in 1905 (Stanton, 1991).

Freud, Ferenczi, and Schreber: homoerotic longings, homophobia, and paranoia

Jewish and German cultural identities carried serious implications with regard to race, gender, sexuality, bigotry, anti-Semitism, and homophobia. We will focus on one incident that occurred in 1910 during Freud and Ferenczi's joint vacation in Palermo as they collaborated on writing the Schreber case. Freud's *Schreber*, "Psychoanalytic notes on an autobiographical account of a case of paranoia," was published in 1911. Although developed in collaboration with Ferenczi, it became derailed over a mutual enactment of dynamics related to racism, anti-Semitism, homophobia, and misogyny. The tense interpersonal incident between Freud and Ferenczi both foreshadowed and shaped Ferenczi's personal analysis with Freud as well as their later theoretical and technical divergence.

In the summer of 1910, Freud traveled to Italy via Paris with Ferenczi, who was then 37 years old and single, although involved since 1900 with the married Frau G., Gizella Pálos. Ferenczi's brief and interrupted analysis with Freud would not begin for four more years. Freud and Ferenczi sailed to Palermo. The trip was marred by unpleasant Sirocco winds, but the personal storm was far worse. On Christmas Day 1921, Ferenczi wrote to Georg Groddeck, with whom he engaged in a manner of mutual analysis for much of his life, a revealing self-analytic letter recalling the incident in Palermo. He wrote,

> I could never be completely free and open with him; I felt that he expected too much of this "deferential respect" from me; he was too big for me, there was too much of the father. As a result, on our very first working evening together in Palermo, when he wanted to work with me on the famous paranoia text (Schreber), and started to dictate something, I jumped up in a sudden rebellious outburst, exclaiming that this was no working together, dictating to me. "So this is what you are like?" he said, taken aback. "You obviously want to do the whole thing yourself." That said, he now spent every evening working on his own, I was left out in the cold – bitter feelings constricted my throat. (Of course I now know what this "working alone in the evenings" and this "constriction of the throat" signifies: I wanted, of course, to be loved by Freud.)
> (Ferenczi, 1921, pp. 8–9)

Comparing Ferenczi's recollections with Freud's contemporaneous description, we can see that both Freud and Ferenczi understood Ferenczi's desires as homoerotic, derivatives of a negative Oedipus complex. From Rome, Freud wrote to Jung, triangulating him with Ferenczi:

> My travelling companion is a dear fellow, but dreamy in a disturbing kind of way, and his attitude towards me is infantile. He never stops admiring me, which I don't like, and is probably sharply critical of me in his unconscious when I am taking it easy. *He has been passive and receptive, letting everything be done for him like a woman, and I really haven't got enough homosexuality in me to accept him as one. These trips arouse a great longing for a real woman. A number of scientific notions I brought with me have combined to form a paper on paranoia,* which still lacks an end, but takes quite a step forward in explaining the mechanism of the choice of neurosis.
>
> (Freud, 1910a, p. 353, emphasis added)

Although Freud accused Ferenczi of being "infantile," inhibited," and "dreamy" (Freud, 1910a, p. 215), and of not asserting his equality, according to Ferenczi's account, Ferenczi had stood up for himself as being not a secretary but a collaborator. Ferenczi protested that he wanted a shared collaboration, but Freud accused him of wanting the whole thing. Freud seems to have been unable to collaborate as an equal, interpreting a demand to participate in partnership as a demand to take over the whole. Ferenczi wrote back to Freud, agreeing that he was infantile and inhibited, adding, "On this occasion I have also rather ruthlessly brought to light the resistance against my own homosexual drive components (and the uncommon sexual overestimation of women which goes along with it)" (Ferenczi, 1910b, p. 217). Ferenczi here explicitly understood his own desires for intimacy with Freud to be homosexual, which he homophobically devalued as infantile, even while recognizing that his own heterosexual excess might be a defense against underlying homoerotic desire. Ferenczi (1910b wrote that he was looking for something more from Freud:

> I did, perhaps, have an exaggerated idea of companionship between two men who tell each other the truth unrelentingly, sacrificing all consideration. Just as in my relationship with Frau G. I strive for absolute mutual openness, in the same manner – and with even more justification – I believed that this, apparently cruel, but in the

> end only useful, clear-as-day openness, which conceals nothing, could be possible in the relations between two Ψa.-minded people who can really understand everything and, instead of making value judgments, can seek the determinants of their Ψa. impulses. That was the ideal I was looking for: I wanted to enjoy the man, not the scholar, in close friendship.
>
> (p. 218)

In his ongoing idealization of telling the truth at all cost, Ferenczi seemed oblivious to the aggression that could be expressed in this way. He was trapped in these dynamics: while seeing himself as longing for genuine equality and mutuality, he was unable to find a third to either competitive aggression (the positive Oedipal – paranoia) or passive submission (the negative Oedipal – hysteria).

Ferenczi (1910b) went on to mention a dream he had in which he saw Freud standing naked before him. Ferenczi analyzed this dream, deriving two motives. The first was unconscious homosexual tendencies. The second was the "longing for absolute mutual openness" (p. 218). Could Ferenczi's longing for openness from Freud simply be explained on the basis of infantile sexual wishes? While recognizing this motive in himself, Ferenczi also believed that the adult wish for personal contact and relatedness should not be reduced to its genetic origins in infantile longings. He longed for Freud to feel comfortable enough with him to expose himself personally, to speak the truth even if it was unpleasant. Ferenczi (1910b) wrote:

> Don't forget that for years I have been occupied with nothing but the products of your intellect, and I have also always felt the man behind every sentence of your works and made him my confidant. Whether you want to be or not, you are one of the great master teachers of mankind, and you must allow your readers to approach you, at least intellectually, in a personal relationship as well. *My ideal of truth that strikes down all consideration is certainly nothing less than the most self-evident consequence of your teachings* ... The final consequences of such insight – when it is present in two people – is that they are not ashamed in front of each other, keep nothing secret, tell each other the truth without risk of insult or in the certain hope that within the truth there

> can be no lasting insult ... according to my Ψα. ideal, there are no halfway standards, all consideration for people and conditions disappear beside my ideal of truth. Please don't misunderstand me. I really don't want to "reform" society, *I am not a paranoiac.* I would only like to see thoughts and speech liberated from the compulsion of unnecessary inhibitions in the relations of Ψα.-minded men. – Unfortunately – I can't begin, you have to! After all, you are Ψα. in person!
>
> (pp. 219–220, emphasis added)

Freud told Ferenczi that his dreams while they were away together were entirely concerned with Fliess, with which he understood it would be difficult for Ferenczi to sympathize. And here Freud's letter quickly turns to his thinking about Schreber. While there is much that could be said about this letter, we want to highlight Freud's denial of his superhero status as well as its impact on those around him; the intricate connections between themes of homosexuality and paranoia in Freud's personal relationships and collaborative work; and Freud's study of Schreber.

> I am also not that Ψα. superman whom we have constructed, and I also haven't overcome the countertransference. I couldn't do it, just as I can't do it with my three sons, because I like them and I feel sorry for them in the process. Not only have you noticed that I no longer have any need for that full opening of my personality, but you have also understood it and correctly returned to its traumatic cause. Why did you thus make a point of it? This need has been extinguished in me since Fliess's case, with the overcoming of which you just saw me occupied. *A piece of homosexual investment has been withdrawn and utilized for the enlargement of my own ego. I have succeeded where the paranoiac fails.*
>
> (Freud, 1910b, p. 221, emphasis added)

In this exchange we can see the clash of contrasting visions as they emerge from complementary personalities. In what follows, we will explicate these dynamics. Ferenczi's uncritical idealism about the psychoanalytic value of mutual and reciprocal openness became more central as his own work evolved, and Ferenczi continued to long for

Freud's openness and personal closeness. He wrote to Freud that he had not given up hope that Freud would

> let a part of your withdrawn homosexual libido be refloated and bring more sympathy to bear toward "my ideal of honesty." You know, I am an unimpeachable therapist. *I don't want to even give up on the paranoiac as a total loss.* So how can I warm up to the fact that you extend your – in part, justified – distrust to the entire male sex! There is certainly much that is infantile in my yearning for honesty – but it certainly also has a healthy core. *Not everything that is infantile should be abhorred.*
>
> (Ferenczi, 1910c, p. 224, emphasis added)

What Ferenczi expected from Freud, the master psychoanalyst, was precisely what some two decades later he attempted to offer his own patients: mutual openness and honesty. What is additionally fascinating is that Ferenczi did not realize that this was his own innovation, but believed it to be the logical and transparent aim of Freud's teachings. Note also the relation of homosexuality and paranoia hovering in the background of these personal exchanges. As we will elaborate, there was an ongoing tension being played out between Freud and Ferenczi, enacting between them the paired binaries: heterosexual/homosexual, active/passive, positive/negative Oedipus, paranoia/hysteria, male/female. Hence, it is understandable that these forces would become explosive in their attempt to collaborate on these very themes, which were elicited by the Schreber case.

The eternal, wandering, "unmanned" Jew

Freud began his theorizing of the relationship between paranoia and repressed homosexuality in 1908, in collaboration with Ferenczi, to whom he was introduced by Jung. In 1910, Jung gave Freud a copy of Schreber's *Memoirs of My Nervous Illness*, although he likely knew of the work as early as 1903–4 (Lothane, 1997). The schism between Freud and Jung that climaxed in 1912 revolved around their differing interpretations of the case of Schreber. Freud used Schreber to highlight the role in paranoia of repressed sexuality, which was central to his theory, and had never been fully accepted by Jung.

In contrast, Ferenczi, who was always ready to understand himself in terms of spiritualized or sublimated homosexuality, argued that what led to paranoia was not homosexuality, but its repudiation. In today's terms, one might read Ferenczi as suggesting that paranoia results from homophobia. Keep in mind that both Freud and Ferenczi's understandings were prior to any formulation of gender identity as distinct from sexuality, and so a man's possession of any culturally designated "feminine" trait was equated with homosexuality. Freud and Ferenczi's works have been used – or rather, misused – for much of the past century, to argue that homosexuality was a pathological and regressed outcome of failed heterosexuality (Phillips, 2003). However, neither Ferenczi nor Freud was moralistic or particularly pathologizing of homosexuality, viewing it as a variation in resolving the Oedipus complex. The pathologizing of homosexuality came later.

Let's return to September 1910 in Palermo, the scene of the primal fight between Freud and Ferenczi. Many of these themes – homoeroticism, homosexuality, homophobia, and paranoia – were brewing in Freud and Ferenczi's minds, leading to this perfect storm. Freud's closeness to and conflict with Ferenczi, his anticipation of Adler's "heresy," his anxious hopes for Jung to become his Aryan successor, reactions stirred by the Wolfman's analysis, and his preoccupation with Schreber, all stimulated in Freud a recurrence of thoughts about his old close friend, Wilhelm Fliess. Freud announced to Jung in December 1910, "My Schreber is finished," but went on to say that he himself could not judge its objective worth "because in working on it I have had to fight off complexes within myself (Fliess)" (Freud, 1910a, p. 380). Freud anticipated an upcoming schism with Adler, which indeed came to full bloom before Schreber was published. Freud (1910a) wrote to Jung,

> I am very glad that you see Adler as I do. *The only reason the affair upsets me so much is that is has opened the wounds of the Fliess affair*. It was the same feeling that disturbed the peace I otherwise enjoyed during my work on paranoia.
>
> (p. 382, emphasis added)

Freud later called Adler paranoid, just as he accused Fliess of becoming paranoid following their break. Freud was preoccupied with mastering his homosexual tendencies, writing to Ferenczi, "I feel myself to be a match for anything and approve of the overcoming of my homosexuality, with the result being greater independence" (Freud, 1910c, p. 227). Ferenczi's appeal for Freud's love conjured the Fliess *dybbuk*, as did Freud's deepening homoerotic ties to Jung. Indeed Jung's paranoid collapse may have been triggered by his break with Freud (Lothane, 1997).

Adler's "heretical" theories matched these dynamics in a way that can only be described as uncanny. Breger (2000) argues that Adler's "concept of the masculine protest – that one exaggerates certain culturally defined masculine traits to repudiate threatening feelings of weakness and helplessness that are seen as feminine – fit Freud all too closely" (p. 204). Neither Breger nor Rudnytsky (2002), however, both of whom have astutely clarified the Freud-Ferenczi relationship, take into consideration that this formulation not only fits Freud and Adler in terms of their idiosyncratic psychodynamics, but also captures precisely the Jewish male cultural response to the prevailing anti-Semitic stereotypes in which they were helplessly trapped – regarded as feminine, circumcised, and thus castrated. While Freud's (1937) notion of "the repudiation of femininity" (p. 252) may seem identical to Adler's "masculine protest," Freud argued from a genitally derived, biological basis that the masculine protest results from castration anxiety, whereas Adler examined social and cultural forces. All of these currents were in the background, as these two wandering Jews, Freud and Ferenczi, traveled intimately together, writing about homosexuality, paranoia, and Schreber's identification with the Eternal Jew. In writing *Schreber*, Freud had to prove Adler wrong: psychosis was not about social issues but about biology, specifically sexuality, and he had to convince Jung that psychosis was rooted in sexual, not spiritual conflict. If in writing *Schreber* Freud was overcoming his homoerotic love of Fliess, then he was also simultaneously enacting the relationship with Ferenczi. Recall James Strachey's comment to Ernest Jones about the redacted Freud-Fliess letters, "It is really a complete instance of *folie à deux*, with Freud in the unexpected role of hysterical partner to a paranoiac" (cited in Boyarin, 1997, p. 194). In Freud's collaboration with Ferenczi, Freud and Ferenczi reenacted the complementary roles of hysteric and paranoiac, but in reverse, with Ferenczi acting as hysterical partner to Freud's paranoiac. The thesis we put forward here is that Freud and

Ferenczi, in a relationship of split complementarity (Benjamin, 1988), divided up between them the two polarized poles of reaction to the anti-Semitism and associated homophobia surrounding them, with Freud reacting along paranoid lines and Ferenczi in his more characteristically hysteric manner. Whereas Freud emphasized his positive Oedipal wishes to repress the negative, Ferenczi highlighted his negative Oedipal wishes, attempting to sublimate them. Whereas Freud tried to emulate the Greek-German ideal of the conqueror-hero, Ferenczi tended toward "ironic obedience," a strategy he would only identify much later (Ferenczi, 1932, p. 19).

In Freud's championing of the positive Oedipus and in his "overcoming" of his homosexuality, Freud was also rejecting what his society viewed, and what he internalized, as the stereotypically Jewish, passive, feminine, masochistic, castrated position. This was precisely the role Ferenczi played in exaggerated caricature. The "repudiation of femininity" became "bedrock," and Freud identified with warriors and conquerors, including Moses, whom he transformed from a self-effacing, reluctant leader into a ruthless man of action. While the rabbis emphasized Moses' humility and caretaking, Freud's (1939) Moses possessed "decisiveness of thought," "strength of will," and "energy of action," exhibiting "autonomy and independence" and "divine unconcern which may grow into ruthlessness" (pp. 109–110). While Freud's notion of the heroic culminated in autonomous ruthlessness, Ferenczi's vision idealized mutual openness, surrender, and forgiveness.

Boyarin (1997) interprets Freud's formulation of Schreber as an autobiographical commentary on Freud's own unconscious dynamics. While Boyarin emphasizes Freud's defensive reaction against his own homosexuality and away from the negative Oedipus, we are expanding Boyarin's analysis by comparing Freud's reactions to those of Ferenczi, who ultimately criticized Freud's "androphile orientation" (p. 187), viewing masculinity itself as a "hysterical symptom" (p. 188). To his patients, Ferenczi directly expressed his pain that as a man, he was taught to suppress his capacities for caretaking and kindness, as these were considered feminine and childish; he held the analyst guilty for his inability to provide maternal care (p. 53). That Freud and Ferenczi differed markedly in their stance toward gender and sexuality is highly significant. Freud and Ferenczi shared the experience of being upwardly mobile, liberal, professional Jews surrounded by a culture of intense anti-Semitism that feminized them, circumcised/castrated them, and rejected them as truly Hungarian, Austrian, or German men. Nevertheless, their individual reactions to these circumstances were dramatically different, because they each had quite distinct childhood experiences with their own mothers and fathers. In other words, their reaction to anti-Semitism is one – but certainly not the only – element involved in shaping Freud and Ferenczi's responses to gender and sexuality and broader aspects of misogyny. To be clear: we are not reducing patriarchy and misogyny to anti-Semitism, but rather are exploring the intersection of misogyny, racism, anti-Semitism, and homophobia. Feminism has exposed the inherent relationship between patriarchy and misogyny, and postcolonial studies have investigated the interrelations between racism, misogyny, and homophobia. A psychoanalytic study of the intersection of anti-Semitism, homophobia, and misogyny enriches the findings of feminism; it does not detract from them. Freud and Ferenczi reacted in opposing ways to their society's anti-Semitism and expectations of normative masculinity; they were both drawn to and made anxious by the other's polar opposite style. This clash of polarities was reflected in their theories and clinical approaches, and in the versions of psychoanalysis that emerged following their work.

The familiar stranger

Ferenczi, while loved by Freud, remained enigmatic and exotic (Erös, 2004). Freud emphasized Ferenczi's Hungarian national character: "Hungary, so near geographically to Austria, and so far from it scientifically, has produced only one collaborator, S. Ferenczi, but one that indeed outweighs a whole society" (Freud, 1914, p. 33). Later, others, too, highlighted Ferenczi's Hungarian national character and gypsy nature (Thompson, 1988). But, as the Hungarian historiographer of psychoanalysis Erös (2004) argues, "Instead of searching for non-existent Hungarian roots, we should emphasize the ethnocultural and linguistic pluralism in Ferenczi's background" (p. 125). This pluralism was typical of assimilationist, middle-class, upwardly mobile Jewish families, such as Freud and Ferenczi's. Ferenczi was Freud's "familiar stranger" (Erös, 2004, p. 125), both *heimlich* and *unheimlich*. It was not

Ferenczi's nationality, language, or culture that evoked this familiar strangeness, but rather his split complementarity with Freud in relation to gender, hysteria, and paranoia. Freud and Ferenczi inhabited the flip sides of positive and negative Oedipal wishes and defenses. Freud's paranoia – his castration anxiety and paternal fear that his sons would band together to kill him – met Ferenczi's hysteria – his excessive "feminine" need to be loved and engaged in direct emotional exchange – even as each unconsciously and ambivalently identified with the other, his uncanny double. Before, during, and after his formal analysis of Ferenczi, Freud repeatedly interpreted to Ferenczi that Ferenczi was trying to obtain the love he missed in childhood from his patients, and via homosexual submission, from Freud. As Ernst Falzeder (2010) puts it,

> Freud did not even dream of giving Ferenczi some of this love himself. No, Ferenczi should get a grip on himself, stop acting like an obnoxious child, and should, as Freud admonished him … "leave the island of dreams which you inhabit with your fantasy children and mix in with the struggle of men."
>
> (p. 401)

Note the equation of femininity and childishness, accepted by both Freud and Ferenczi until Ferenczi began to challenge this assumption in his final years.

In his analysis of Schreber, Freud focused exclusively on Schreber's dynamic conflicts about his longings for his father's love, the negative Oedipus complex – with not a single mention of Schreber's relation to his mother. The neglect of the maternal is characteristic of Freud's work, reflecting, among other things, his own lack of insight into his conflicts concerning his own mother. Not only is the mother neglected, only present as the object of the child's desire, but so too are the loving relations of the boy to his father. Only the competitive and murderous side of the ambivalence is present within the positive Oedipus. Significantly, also neglected in Freud's work was the theme of anti-Semitism, including his society's assumption of the passive, effeminate, perverse, homosexual, castrated nature of Jewish men. Freud made no mention of Schreber's incorporation of the rhetoric of anti-Semitism into his delusional system. Schreber constructed a complex theology involving a divided God with dark and light incarnations, whose "rays" and "nerves" would sexually violate him. Schreber believed that he was being literally "unmanned," an Eternal or Wandering Jew who was being transformed into a woman, so that God could sexually violate him and conceive a new human race. As part of his transformation, he felt his stomach being replaced with an inferior "Jew's stomach." Unmanning and Jewification are equivalent. Examining the margin comments on Freud's copy of Schreber's book, Gilman (1993) demonstrates that Freud was well aware of this rhetoric. But if Freud commented on Schreber's identification with the Wandering Jew, he would draw attention to the most obvious marker of his own Jewishness, and undercut his credibility as a neutral (read non-Jewish) scientist. It was therefore important for Freud to present his data as uncontaminated by anything that might inscribe them as Jewish. The image of the Wandering or Eternal Jew converged with "the eternal feminine"[2] to mark or circumcise the Jew as racially/sexually different (Pellegrini, 1997).

Paranoia and anti-Semitism were closely related. In fin de siècle Germany and Austria, paranoia was often centered on the perceived danger of a Jewish conspiracy. Gilman (1993) contends that Freud displaced the perceived danger from Jews to homosexuals. Similar to his rejection of the hereditary etiology Charcot had championed, Freud rejected Kraft-Ebbing's theory that homosexuality, like Jewishness, was an innate biological flaw. Instead, Freud viewed it as a developmental arrest, not as degenerate, but as atavistic or primitive. When Freud and Ferenczi stayed together in Palermo to collaborate on the case of Schreber, the deck was stacked for an enactment of the very content they were immersed in writing about – homosexuality, paranoia, and homophobia. Here were two Jewish men, viewed by their society as castrated, homosexual, and feminine, collaborating together in partnership, writing about the themes that were intensely preoccupying them. Freud was determined not to relive his love of Fliess, while Ferenczi, longing for love and intimacy, dreamed of seeing Freud naked.

Freud's (1911) formulation of Schreber was inextricably linked with his own internalized homophobia, stemming from his identity as a feminized Jew living in the larger context of an anti-Semitic and homophobic milieu, just at a time when homosexuality was being transformed into a distinct identity. Freud's recognition of Schreber's desire to be transformed into a woman meant facing his own unresolved feminine desires, which in their society was equated with homosexuality. Anxious to overcome the pathology of feminization and homosexuality that fin de siècle Europe attributed to Jews, Freud proceeded to pathologize them, or at the very least to characterize them as developmentally primitive.

Whereas Freud began his career focusing on hysteria in men (including in himself), now a new pathology became central – paranoia – and hence a new binary emerged. With paranoia as the new prototype of male psychopathology, hysteria returned to its pre-Freudian position as quintessentially female. Vulnerability was displaced from circumcised Jewish men onto hysterical women and paranoid men – men who were unconsciously homosexual. Hysteria and paranoia, caricatures of femininity and masculinity, were explained by positing universal anxieties: penis envy, castration anxiety, and the repudiation of femininity became psychological bedrock. The negative Oedipus was pathologized and men's wish for penetration was repressed. All differences, including race and religion, became minor differences, except for the one big universal difference–the phallic difference – the difference between the sexes (Pellegrini, 1997). This formulation is not meant to imply that misogyny is secondary to racism or religious hatred; rather, we believe that each of these displaces and disguises the others.

Let's examine how the inventor of the term "introjection" (Ferenczi, 1909a) and the first analyst to examine the dynamic of "identification with the aggressor" (Ferenczi, 1933a) dealt with the anti-Semitism that surrounded him. This is a striking illustration of how a colonized people introject the views of the colonizer – how they identify with the aggressor, albeit with disguised ambivalence, or with what Ferenczi (1913) described as "mockery and scorn concealed behind the blind belief" (p. 443). Let's return to Ferenczi's 1921 Christmas day letter to Groddeck, in which he recalled the incident in Palermo.

Georg Groddeck, the self-proclaimed "wild analyst" (Groddeck, 1977, p. 7) was a pioneer in psychosomatic medicine, and practiced at Baden-Baden. After Freud introduced Ferenczi to Groddeck in 1917, Ferenczi became enamored of him and, as was his wont, opened himself up to obtain Groddeck's love. In fact, for the rest of his life, Ferenczi spent summers at Groddeck's sanatorium and the two engaged in something of a mutual analysis. Ferenczi was resentful of Freud because he allowed himself to be pressured by Freud to marry Gisella, a woman older than he who was no longer able to bear children.[3] Ferenczi never felt sexually satisfied in his marriage, writing to Groddeck, "I, my 'It', isn't interested in analytic interpretations, but wants something real, a young wife, a child!" (Fortune, 2002, p. 11). Immediately, Ferenczi shifted to his feelings about Groddeck. "Are you by any chance this female friend for me, or am I using your friendship in a homosexual way to replace her?" (Fortune, 2002, p. 11) Pay attention here to the flow of associations and the emerging themes of heterosexuality and homosexuality, positive and negative Oedipus complex, and Jewishness and anti-Semitism. Ferenczi next told a dream, which he called an "entirely 'Hungarian' dream," illuminating his Hungarian experience and identity. In the dream, Ferenczi was happily singing a Hungarian folksong, the words of which he recalled:

> This is what the old Jew tells me.
> Here! – it's from my market stall.
> I want nothing from your stall,
> I don't want you, old Jew, either.
> This is what Fay Gyula tells me (name of a dashing man)
> I'll buy you, dearest, dresses, ribbons,
> Don't need your dresses, ribbons, Fay,
> All I want is you.

Ferenczi does not hesitate to provide his associations to the dream. On Christmas Eve, he had a small dinner with his family and there were two "servant-girls," sisters, singing and laughing with their friends. The younger one is 16 and has "remarkably red lips." The older is 19 or 20 and Ferenczi writes, "She has, as I was able to establish during the course of a medical examination, remarkably firm, ripe breasts, with enormous nipples which become erect during the examination. Interpretation: these pretty girls didn't want an old Jew like me!" (Fortune, 2002, p. 13) Ferenczi notices that he is growing gray while a friend of his still has black hair and his wife is a "fresh young blonde."

Ferenczi says that he picked up that folksong as a child when he visited the vineyard with his father and heard the peasant women singing it. Strikingly, Ferenczi recalls that he also heard his own parents sing the song. He remembers yearning for the "earthly charms of those peasant girls in that vineyard." Ferenczi then adds that the song was somehow "bisexual" and that the "dashing man" Fay Gyula was simultaneously also a beautiful lady.

In our view, the dream reflects Ferenczi's internalization of the anti-Semitism surrounding him, magnified by his identification with his parents' introjections of these same attitudes. That he could happily sing and laugh about these blatantly anti-Semitic images is an illustration of his and his family's identification with the aggressor. It also speaks to their Hungarian nationalism, their longing for acceptance by the culture, and their belief that they would in fact be absorbed as Hungarians of Jewish faith, a hope that would soon be crushed. Perhaps Ferenczi and his parents happily singing this anti-Semitic folksong reveals the workings of dissociation, illustrating Homi Bhabha's (1984) formulation of the ambivalence of colonial mimicry, including the wavering between mimicry and mockery, resemblance and menace. Anticipating Bhabha's insight, Ferenczi contended that identification with the aggressor is never complete (Frankel, 2002). The split-off ego is dissociatively contemptuous and sarcastic, and displays what Ferenczi importantly designated "ironic obedience." As he elaborated, "The mentally ill person has a keen eye for the insanity of mankind" (Ferenczi, 1932, p. 19).

In March 1919, Ferenczi was appointed as the first university professor of psychoanalysis. On April 29, Ferenczi wrote to Freud announcing it as official. The significance of this appointment has been romanticized, as by that time the independence of the university had been suspended under the Hungarian Republic of Councils (Erös, 2004). With the victory of the counterrevolutionary Horthy regime, there were numerous mass executions and arbitrary arrests. Jews were accused of collaborating with the communists. By August, Ferenczi's professorship was annulled and soon he was also excluded from the Budapest Medical Association (Giamppieri and Erös, 1987). Ferenczi (1919) wrote to Freud,

> The ruthless clerical anti-Semitic spirit seems to have eked out a victory. If everything does not deceive, we Hungarian Jews are now facing a period of brutal persecution of Jews. They will, I think,

> have cured us in a very short time of the illusion with which we were brought up, namely that we are "Hungarians of Jewish faith." (p. 365)

Ferenczi then added a line that, from our perspective, is bitterly ironic. "I picture Hungarian anti-Semitism – commensurate with the national character – to be more brutal than the petty-hatred of the Austrians." He continued, "Personally, one will have to take this trauma as an occasion to abandon certain prejudices brought along from the nursery and to come to terms with the bitter truth of being, as a Jew, *really* without a country." An eternally wandering Jew. "The blackest reaction prevails at the university. All Jewish assistants were fired, the Jewish students were thrown out and beaten" (pp. 365–366). Freud (1919a) responded with "burning disappointment for you, one which has robbed you of a fatherland" (p. 367). Ferenczi found himself *unheimlich*, uncanny, without a home – a familiar situation for a Wandering Jew.

Never giving up his love for Freud, in one of his last letters, March 29, 1933, Ferenczi wrote to Freud, "Short and sweet: I advise you to make use of the time of the not yet impending dangerously threatening situation and, with a few patients and your daughter Anna, to go to a more secure country, perhaps England" (Ferenczi, 1933b, p. 448). Freud responded that it was not certain that Hitler will overpower Austria, and if he does it will not reach the level of brutality as in Germany, and in any event his own life is secure, and besides being an immigrant is not easy, and even if they kill you, one kind of death is as good as another!

On May 4, 1933, as he was dying, and with almost no strength left to hold the pen, Ferenczi wrote to wish Freud a happy birthday. Sándor Ferenczi died in Budapest on May 22, 1933. Ferenczi's younger brother, Karoly, and his wife Vilma Klar died in Auschwitz in 1944. His younger sister Zsofia had an inscription carved in a gravestone in the cemetery of Miskolc. After their names, it reads, "I will keep hold of your memories for ever. Your mourning sister."[4]

Conclusion

We are all deeply embedded in social and cultural assumptions and biases that are well beyond our capacity to observe. These include prejudices that are unjust and dangerous, and that influence both our self-understandings and our clinical practices. The mutual enactment in Palermo and the history of the Freud-Ferenczi relationship illustrates how these pre-reflective beliefs and related unconscious dynamics are inevitably enacted in our relationships, particularly as we actualize the very content we are formulating in words. Our hope is that this study of the context beyond the psychoanalytic text will serve as an example of the critical importance of studying the development of psychoanalytic ideas, including our fundamental clinical concepts, within the larger framework of the social, cultural, political, economic, and religious surround.

Notes

1 This chapter is adapted from Aron and Starr's (2013) *A Psychotherapy for the People: Toward a Progressive Psychoanalysis*. New York: Routledge. An earlier version was presented by Lewis Aron as the Keynote Address to the Spring Meeting, Division of Psychoanalysis (39), American Psychological Association, New York City, April 15, 2011.

2 "The eternal feminine" is a cultural archetype, much invoked by Symbolist artists and writers of the late nineteenth century, whereby a woman was an instinctual or spiritual being, whether a wicked temptress or a saintly virgin.

3 A review of the Freud-Ferenczi correspondence makes it abundantly clear that even while claiming to remain neutral, Freud admitted to Gisella that he was doing all he could, both in and out of the analysis, to persuade Ferenczi to marry her. For a thorough account of the quadrangle between Freud and Ferenczi, Ferenczi's wife Gisella, and her daughter Elma, see Berman (2004).

4 For the tragic story of the anti-Semitic and communist persecutions of Hungarian analysts throughout the twentieth century, see the review by Judit Mészáros (2010).

References

Aron, L., & Starr, K. (2013). *A Psychotherapy for the People: Toward a progressive psychoanalysis*. New York: Routledge.

Benjamin, J. (1988). *The Bonds of Love*. New York: Pantheon.

Berman, E. (2004). Sándor, Gizella, Elma. *International Journal of Psychoanalysis*, 85: 489–520.

Bhabha, H. (1984). Of mimicry and man: The ambivalence of colonial discourse. *Discipleship: A Special Issue on Psychoanalysis*, 28: 125–133.

Boyarin, D. (1997). *Unheroic Conduct: The rise of heterosexuality and the invention of the Jewish man*. Berkeley: University of California Press.

Breger, L. (2000). *Freud: Darkness in the midst of vision*. New York: John Wiley.

Erös, F. (2004). The Ferenczi cult: Its historical and political roots. *International Forum of Psychoanalysis*, 13: 121–128.

Falzeder, E. (2010). Sándor Ferenczi between orthodoxy and heterodoxy. *American Imago*, 66(4): 395–404.

Ferenczi, S. (1909a). Introjection and transference. In J. Rickman (ed.) & J.I. Suttie (trans.), *First Contributions to Psycho-analysis*. London: Hogarth Press, 1952, chapter 2.

Ferenczi, S. (1909b). Letter from Sándor Ferenczi to Sigmund Freud, October 30, 1909. In E. Brabant, E., Falzeder, & P. Giampieri-Deutsch (ed. & trans.), *The Correspondence of Sigmund Freud and Sándor Ferenczi, 1908–1914*. Cambridge, MA: Belknap Press/Harvard University Press, 1993, vol. 1, pp. 91–92.

Ferenczi, S. (1910a). Letter from Sándor Ferenczi to Sigmund Freud, March 22, 1910. In E. Brabant, E., Falzeder, & P. Giampieri-Deutsch (ed. & trans.), *The Correspondence of Sigmund Freud and Sándor Ferenczi, 1908–1914*. Cambridge, MA: Belknap Press/Harvard University Press, 1993, vol. 1, p. 153.

Ferenczi, S. (1910b). Letter from Sándor Ferenczi to Sigmund Freud, October 3, 1910. In E. Brabant, E., Falzeder, & P. Giampieri-Deutsch (ed. & trans.), *The Correspondence of Sigmund Freud and Sándor Ferenczi, 1908–1914*. Cambridge, MA: Belknap Press/Harvard University Press, 1993, vol. 1, pp. 217–221.

Ferenczi, S. (1910c). Letter from Sándor Ferenczi to Sigmund Freud, October 10, 1910. In E. Brabant, E., Falzeder, & P. Giampieri-Deutsch (ed. & trans.), *The Correspondence of Sigmund Freud and Sándor Ferenczi, 1908–1914*. Cambridge, MA: Belknap Press/Harvard University Press, 1993, vol. 1, p. 224.

Ferenczi, S. (1913). Belief, disbelief, and conviction. In J. Rickman (ed.) & J. I. Suttie (Trans.), *Further Contributions to Psycho-analysis*. London: Hogarth Press, 1950, pp. 437–450.

Ferenczi, S. (1915). Letter from Sándor Ferenczi to Sigmund Freud. In E. Brabant, E., Falzeder, & P. Giampieri-Deutsch (ed. & trans.), *The Correspondence of Sigmund Freud and Sándor Ferenczi*. Cambridge, MA: Belknap Press/Harvard University Press, 1996, vol. 2, p. 80.

Ferenczi, S. (1919). Letter from Sándor Ferenczi to Sigmund Freud, August 28, 1919. In E. Brabant, E., Falzeder, & P. Giampieri-Deutsch (ed. & trans.), *The Correspondence of Sigmund Freud and Sándor Ferenczi*. Cambridge, MA: Belknap Press of Harvard University Press, 1996, vol. 2, p. 365.

Ferenczi, S. (1921). Letter from Sándor Ferenczi to Georg Groddeck, December 25, 1921. In C. Fortune (ed. & trans.), *The Sándor Ferenczi-Georg Groddeck Correspondence*. London: Open Gate Press, 2002, pp. 8–9.

Ferenczi, S. (1932). *The Clinical Diary of Sándor Ferenczi*, ed. J. Dupont, trans. M. Balint & N.Z. Jackson. Cambridge, MA: Harvard University Press, 1988.

Ferenczi, S. (1933a). The Confusion of Tongues between adults and children: The language of tenderness and of passion (M. Balint, Ed.). *International Journal of Psycho-Analysis* 30(4): 1949.

Ferenczi, S. (1933b). Letter from Sándor Ferenczi to Sigmund Freud, March 29, 1933. In E. Brabant, E., Falzeder, & P. Giampieri-Deutsch (ed. & trans.), *The Correspondence of Sigmund Freud and Sándor Ferenczi*. Cambridge, MA: Belknap Press/Harvard University Press, 1996, vol. 3, p. 448.

Fortune, C. (ed.) (2002). *The Sándor Ferenczi–Georg Groddeck Correspondence, 1921–1933*, trans. J. Cohen, E. Petersdorff, & N. Ruebsaat. New York: The Other Press.

Frankel, J. (2002). Identification and "traumatic aloneness." *Psychoanalytic Dialogues*, 12: 159–170.

Freud, S. (1910a). Letter from Sigmund Freud to Carl Jung. In W. McGuire (ed.), *The Freud/Jung letters: The correspondence between Sigmund Freud and C.G. Jung*. New Jersey: Princeton University Press, 1974, pp. 1–592.

Freud, S. (1910b). Letter from Sigmund Freud to Sándor Ferenczi, October 6, 1910. In E. Brabant, E., Falzeder, & P. Giampieri-Deutsch (ed. and trans.), *The Correspondence of Sigmund Freud and Sándor Ferenczi, 1908–1914*. Cambridge, MA: Belknap Press/Harvard University Press, 1993, vol. 1, pp. 221–222.

Freud, S. (1910c). Letter from Sigmund Freud to Sándor Ferenczi, October 17, 1910. In E. Brabant, E., Falzeder, & P. Giampieri-Deutsch (ed. and trans.), *The Correspondence of Sigmund Freud and Sándor Ferenczi, 1908–1914* Cambridge, MA: Belknap Press /Harvard University Press, 1993, vol. 1, p. 227.

Freud, S. (1914). On the history of the psycho-analytic movement. In J. Strachey (Ed. & Trans.), *The Standard Edition of the Complete Psychological Works of Sigmund Freud* (Vol. 14, pp. 1–66). London: Hogarth Press, 1957.

Freud, S. (1919a). Letter from Sigmund Freud to Sándor Ferenczi, September 5, 1919. In E. L. Freud (ed.), *Letters of Sigmund Freud, 1873–1929* (p. 367). London: Hogarth Press, 1961.

Freud, S. (1919b). The "uncanny". In J. Strachey (ed. & trans.), *The Standard Edition of the Complete Psychological Works of Sigmund Freud*. London: Hogarth Press, 1955, vol. 17, pp. 219–256.

Freud, S. (1937). Analysis terminable and interminable. In J. Strachey (ed. & trans.), *The Standard Edition of the Complete Psychological Works of Sigmund Freud*. London: Hogarth Press, 1964, vol. 23, pp. 216–253.

Freud, S. (1939). Moses and monotheism. In J. Strachey (ed. & trans.), *The Standard Edition of the Complete Psychological Works of Sigmund Freud*. London: Hogarth Press, 1964, vol. 23, pp. 1–138.

Gaztambide, D. (2011, April 28). "A psychotherapy for the people": Freud, Ferenczi, and psychoanalytic work with the underprivileged. Paper presented at the Ferenczi Center at the New School for Social Research, New York.

Giamppieri, P., & Erös, F. (1987). The beginnings of the reception of psychoanalysis in Hungary 1900–1920. *Sigmund Freud House Bulletin*, 11(2): 13–28.

Gilman, S.L. (1993). *Freud, race, and gender*. Princeton, NJ: Princeton University Press.

Groddeck, G. (1977). The meaning of illness. *International Psycho-Analytic Library*, **105**: 1–266. London: Hogarth Press/Institute of Psycho-Analysis.

Kapusi, K. (2010). Toward a biography of Sándor Ferenczi: Footnotes from Miskolc. *American Imago*, 66: 405–410.

Lothane, Z. (1997). The schism between Freud and Jung over Schreber. *International Forum of Psychoanalysis*, 6: 103–115.

Lukacs, J. (1988). *Budapest 1900: A historical portrait of a city and its culture*. New York: Grove Press.

Mészáros, J. (2010). Progress and persecution in the psychoanalytic heartland: Anti-semitism, communism and the fate of Hungarian psychoanalysis. *Psychoanalytic Dialogues*, 20: 600–622.

Pellegrini, A. (1997). *Performance Anxieties*. New York: Routledge.

Phillips, S.H. (2003). Homosexuality: Coming out of the confusion. *International Journal of Psychoanalysis*, 84: 1431–1450.

Rozenblit, M.L. (2001). *Reconstructing a National Identity: The Jews of Habsburg Austria during World War I*. Oxford and New York: Oxford University Press.

Rudnytsky, P.L. (2002). *Reading Psychoanalysis*. Ithaca, New York: Cornell.

Stanton, M. (1991). *Sándor Ferenczi: Reconsidering active intervention*. London: Free Association Books.

Sziklai, A. (2009). *The Jewish theme in the relationship of Sigmund Freud and Sándor Ferenczi: Between the state and the public sphere*, vol. 84 of working paper. Jerusalem: European Forum at the Hebrew University.

Thompson, C.M. (1988). Sándor Ferenczi, 1873–1933. *Contemporary Psychoanalysis*, 24: 182–195.

Chapter 7

The dimensions of the Freud/ Ferenczi correspondence

Peter Hoffer

The correspondence between Sigmund Freud and Sándor Ferenczi is arguably the richest in content of Freud's major correspondences. Spanning a period of some twenty-five years, it is a chronicle of the relations between two of the founders of psychoanalysis during one of the most eventful formative periods of its existence. As such, it presents the history of a relationship unique in its depth of personal intimacy and intellectual ferment. It would be impossible to do justice to the richness of this history in the brief space and time allotted to me. Even a close reading of the correspondence itself would only begin to do so. Mindful of these limitations, I will attempt in the following to characterize, in the form of a narrative, the overlapping scientific, personal, and historical dimensions of this intimate, complex, and often troubled relationship, as revealed in the correspondence, with a view toward elucidating the transformations that it underwent in the personal lives of the principals and in the history of psychoanalysis.

Freud and Ferenczi had already become well acquainted when, in September of 1910, they embarked on one of the many holidays they would spend together, in Palermo, Italy, which provided the occasion for what would prove to be a defining moment in their relationship. Their oft-cited altercation over the writing of the Schreber case, which Ferenczi described eleven years later in a letter to Groddeck (see Fortune, 2002, pp. 8–9), set the tone for a change in their relations, in the form of a pact – which could be described as Faustian – conceived by Ferenczi and tacitly agreed to by Freud. In an animated exchange of letters following the event, Freud remarks: "I would have wished for you to tear yourself away from the infantile role next to me as a companion with equal rights, which you did not succeed in doing"

(Brabant, Falzeder, and Giampieri-Deutsch, 1993, p. 215). In his lengthy reply of October 3, Ferenczi attempts to balance his emotional account with Freud by entering a plea for "absolute mutual openness" based upon an understanding whereby they "*are not ashamed in front of each other, keep nothing secret, tell each other the truth without risk or insult*" (ibid., p. 220; emphasis in the original), adding, "If you had scolded me thoroughly instead of being eloquently silent! I would have perhaps felt grievously wounded in the first instant, but ... I would have owed you a very large debt of gratitude for it" (ibid.).

In his reply of October 6, Freud immediately picks up on this last remark: "Why didn't I scold you and in so doing, open the way to an understanding? Quite right, it was a weakness on my part; I am also not that ψα superman whom we have constructed, and I also haven't overcome the countertransference. I couldn't do it, just as I can't do it with my three sons, because I like them and I feel sorry for them in the process" (ibid., p. 221). In his letter of October 12, Ferenczi reiterates his plea in the form of an "ideal of honesty," with the assertion that "Not everything that is infantile should be abhorred ... I still hold firm to the conviction that it is not honesty but superfluous secrecy that is abnormal ... I am grateful to you for every word that you say about my behavior, no matter how unpleasant it may be" (ibid., p. 224).

The forgoing exchange may serve to illustrate how, from this point on in the correspondence, the relationship between Freud and Ferenczi began to take on a quintessentially psychoanalytic character (see Dupont, 1994; Grubrich-Simitis, 1986; Hoffer, 1991), spurred on by Ferenczi and perpetuated by Freud's – often reluctant – acquiescence, which laid the foundation for a friendship unique among all of Freud's relationships with his collaborators in its depth of personal intimacy and engagement.

Although the personal and scientific dimensions of their relationship often coexisted independently of one another, as is exemplified by their mutual interest in thought transference, homosexuality, paranoia (See Ferenczi's letter of May 13, 1911, Brabant et al., 1993, pp. 276–277), among other pursuits, they began to merge intermittently as Ferenczi became increasing absorbed in revealing his dreams, associations, parapraxes, and other private matters to Freud. Ferenczi waxes rhapsodic as he reports to Freud from Budapest shortly after their return from a holiday spent together in Bolzano:

> [The] joy of being able to spend two days with you again in intimate conversation, free from the obligations of work, seems to me here in my isolation to be so improbable that the impression of the fairy-tale-like quality of our splendid excursion is enhanced even more by it. Incidentally, I never depart from you without benefit. I mean by that not an increase in my understanding of mental activity in general but rather a deepening of insight specifically into my own mental life, without which there can be no true knowledge – but especially no true *faith*.
>
> (letter of April 24, 1911, ibid., p. 270; emphasis in original)

Ferenczi's urge for a further deepening of insight into his mental life becomes more acute, when, after his decision to take Elma, the daughter of his mistress and long-time companion, Gizella Pálos, into analysis, he falls in love with her shortly after the suicide of one of her suitors, proposes marriage, reconsiders his decision and subsequently persuades Freud to take Elma into analysis himself. The details of this episode in Ferenczi's life and its impact on his already complicated relationship with Freud have been described by numerous commentators (Berman, 2004; Bokanowski, 1996; Dupont, 1995; Gabbard, 1995; Haynal and Falzeder, 1991; among others). Its significance, however, for exacerbating the conflictual aspects of their relationship lies in the fact that it led directly to Ferenczi's frequent urgings that Freud take him into a formal analysis, the prospect of which Freud always greeted sympathetically but with considerable reservation. After one such plea from the former in the form of a "stay in Vienna with combined psychic-somatic treatment," Freud writes:

> I am always glad to hear about how you are, even if you can't report the best. What consoles me is the extraordinary elevation of your intellectuality at this time … But I know that four or six weeks of analysis would be much too insufficient. For that reason, something else comes into consideration, namely, my dearth of inclination to expose one of my indispensable helpers to the danger of personal estrangement brought about by the analysis.
>
> (letter of May 4, 1913, Brabant et al., 1993, pp. 481–482)

This declaration, in all its benevolent succinctness, speaks volumes, in that it not only reveals a reluctance on Freud's part to unleash the "negative transference" that would become a bone of contention between Freud and Ferenczi in the personal and scientific dimension of the correspondence during the later stages of their relationship, but it also highlights Ferenczi's importance to Freud as a loyal supporter of "the cause" (*die Sache*) of psychoanalysis, which often took precedence over personal considerations, not only in Ferenczi's case, but in Freud's relations with his other collaborators as well.

Despite Freud's reservations, Ferenczi was able to persuade Freud to undertake a formal analysis with him, which began on September 30, 1914 but was interrupted by Ferenczi's conscription into the Hungarian Hussars after the outbreak of World War I (Stanton, 1991, p. 24). It is noteworthy in this context that on the day he was to arrive in Vienna for his first session, Ferenczi missed his train and requested a postponement for the following day (Brabant and Falzeder, p. 19). This mistake is not an isolated incident in his relations with Freud, but is typical of numerous symptomatic acts and parapraxes of a transferential nature, some of which Ferenczi attempted to analyze in his letters to Freud, and which signaled an intensification of the analytical tenor of the correspondence, which was increasingly assuming the role of a substitute for a formal analysis. On October 27, Ferenczi writes to Freud: "I will – I believe – have to conduct our correspondence, at least in part, on an analytical basis; the sudden breaking off of our doctor-patient relationship (you see, I am writing as if in free association) would otherwise be all too painful for me. In addition, difficult to carry out." (ibid.). As is generally well known, the analysis was resumed in 1916, from June 14 to July 5, and again from September 26 to October 9 (Kilborne, 2008, p. 6).

The immediate occasion for the resumption of Ferenczi's analysis centered around the intensification of Ferenczi's conflict in his love relations and his painful indecision over whether to propose marriage to Gizella, exacerbated in no small part by Freud's urgings in its favor. Freud's decision to terminate the analysis prematurely has become the subject of continuing controversy, and his motives for doing so remain clouded, notwithstanding his attempt to explain them publicly in his essay "Analysis Terminable and Interminable" (1937), published four years after Ferenczi's death. His explanation to Ferenczi for his decision to terminate the analysis is given directly in a letter of November 16, 1916:

> You know that I consider your attempt at analysis finished, – finished, not terminated [*abgeschlossen, nicht beendet*], but rather broken off because of unfavorable circumstances. If you were still able to make your decision [to marry Gizella] dependent on the continuation of the analysis, then you would have forced it into the service of delay, which shouldn't be.
> (Falzeder and Brabant, p. 153)[1]

Whether or not it was justified by "circumstances," Freud's decision to terminate Ferenczi's analysis as he did had a profound impact on Ferenczi's life, his sense of self, and his continuing relations with his family, with Freud, and with other members of the psychoanalytic movement.

The end of World War I ushered in a period of intense productivity and transformation within psychoanalysis, in which Ferenczi played a major role. As one of the founders of the International Psychoanalytic Association (IPA) and a charter member of the "secret committee" spawned in the aftermath of the defections of Jung and Adler, Ferenczi continued to enjoy a privileged position among Freud's closest associates, which was enhanced by his election to the presidency of the IPA and his appointment as the first Professor of Psychoanalysis of Budapest University (Stanton, 1995, p. 29). These elevations were short-lived, however, in consequence of the overthrow of the forward-looking revolutionary socialist regime of Béla Kun by the anti-Semitic fascist dictatorship of Admiral Miklós Horthy. In the midst of the ensuing political turmoil, it was decided that Ferenczi should resign the presidency of the IPA, to be replaced in the post by Ernest Jones (ibid., p. 30).

Ferenczi's already substantial scientific productivity increased during the beginning decade of the '20's and continued to find favor with Freud, whose own productivity increased proportionally, with the publication of such monumental works as "Beyond the Pleasure Principle" (1920) and *The Ego and the Id* (1923). But the year 1924 saw an increase in tension in the personal and scientific dimensions of their relationship, which was fueled in part by dissensions in the secret committee over the publication of *The Development of Psychoanalysis*, written jointly by Ferenczi and Rank. The controversy over its publication and the work by Rank that followed on its heels, *The Trauma of Birth* (1924), rocked the psychoanalytic community. Much has been written about it by numerous commentators (Hoffer, 2008; Lieberman, 1985; Rachman, 1997a; Wittenberger, 1995, among others), and limitations of time and space prevent me from discussing it here in detail. Suffice it to say, it left an indelible imprint on the lives and careers of many of the principals and produced major ramifications in the theory and practice of psychoanalysis that are still evident today.

Although Ferenczi ultimately distanced himself from Rank, the reverberations of the controversy that surrounded their collaboration left an indelible imprint on the former's continuing relations with Freud and on the history of psychoanalysis.

To all outward appearances, relations between Freud and Ferenczi remained amicable during the years immediately following the Rank crisis, with no let-up in Ferenczi's productivity and Freud's concomitant encouragement of his scientific pursuits, with the publication of Ferenczi's *Thalassa: A Theory of Genitality* (1989 [1924], which had been the subject of an earlier collaboration between Ferenczi and Freud and the significance of which had been eclipsed by the controversy surrounding *The Trauma of Birth*. But a close reading of their correspondence during the mid-1920s indicates that a subtle shift in their personal and intellectual relations was taking place in connection with Ferenczi's ongoing explorations in the sphere of technique. In "Contra-Indications to the 'Active' Psycho-Analytical Technique" (1926), a paper read at the Ninth International Psychoanalytic Congress in Bad Homburg in September 1925, Ferenczi begins to question aspects of his own "active" technique, which had been influenced to a large extent by his observations of Freud's technique and supported by Freud himself (see Freud, 1919):

> ["Activity"] unquestionably stimulates the resistance of the patient in so far as it seeks to increase the psychical tension by painful frustrations, injunctions, and prohibitions, and so gain new material. That is to say, the ego of the patient runs counter to the analyst … [F]rom this relation of the ego to frustration, it follows that the analysis ought never to begin with active measures. On the contrary, for a long time the ego must be treated with forbearance or at least treated with circumspection, for otherwise no working positive transference will occur.
>
> (Ferenczi, 1926, pp. 218–219)

On New Year's Day 1928, Ferenczi sent Freud a "little paper," called "The Elasticity of Psychoanalytic Technique" (Ferenczi, 1928), which elaborated on the lines of thought cited above. In his reply of January 4, Freud is effusive in his praise, commenting that the paper "testifies to that superior maturity that you have acquired in the last few years and in which no one approaches you" (Falzeder and Brabant, 2000, p. 332). In the next paragraph, however, he raises an "objection" to one of the central ideas presented in the paper, the analyst's exercise of "tact" in the analytic situation:

> All those who have no tact will see in this a justification of arbitrariness, i.e., of the subjective factor, i.e., of the influence of one's own unrestrained complexes. What we undertake in reality is a weighing out, which remains mostly preconscious, of the various reactions that we expect from our interventions, in the process of which it is first and foremost a matter of the quantitative assessment of the dynamic factors in the situation. Rules for these measurements can naturally not be made; the analyst's experience and normality will have to be the decisive factors. But one should thus divest "tact" of its mystical character for beginners.
>
> (ibid.)

In his reply of January 15, Ferenczi respectfully acknowledges Freud's critique of the paper, which he had earlier presented to the Budapest Society, remarking that

> I endeavored ... to prove that there is essentially no difference between your conception and mine. I know that you occasionally told me that I strive all too much to produce complete identity between your views and mine. But I believe that this time I am in the right ... I only think that one should put oneself first and foremost into the patient's position, one must "empathize" [*einfühlen*], but I am completely of your opinion regarding the topography of this psychic process ... In conclusion, I also agreed with the assertion that, despite all precautions, a misuse can occur, even with these technical recommendations. I prophesied directly (after the

> sadistic "active") the possibility of a "masochistic" period of analysis, of which I warned our members.
>
> (ibid., p. 334)

The subtle tone of disagreement in these utterances contains a foreshadowing of what was to come, as is demonstrated in the personal, scientific, and historical dimensions of the ensuing correspondence.

Much has been written from various perspectives about the apparent deterioration of relations between Freud and Ferenczi and the events leading up to the controversy within the psychoanalytic community surrounding Ferenczi's presentation of the "Confusion of Tongues" paper (Ferenczi, 1933) at the Twelfth International Psychoanalytic Congress in Wiesbaden, Germany in September 1932 (see Blum, 1994; Fromm, 1959; Grünberger, 1980; Hoffer, 2010; Rachman, 1997b, among others). I have little of substance to add in this brief narrative that will further influence the ongoing debate, other than to observe, as others have done, that the continuing painfully strained personal and intellectual relations between Freud and Ferenczi did not meet a similar fate as did those between Freud and some of his former colleagues (cf. Rank, Jung, Adler, Fliess, among others). This is due in no small part to Ferenczi's dogged insistence that the technical experimentation that was arousing so much consternation in Freud, however flawed, was not in vain. After a particularly intense exchange that took place during a three-day visit with Freud in Vienna in late October 1931, following a lengthy hiatus in their correspondence, Ferenczi writes:

> [Such] a far-reaching and first-time examination of the differences in our views … needs time to be settled. We are of one mind in principle as well as in the manner of acting. No less than you do I want to circumvent unnecessary and avoidable dangers; it is only a matter of a difference in the pace of what is *unavoidably* to be communicated and in the conception of the duty of science to communicate everything, even what is risky (if it is true) in the hope that from truth, ultimately only good can sprout.
>
> (letter of December 5, 1931, Falzeder and Brabant, 2000, p. 421; emphasis in original)

What followed on Freud's part was his well-known letter of December 5, 1931, in which, mobilizing "the brutal fatherly side," he excoriates Ferenczi for reviving the "kissing technique," reminding him that "the inclination toward sexual games [*Spielerei*] was not alien to [him] in pre-analytic times, so that one could put the new technique into context with the old misdemeanor" (ibid., p. 423).

On January 7, 1932, Ferenczi writes the first entry in what would become his *Clinical Diary* (Ferenczi, 1932), titled "Insensitivity [*Fühllosigkeit*] of the analyst". One may ask, *en passant*: "who is the analyst here?"

Both the letters that follow and the clinical diary – the writing of which can be viewed as an attempt on Ferenczi's part to continue his side of the correspondence, along with his own self-analysis, without Freud's knowledge or participation – are testimony to the fact that their relationship, as strained as it was, remained intact up to Ferenczi's untimely death on May 22, 1933. Although there is much more to be said on the subject of their continuing relations following their last face-to face meeting – both positive and negative – and, mindful that there are numerous historical omissions in my narrative, I would like to draw it to conclusion with the general observation that, despite the bitter animosity that would surface periodically in connection with the content of the "Confusion of Tongues" paper, the bond of friendship that had existed between them from the beginning was strong enough to resist all the forces, internal and external, that were working to sever it.

As an epilogue to this narrative, I would like to offer a possible approach to interpreting the complexities of their relationship by raising some questions that can only be answered when one takes into account the totality of the historical, personal, and scientific dimensions of the correspondence[2]: The pact that Freud and Ferenczi had made some twenty years earlier as a consequence of their portentous encounter in Palermo was grounded in Ferenczi's insistence that they "*not* [*be*] *ashamed in front of each other, keep nothing secret, tell each other the truth without risk or insult*" with the addendum, "If you had scolded me thoroughly instead of being eloquently silent! I would have perhaps felt grievously wounded in the first instant, but ... I would have owed you a very large debt of gratitude for it." If we now fast-forward to the turbulent weeks and months that preceded the presentation of the "Confusion of Tongues" paper, we may observe that there are numerous instances in which Freud demonstrated the "brutal fatherly side" of his temperament when he "scolded" Ferenczi for his supposed "misdemeanors," both personal and professional. From a psychoanalytic perspective, we may theorize that Freud was – perhaps unconsciously – mobilizing the sadistic "active" technique in his approach to helping Ferenczi resolve his personal conflicts, acting in the service of the "absolute mutual openness" that Ferenczi so fervently desired. Was Ferenczi, for his part, enacting the masochistic side of this technique when he did, in fact, feel "grievously wounded" by the treatment accorded to him? Was he perhaps altering the terms of the pact that had been set in Palermo when he commenced writing his clinical diary, in the process concealing from Freud numerous criticisms and expressions of affect representing his "unanalyzed negative transference," which, had they been subjected to analysis, might have "open[ed] the way to an understanding"? Would such an understanding have even been possible "considering the limited horizon of analysis in those early days" (Freud, 1937, p. 222)?

I defer to the readers of the correspondence between Freud and Ferenczi to formulate their own answers to these questions.

Notes

1 According to Ernst Falzeder (personal communication), the juxtaposition of the words "*abgeschlossen*" and "*beendet*" was a deliberate ambiguity on Freud's part, since they are virtually synonymous in German. It is also noteworthy that a literal translation of Freud's essay "Die endliche und die unendliche Analyse" would read: "Analysis with and without End."

2 For an interpretation of their relationship based on Ferenczi's supposed "regressive behavior," see Nemes (1988).

References

Berman, E. (2004). Sándor, Gizella, Elma: A biographical journey. *International Journal of Psychoanalysis*, 85: 489–520.

Blum, H. (1994). The Confusion of Tongues and psychic trauma. *International Journal of Psychoanalysis*, 71: 871–882.

Bokanowski, T. (1996). Sándor Ferenczi: Negative transference and transference depression. In P. Rudnytsky, A. Bókay, & P. Giampieri-Deutsch (eds.), *Ferenczi's Turn in Psychoanalysis*. New York: New York University Press, pp.120–144.

Brabant, E., Falzeder, E., & Giampieri-Deutsch, P. (eds.) (1993). *The Correspondence of Sigmund Freud and Sándor Ferenczi, vol. 1, 1908–1914*. Cambridge, MA: Harvard University Press.

Dupont, J. (1994). Freud's analysis of Ferenczi as revealed by their correspondence *International Journal of Psychoanalysis*, 75: 301–320.
Falzeder, E., & Brabant, E. (eds.) (1996). *The Correspondence of Sigmund Freud and Sándor Ferenczi, vol. 2, 1914–1919*. Cambridge, MA: Harvard University Press.
Falzeder, E., & Brabant, E. (eds.) (2000). *The Correspondence of Sigmund Freud and Sándor Ferenczi, vol. 3, 1920–1933*. Cambridge, MA: Harvard University Press.
Ferenczi, S. (1926). Contra-indications to the "active" psychoanalytical technique, In: *Further Contributions to the Theory and Technique of Psycho-Analysis*. London: Hogarth Press, pp. 217–230.
Ferenczi, S. (1933). Confusion of Tongues between adults and the child. In *Final Contributions to the Problems and Methods of Psycho-Analysis*. London: Hogarth Press, pp. 217–230.
Ferenczi, S. (1989 [1924]). *Thalassa: A Theory of Genitality*. London: Karnac Books.
Fortune, S. (ed.) (2002). *The Sándor Ferenczi-Georg Groddeck Correspondence, 1921–1933*. London: Open Gate Press.
Freud, S. (1919). Lines of advance in psychoanalytic therapy. *Standard Edition*, 17: 157–168. London: Hogarth Press.
Freud, S. (1920). Beyond the Pleasure Principle. *Standard Edition*, 18: 7–64. London: Hogarth Press.
Freud, S. (1923). *The Ego and the Id*. *Standard Edition*, 17: 3–68. London: Hogarth Press.
Freud, S. (1937). Analysis terminable and interminable. *Standard Edition*, 23: 211–253. London: Hogarth Press.
Fromm, E. (1959). *Sigmund Freud's Mission*. New York: Harper, pp. 62–67.
Gabbard, G. (1995). The early history of boundary violations in psychoanalysis. *Journal of the American Psychological Association*, 43(4): 1115–1136.
Grubrich-Simitis, I. (1986). Six letters of Sigmund Freud and Sándor Ferenczi on the interrelationship of psychoanalytic theory and technique. *International Review of Psycho-Analysis*, 13: 259–277.
Grünberger, B. (1980). From the "active technique" to the "confusion of tongues." On Ferenczi's deviation. In S. Lebovici & G. Widlöcher (eds.), *Psychoanalysis in France*. New York: International Universities Press, pp. 127–152.
Haynal, A., & Falzeder, E. (1991). "Healing through love"? A unique dialogue in the history of psychoanalysis. *Free Associations*, 21: 1–20.
Hoffer, A. (1991). The Freud-Ferenczi controversy – a living legacy. *International Review of Psychoanalysis*, 18: 465–472.
Hoffer, P.T. (2008). Ferenczi's collaboration with Rank: On paradigm shift and the origins of complementarity in psychoanalysis. *American Journal of Psychoanalysis*, 68: 128–138.
Hoffer, P.T. (2010). From elasticity to the confusion of tongues: A historical commentary on the technical dimension of the Freud/Ferenczi controversy. *Psychoanalytic Perspectives*, 7 (1): 90–103.
Kilborne, B. (2008). Human foibles and psychoanalytic technique: Freud, Ferenczi, and Gizella Palos. *American Journal of Psychoanalysis*, 68: 1–23.
Leitner, M. (1998). *Freud, Rank und die Folgen*. Vienna: Turia & Kant.
Lieberman, E.J. (1985). *Acts of Will: The life and work of Otto Rank*. Amherst: University of Massachusetts Press.
Nemes, L. (1988). Freud and Ferenczi: A possible interpretation of their relationship. *Contemporary Psychoanalysis*, 24 (2): 240–249.

Rachman, A. (1997a). *Sándor Ferenczi: The psychotherapist of tenderness and passion*. Northvale, NJ: Jason Aronson.

Rachman, A. (1997b). The suppression and censorship of Ferenczi's Confusion of Tongues paper. *Psychoanalytic Inquiry*, 17: 459–485.

Stanton, M. (1991). *Sándor Ferenczi: Reconsidering active intervention*. Northvale, NJ: Jason Aronson.

Wittenberger, G. (1995). *Das "Geheime Komitee" Sigmund Freuds: Institutionali sierungsprozesse in der Psychoanalytischen Bewegung zwischen 1912 und 1927*. Tübingen: Edition Diskord.

Chapter 8

The Budapest School's concept of supervision

Michael Balint's legacy to the development of psychoanalytic specificity theory

Howard Bacal

Michael Balint trained with Sándor Ferenczi in Budapest and had already assumed a leading role in Hungarian psychoanalysis when he immigrated to England in 1939 with his wife, Alice, also a psychoanalyst. Balint made original and important contributions to psychoanalytic theory, therapy, research, and training (see Bacal and Newman, 1990). To mention only a few: Balint (1935) proposed a radical, relational revision of Freud's theory of psychosexual stages of development; Michael and Alice Balint (1939) described the psychoanalytic situation as a reciprocal process, in effect anticipating contemporary theories of intersubjectivity by almost half a century; and in 1968, building upon his concept of "primary object love" (1937), Balint (1968) elaborated his idea of "the basic fault", breaking deep new ground in the understanding and treatment of early psychological trauma (see also Balint, 1969b).

Balint is perhaps best known for his pioneering work in bringing a psychoanalytic perspective to medical practice (Balint, 1957). The "Balint Group", a seminar-based clinical training whose aim is to enhance doctors' therapeutic responsiveness to the psychological problems of their patients, began at the Tavistock Clinic in the early 1950s, and continues to be offered worldwide under the auspices of the International Balint Federation and the American Balint Society.

What is less well-known is that this method of training general physicians for psychotherapeutic work was Balint's application of the unique approach to supervision of the Hungarian Psychoanalytic Society, that Balint offered in its original form[1] to his analysands at the Institute of Psychoanalysis in London.

In this chapter, I describe my experience of the Budapest model in psychoanalytic supervision with Michael Balint, and its application in "Balint Groups", which I led at the Tavistock Clinic, and in which I participated with Michael and Enid Balint in a research project at University College Hospital in London.[2] I then trace the influence of the Budapest model on the development of psychoanalytic supervision, in particular how it has influenced my conceptualizing psychoanalytic treatment and supervision as *the specificity of dyadic process*. The chapter concludes with an example of the application of *specificity theory* in my own supervisory work.[3]

My experience of the Budapest model of supervision

Balint supervised my first analytic control case for seven and a half years according to the Hungarian psychoanalytic supervisory method, wherein the candidate's training analyst supervises his first case within the candidate's own analysis as he shares his experience of his patient in the course of his associations. No separate session is set aside for this supervision. When the student, whose analysis is five times a week,[4] spontaneously talks about his experience of working with his "control case", his analyst responds as "supervisor". The London Institute of Psychoanalysis permitted Balint to offer the Budapest School's model of supervision, providing that it was voluntarily undertaken, and that the candidate undertook supervision of an additional case according to the traditional model.

I was eager to begin my first analytic training case in this way; but I conveyed to Balint that I was also feeling curiously ambivalent about starting the work with the patient I had selected – an interesting but apparently "difficult" young woman who, I noted during my associations in an analytic session, was around the same age as my younger sister. My resistance began to fade when Balint interpretively inquired whether I was ready for a little sister. His interpretation derived from my having told him earlier that, when my sister's nurse left when she was one year old, I (four and half, at the time) was heard to ask why she was not taking the baby with her; after all, she had arrived with her! Such observations, traditionally regarded as designating countertransference, constituted the focus of the Budapest supervisory model. This focus constituted the reason why, in this model of supervision, it is the first control case that is done with the candidate's own analyst "so that obstructions that stem from his own personality but are not yet revealed would be able to come to the surface as soon as possible" (Mészáros, 2010, p. 85).

The Hungarian method of supervising, however, transcended a focus on countertransference to encompass a particular form of interaction. It enabled me to appreciate, with striking immediacy, *how specific aspects of who I was in relation to my particular patient as our process unfolded,* affected my responses to her.[5] During another analytic session, I anxiously conveyed to Balint that I was having trouble working with another patient, as she seemed to be uncomfortably like me in some respects. I was startled – but enormously helped – to hear him say, "Every patient is the same as every other, yet completely different." Balint was, in effect, according recognition to the uniqueness of every analysis, which was a major theme of the paper he co-authored with Alice Balint in 1939. In that paper, the Balints also offered what was at that time a radically new view of psychoanalytic practice – that "The analytical situation is the result of an interplay between the patient's transference and the analyst's counter-transference, complicated by the reactions released in each by the other's transference on to him" (Balint and Balint, 1939, p. 227). The same awareness – that psychoanalytic practice is dyadically co-constructed, and specific to its participants – is implicit in the Budapest school's view of what constituted optimal supervisory work: the supervision by the candidate's analyst in the setting of the analytic situation. The model was unique in the psychoanalytic world in its focus on *the unique world of that analyst and that analysand in their emergent process.*

What I experienced as pivotal in the Budapest model in psychoanalytic supervision with Balint, and in the setting of its application in the "Balint Group" (Bacal, 1972, 1975), constituted a significant influence in my development of *specificity theory.*

Specificity theory

Specificity theory (Bacal, 2006, 2011a, 2011b) is a contemporary psychoanalytic systems theory that regards therapeutic effect as being centrally a function of the therapeutic capacities of each analyst–patient pair as they emerge within a unique reciprocal relational process in the moment and over time.

Therapeutic possibility unfolds within the co-created, unpredictable process of any particular dyad. It is, ultimately, determined by "dyadic fit" – by the capacities and limitations of that therapist and that patient to understand and respond to each other. Specificity theory does not provide the practitioner with dos and don'ts. Rather, through its in-depth focus on process, it illuminates how a therapist may practice as best she or he can with each particular patient.

Structured psychoanalytic theories prescribe and proscribe responses and designate techniques that offer methods and guidelines in order to obtain foreseen results. In contrast, specificity theory holds that focusing on the emergent process of the particular dyad can optimally illuminate how such structured concepts may come more usefully into play. When a therapist fully comprehends and privileges the specificity of human relatedness at every level and at every moment in time, the application of both explicitly formulated concepts, as well as implicitly held "theory", within the clinical situation becomes more apparent, and is enhanced.

Specificity theory also offers a valuable new dimension to the education of the psychoanalytic therapist. Focusing on the specificity of process within supervisory situations – both individually and in groups – which was, in effect, how Balint implicitly worked, without actually conceptualizing it as such – educates the practitioner not only about how to become the clinician he or she can be with a particular patient, but also how she or he may become a better therapist for all of them.[6]

The specificity of the Budapest model as applied to Balint Group training

Balint Group work encourages its participants to explore in depth how aspects of the particular doctor–patient relationship can affect the patient's illness and its treatment. The title of Balint's groundbreaking book in this area is *The Doctor, His Patient, and the Illness* (1957). The Balint Group approach to consultation in effect gave substance to a systems (see Coburn, 2002, 2014) understanding of "illness" and its treatment that was remarkably ahead of its time. It exemplified the application of a dyadic process approach to supervisory work in a group setting that derived from the Budapest model of supervision. Discussion of patients in the Balint Group emphasizes the exploration of therapeutic possibility between that particular doctor and that particular patient (see also Balint, 1969a; Balint and Norell, 1973). The group leader encourages the sharing and discussion of how particular predilections and issues of individual doctors may emerge to interfere with or to enhance therapeutic effect for that patient.

In a book written with members of a research group twenty years after Michael Balint's death, Enid Balint (Balint, Courtenay, Elder, Hull and Julian, 1993) summarized developments in the psychological aspects of general practice since Michael first elaborated his ideas. Both the group's way of working and what they discovered about the doctors' capacities for therapeutic work underscore the uniqueness and specificity of supervisory, as well as therapeutic, process.

> [Our aim was] to have a wider look at the … uncertainties which abound in working with patients; while at the same time not attempting to reduce them to neat patterns, leaving the perspectives as wide as possible in the realization that what one person sees from one angle cannot be seen from another's … the doctors [came to] realize that their healing powers were strictly limited, but … on the other hand, observed that very small changes in a person can produce amazingly large effects on the life of an individual. It seems that the unique relationship which occurs in the general practice setting informs us as to what the work is really about.
>
> (pp. 98–99)

The traditional psychoanalytic training model keeps supervision and personal analysis separate. Within the setting of supervision, responses that an experienced supervisor may recommend to his supervisee may be helpful, yet may not address specific personal issues that are significantly affecting the therapy at the time. While personal therapy may enable the student therapist to come to know himself better, help him to "change", it may not enable him to address particular issues that are currently emerging with regard to his control case. In other words, neither the setting of traditional supervision nor personal analysis alone reliably offers the opportunity to address actively relevant dyadic process between the supervisee and her patient. The Budapest model does this directly, by illuminating not only what may be therapeutically optimal, but also therapeutically workable, between the student analyst and her particular patient.

The Budapest model has had a profound, though largely unnoticed, effect upon contemporary perspectives on psychoanalytic supervision, even though it was officially banned by the International Psychoanalytic Association in 1947.

The evolution of psychoanalytic supervision

Supervision has come to be accepted by a number of contemporary analysts as a curious kind of hybrid that variously comprises teaching, training and, in some ways, treatment. Kindler (1998) observes that a good supervisor contributes in more diverse ways to the effectiveness of the treatment under supervision "[than through his] traditional roles of imparting technique, teaching theory, and formulating the psychodynamic meaning of the patient's communications" (p. 376). Yet, how many psychoanalytic educators even now would agree with Wolf that supervision constitutes a process in which learning depends upon the active participation of both participants in a mutually responsive relationship that entails "not only [sharing and creating] information ... but simultaneously and necessarily also [sharing, creating, and participating] in each other's inner experience of themselves and of the other" (Wolf, 1995, pp. 261–262]? "The purpose of so-called supervision", Wolf maintains, "is [not only] to facilitate the emergence of ... psychological skills and talents [but also] to strengthen ... those personality traits that will enable the student-analyst to perform and to improve his psychoanalytic work" (p. 259). Yet, almost forty years earlier, Michael Balint asserted that "the acquisition of therapeutic skill does not consist only of learning something new: it inevitably also entails a limited, though considerable, change in the [therapist's] personality" (Balint, 1957, p. 299).

The backstory to how psychoanalysts arrived at contemporary views on supervision comprises a tale of battling perspectives and, at times, confusion about just what supervision is or should be.

For some while, Freud and his early followers informally offered instruction to their analysands who were interested in practicing psychoanalysis. The three-column model – the so-called Eitingon model – for the training of analysts: theoretical courses, personal analysis, patients under supervision, was introduced at the Berlin Psychoanalytic Institute in the early 1920s and was later adopted by most other training centres. Ferenczi, however, felt that separating supervised analytic work from the candidate's analysis would limit the student's "opportunity for continuous development through various methods of teaching" (Fleming and Benedek, 1966, p. 12).

The earliest, and most famous, proponent of "teaching" the student how to practise psychoanalysis was Max Eitingon. Eitingon felt that characteristic inadequacies and learning problems of the beginner required that he be taught the technique of psychoanalysis. Eitingon maintained that it was "necessary to teach the technique of psychoanalysis through another method" (i.e., through a method other than the Budapest model) (Fleming and Benedek, 1966 p. 11). While the Budapest analysts did not forgo the teaching of "psychoanalytic technique", they saw their pedagogic task somewhat differently. They emphasized the effect of the analyst's character on the analytic situation (A. Balint, 1935), particularly when he is a beginner. "[The analyst's] technique and improvements in it", according to Kovacs, "are ... directly related to the analyst's personality" (Kovacs, 1936, p. 348). Kovacs underscored the importance of Freud's assertion, in 1910, "that the pre-requisite for a successful application of psycho-analytical technique is that the physician should begin his analytical training by being analyzed himself" (quoted in Kovacs, 1936, p. 348). The Budapest analysts advocated that the student continue in analysis while he is treating his patients. They also considered it important that the candidate's training analyst supervise his work, in effect giving substance to the designation, "training analyst". They were asserting that self-understanding was maximally usable when it is perceived as relevant to the patient with whom the student analyst is currently working.

At the "Four Countries Conference" in the 1930s, where European analysts met to present papers and to discuss problems,[7] it was agreed that in psychoanalytic training attention should be focused on two areas – the student's reactions to the patient's transference, and the teaching of analytic technique – and that more attention should be paid to the first of these than had hitherto been the case. To emphasize the difference between the two, the focus on the student-analyst's countertransference was termed "Kontrollanalyse", and the focus on teaching the student how to conduct analysis, i.e. "technique", was called, "Analysenkontrolle" (Balint, 1948, p. 165; see also Fleming and Benedek, 1966, p. 14).[8] There was supposedly universal agreement about the nature of the latter and that it did not involve the student's countertransference. Yet, confusingly, the participants at the Four Countries Conferences also agreed that the two tasks of training "could not be divided" (Balint, 1948, p. 165). This seemed to imply that both the supervisor and the student's analyst were expected to address both areas, but it was not made clear just how this recommendation should be implemented.

At one of the conferences, in 1933, Kovacs (1936) reported that, in supervising candidates who were not in analysis – even those who had been in analysis with her but who presently were not – she had difficulty orienting herself adequately to the material in order to carry out her supervisory tasks: "I did not know the candidate's character and his modes of reaction, and so I could not say from what point of view he was judging the various situations he encountered" (p. 352). In Kovacs's experience, "Analysenkontrolle" without "Kontrollanalyse" was superficial and unsatisfactory; that is, she felt that she could not adequately supervise someone who was not simultaneously in analysis with her.

In their 1939 paper "On Transference and Counter-transference", Alice and Michael Balint described the great variation in so many of the supposedly universal ways that analysts work, which suggested that, despite efforts to adhere to Freud's technical recommendations, analytic technique was far from universally the same. This would imply that, in teaching candidates how to conduct an analysis, we should not ignore an omnipresent variable: who the analyst is. In the same paper, the Balints conveyed that we should pay closer attention to the vicissitudes of the analytic dyad. Their remarkable assertion, that "the analytical situation is the result of an interplay between the patient's transference and the analyst's counter-transference, complicated by the reactions released in each by the other's transference on to him" (p. 227), further underscored the relevancy for analytic training of the Budapest supervisory approach wherein the candidate's work is supervised in the setting of his analysis.

Balint (1948) reports that, while the participants at successive Four Countries Conferences "[agreed that] analysis of the counter-transference must form an essential part of the training, i.e., [analysis and supervision] cannot be divided, no decision could be reached on the point whether the training analyst or another should begin the supervision with the candidate" (p. 165). Eventually it was agreed that further experience was needed before this could be decided. However, without further observation or published discussion, the new London Standing Rules – according to Balint, Ernest Jones's rules – were authoritatively proclaimed: "'The analyst undertaking the student's personal analysis does not undertake the supervision of his cases'" (Balint, 1948, p. 165).

At that point, the "tripartite" system of psychoanalytic training officially came into being, entailing strict separation of its three modalities: the analysis of the candidate, the treatment of cases under supervision, and theoretical lectures and seminars. In Hungary, however, this did not quite happen. Balint (1948) explicitly stated the view of the Hungarian school that the candidate's clinical training can be best done if the personal analysis and the supervision are carried out by the same person, that is, the candidate's analyst, at least with the first case. In other words, the optimal situation for "supervising" the candidate, according to the analysts in the Budapest Institute, is the one in which the supervisor is in the best position to address personal issues of the candidate as they may be affecting his work with his patient.

As far as I know, every psychoanalytic training organization apart from the institute in Budapest complied with Jones's edict. The "training" analyst just analysed the candidate, and the supervisor just taught him "how to do analysis". Yet, while everyone except the Hungarians seemed to welcome this arrangement, the appearance in the literature of many papers in which analysts continued to debate what constitutes optimal supervision suggests that the controversy that began in the 1930s which supposedly ended with the implementation of the "London Rules" in 1947 had not cooled down all that much. It also implied that the implementation of these rules may not have delivered the educational yield that Jones and his faithful followers assumed it would.

Four main themes have emerged in the psychoanalytic literature about supervision. These themes in effect address and elaborate the same issues debated by the attendees at the Four Countries Conferences in the 1930s. They essentially comprise the following questions: (1) Should the supervisor primarily be "teaching" the supervisee how to conduct a psychoanalysis, explicitly focusing on principles of analytic conduct and, implicitly – and inevitably – emphasizing the relevance of particular analytic theory? (2) Should the focus of supervision primarily be on the supervisee's patient or on the supervisee and his characteristic problems? (3) Should the focus be on process – between the supervisee and his patient, or/and between the supervisor and the supervisee? (4) In what ways and how personally should the supervisor engage the supervisee in addressing "transference-countertransference", or "relational", issues, either between her and her patient or/and between her and the supervisor?

Despite recognition by many analysts that "supervision is more than education and less than treatment" (Solnit, 1970, p. 359), discussion in the psychoanalytic literature about the Budapest supervisory model since Balint's 1948 paper was relatively sparse. (Some examples were Ekstein and Wallerstein, 1958; Fleming and Benedek, 1966; Bacal 1972, 1975; and, more recently, Bacal, 2011a, 2011b; Gabor, 2014).

A number of contributions to the literature do, however, indicate the influence of the Hungarian analysts' perspectives. In his presentation to the Third Pre-Congress on Psychoanalytic Training, Solnit (1970) reported that "Although there [was] general agreement that the resolution of countertransference was the task of the student's own analysis, most institutes expect the supervisor to take it up tactfully and to deal with its educational implications if that is feasible" (p. 359). Pulver's (1984) view is that the ongoing debate as to whether supervision "should be considered purely an educational experience or whether it should, in addition, be therapeutic" is spurious[9]; he concludes that "the question … can be answered solely from the dynamics of the supervisory situation" (p. 489). Pulver "[disagrees] with Keiser (1969) that [Fleming and Benedek] are much too therapeutic in their approach" (p. 490). He conveys that what may be identified as therapeutic work for the supervisee can be very useful for his analytic work with his patient (see also Bromberg, 2013; Levy and Parnell, 2001). Pulver concurs with Ekstein and Wallerstein that it is the purpose to which the supervisor's responses are put that render them appropriate. For Pulver, "[Supervision] is a powerful interaction, filled with emotions and made even more complex by the fact that it is an interaction about an interaction" (Pulver, 1984, p. 489; see also my comments about Bromberg's supervision of a candidate, on p. 155). Dewald (1981), anticipating Kantrowitz's findings, draws attention to the importance of the supervisor's "[making] an assessment of the candidate's needs and vulnerabilities ... as a guide for interventions" (p. 80).

Supervision as process: its uniqueness and specificity

Even earlier, Fleming and Benedek (1966) recognized the usefulness of a systems, or process, perspective in supervision.

> Supervisory work requires an even greater span of system sensitivity than is necessary for analytic treatment ... [The supervisor must be] attuned to the patient and the analyst, the relationship between them and to the progress of the analytic process, [as well as to the relationship between himself and the supervisee].
>
> (p. 56)

In their study of supervision transcripts, the goal of teaching the students about *process* was common to all supervisory activity. Their view is that "[teaching] the student to regard psychoanalysis as a process is the most important and probably the most difficult of the supervisory tasks" (p. 53). I have indeed found that when offering case examples in clinical seminars and at psychoanalytic conferences for the purpose of studying the uniqueness of dyadic process, participants tend to wander away from a focus on process to talk about the psychodynamics of the case based on one theory or another and how the analyst might on that basis intervene effectively.

Fleming and Benedek also in effect imply that the recognition of dyadic process as unique and specific meant that "What the student learns in one supervisory session about his patient and/or about himself, he can apply only in the future to situations which are similar but never identical ...The 'experience' itself can never be repeated" (p. 238) (see also Kindler, 1998).

Kantrowitz (2002b), on the basis of her research, arrives at analogous conclusions (see also Coburn, 1997):

> The interaction of the characteristics of candidate, supervisor, and patient [affects] the candidate's learning and analytic work ... The particular gains candidates derive from working with particular

> supervisors is a function of the specific needs arising from their stage of training, their previous experience, their character traits and conflicts, and their interaction with the character and conflicts of their patients.
>
> (2002b, p. 966)

The application of specificity theory to supervision gives further substance to this (see Bacal, 2011a, chapter 10). In addition, it directs its participants to address, in the particularity of *their* process, not only what constitutes optimal ways of learning, for that supervisee, with regard to the treatment of that patient, but also what is possible for them to accomplish together. Specificity theory makes the latter explicit in its emphasis on the importance of "fit" in supervision, as well as in treatment.

The specificity of fit and the supervisory process

We need to give more consideration to the importance of "fit" between particular supervisors and particular supervisees. Aronson (2000) writes trenchantly about his experience with three different supervisors whose quite different responsiveness to him and to his work with his patient resulted in quite different experiences of fit and concomitantly of the usefulness of the supervision. My experience affirms Kantrowitz's (2002b) finding that a good "match" between supervisor and supervisee and the supervisee's patient enhances the supervisee's learning experience. It is useful to be aware of when the fit within the educational dyad, or triad, may be significantly less than optimal.

Kantrowitz's (2002a, 2002b,) research indicates that a "felicitous match [between candidate, supervisor, and patient] can aid professional and personal analytic development [and that a] clash of characteristics … can slow or impede learning and adversely affect analytic work" (2002b, p. 938).[10] My own experience affirms this: I have worked with supervisees with whom the fit or lack thereof made a considerable difference to what we could do together (Bacal, 2011a, chapter 10). Yet Kantrowitz also emphasizes the unpredictability of (triadic) process:

> …[The] nature and helpfulness of the match cannot be predicted in advance, for several reasons. One is that what is manifest in

> each of the participants does not reveal all that potentially may emerge; different people bring out different aspects of each other. Another reason is that interactions among the three participants and their specific characteristics evolve and change over the course of the work.
>
> ...The dynamic interplay of patient and candidate may yield surprises. Patients may evoke conflicts in candidates that were insufficiently analyzed, or that did not emerge in their analyses.
>
> (pp. 964, 960)

A most interesting finding, which recalls Vilma Kovacs' observation of the importance to her of having the candidate in analysis with her during the supervision (Kovacs, 1936).

The specificity of process and parallel process

I have wondered whether the traditional arrangement of separating the modalities of "training" and "treatment" are in some measure responsible for the phenomenon of parallel process. Why does the student therapist bring to supervision an unconsciously disguised representation of the problem with his patient, yet one that is curiously revealing to the supervisor or, as characteristically happens, to a supervisory group? Could this possibly be because he is unconsciously, though ambivalently and "resistively", seeking help with a specific problem in relation to his patient that feels "personal" and similar, a problem that his therapist may not have responded to, but for which he does not anticipate adequate help either, from the supervisor, in that setting?

From the perspective of specificity theory, recognizing and attending to the possible effect of one system operating on another, how in particular supervisory situations specific issues that remain unaddressed in other systems may play out, can be productive. Sometimes the parallel is "seen" at the outset, sometimes not. In my experience, especially in experiential supervisory groups (and in particular where group therapists discuss their experience in their own groups), this can be a useful teaching tool. The important consideration is whether and, if so how, the particular supervisee and that supervisor, or supervisees, can deal effectively with them.

Specificity theory regards the supervisory situation as a process that is constituted by the emergence of dyadic specificities in at least the two situations – of supervisor and supervisee, and of the supervisee and his patient,[11] each of which may reciprocally affect the other. Other systems – the student analyst and his analyst, the supervisor and the student's analyst – as well as those within the psychoanalytic training institute may, implicitly, sometimes also explicitly, come into play. Ultimately, the dyad comprising supervisor and supervisee, variously affected by these adjacent systems, will discover, within the specificity of their process, what constitutes possibilities for optimal supervisory work for the particular candidate's educational needs. What that student needs, and what he or she can use from that supervisor at that time, and how this matches the supervisor's views and capabilities, will unfold within their unique pedagogic process. Supervisee and supervisor must learn together how they can best learn, work, and – as Aronson (2000) suggests – play together.

Aronson (2000) has offered a Winnicottian perspective on supervision that very much matches mine. He characterizes an optimal supervisory process as a

> playful, creative experience … [a] "to and fro", in which … each participant [places] his particular stamp on the material and process, creating an exchange of sorts. In essence, the supervisee develops the capacity to discover – himself, the patient, the process of psychoanalysis – while concurrently allowing himself to be found by the patient, by himself, and by the supervisor.
>
> (p. 125)

Ekstein and Wallerstein (1958) recognize that supervisors have particular predilections and preferences for how they supervise, partly as an expression of their personalities. Some supervisors feel comfortable discussing countertransference issues with their supervisees at a personal level and interacting with them around these issues as they emerge, either in relation to the patient or/and in relation to themselves. Some supervisors do not, however, and prefer to address them in general terms, or only didactically, or not at all, and may refer the student back to her analyst for more personal analysis.

Ekstein and Wallerstein express the hope that supervisors "could make choices ... which derive from the specific problems and needs of the learner rather than from their personal preferences and their personal security as teachers" (1958, p. 261). While I resonate with their "hope", I think that the way we could most usefully approach this challenge is by training supervisors to recognize the possibilities and limitations of the particular dyad of that supervisor with that supervisee as they emerge in process, just as we recognize these with regard to the specificity of the process between the trainee-analyst and her patient.

Specificity theory does not pre-empt how supervision "should" be done, or "can" be done, nor what kind of analyst that student should become. Rather, the supervisor and supervisee will optimally "teach" each other by becoming aware of what the supervisee's learning needs are at that time, in relation to that patient, as they become specifically evident, either in the process between her and her patient or/and between her and the supervisor. Intrinsic to specificity theory is its emphasis on uniqueness, unpredictability and the specificity of process. While the supervisor will inevitably – and *perhaps* usefully – have in mind, consciously or unconsciously, what it means to work in the "right" way as a psychoanalyst, specificity theory allows that neither the supervisor nor the supervisee knows in advance the optimal ways for the supervisor to respond to that student, or what he or she should learn. They can, however, discover this – and how effectively this can be carried out within that supervisory dyad – by attending to the specificity of their unfolding process. In effect, any or all of the four themes described above may variously emerge as *specifically* relevant in any particular supervision.

While the Budapest model of supervision is not formally recognized in any of the four analytic institutes where I supervise candidates, it had not been explicitly interdicted, either, until recently. I offer this kind of supervision informally in two settings, if the fit is right: with my trainee analysands, within their analytic sessions; and with supervisees, in the supervisory situation. With regard to the former setting, I am responsive to my analysand's requests for help with their control cases. My analysand's work with her patient is one of the most important activities in her life. It is a part of who she is, of her personal as well as of her professional development. In addition, my awareness that our shared outside system – our psychoanalytic institute – regards our psychoanalytic work as central to his or her development as an analyst also inclines me to believe that it would be remiss of me not to respond as helpfully as I can to a request for assistance in the treatment of her patient. The alternatives of "just listening", or interpreting associations about her patient only as they may personally relate to her, or suggesting she take the problem she is having with her patient to her supervisor, fall just as short as the traditional recommendation of the supervisor that the supervisee take her "countertransference" problem up with her analyst.

Ekstein and Wallerstein (1958) emphasize the importance of adhering to the educational purpose of supervision: "leading [the student] toward greater skill in his work with his patients" (p. 254). They express concern that, if training and treatment are carried out in the same setting, the educational purpose of supervision could become subverted. Yet they simultaneously recognize that

> supervision – that is, the supervisory process – [is] not simply … the transmission of knowledge and skills, but rather … a complex process that goes on between the supervisor and his student. This process is a helping process in which the student is being helped to discover his problems as a psychotherapist, to resolve them with the help of the supervisor … This process includes affective problems, interpersonal conflicts, problems in being helped, as well as in helping, and is truly itself a helping process (p. 251).

Ekstein and Wallerstein's view of the supervisory process so substantially endorses the Budapest model, one might question whether their concern has more to do with its non-adherence to established tradition than about its not effectively adhering to the educational purpose of supervision. Recently, Bromberg (2013, p. 12) describes how he struggled during the process of discovering that, in order to help his supervisee treat her patient effectively, he had to expand his role as supervisor to that of therapist. Perhaps this role expansion might not have entailed such a struggle for Bromberg had he been familiar with the Budapest model of supervision.

The point, it seems to me, that Ekstein and Wallerstein effectively make, and Bromberg's example vividly depicts, is that the path along which any particular supervisory dyad must travel in order to achieve its educational purpose is variegated and unpredictable. Specificity theory underscores both Ekstein and Wallerstein's, and Fleming and Benedek's, view of supervision as process, but adds that the nature and effectiveness of such a process will be specific for that supervisory dyad.

My way of working with supervisees has significantly changed under the influence of specificity theory. Apprehending the nature of the potential and limitations that my supervisee and I encounter and co-create as a particular supervisory couple enables us to discover more clearly what *we* can, and cannot, do together in our process. In particular, when my supervisee and I find ourselves mutually receptive to talking about emotional issues – sometimes even quite personal ones – that arise between her and her patient, or/and between her and me, we may even be able to exceed the expectations for learning ordinarily inherent within traditional supervision and, in this way, potentially enhance the treatment of the patient.

I will conclude with an example of how one of my supervisees and I worked together within the traditional framework of supervision. Our work reflects not only the systems perspective of Fleming and Benedek; it advances the concept of the Budapest model of supervision. In this example, the supervisor's process of listening to himself after responding in a particular way to his supervisee, and then sharing this with her led to interactions with this supervisee that in turn led to a significant educational experience – for both of them.[12]

Illustration

Dr P. is an advanced analytic candidate at the Institute of Contemporary Psychoanalysis in Los Angeles, whose third control case I was supervising. Dr P. was in analysis with a colleague, and conveyed how important that work continued to be for her. Yet she valued the opportunity to present her analytic work with the "free-associative" openness that characterized the Budapest supervisory model.

I would emphasize that, in my experience as a supervisor, the way Dr P. and I worked together does not ubiquitously happen, even with candidates at this Institute. I have found myself working with supervisees in ways that range from the formal presentation by the student of her account of the analytic hour as she has recorded it to what an observer would find similar in tone and ambience, and to some extent in content, to an analytic session.

Specificities resembling the latter emerged as salient in substantial measure for Dr P. and myself in our process. A specific aspect of fit between Dr P. and myself that contributed to the productive operation of our particular supervisory process was our ability to co-create an ambience in which we could comfortably discuss personal aspects of who we are that emerged in a process that might be affecting our supervisory work, and their possible effect on the therapeutic process of Dr P. with her patient. This does not necessarily mean that this way of working is "better" than others. It does mean that this is the way Dr P. and I worked best together.

As Dr P. was about to leave after a supervisory session, I found myself telling her about my work with a patient that reflected problems similar to those with which she was struggling with her patient, N. I was at the time aware of a certain internal pressure to share my experience with her.

After Dr P. left, I reflected on what I had done, and as we began our next supervision session I shared my thoughts with Dr P. – that it seemed to be a curious kind of "narcissistic" behaviour. I had felt a need to have her hear what *I* had to say, since she had done virtually all the talking in that session. I added that I was also wondering whether this was what Dr P. needed to do in that session. I told her that, in my view, she was doing excellent analytic work as she struggled with the problems presented by her patient, and that what she may have indeed needed from me during the last supervision session was in fact to listen to her, and to experience my quiet validation. I wondered, too, whether my reaction could also be understood as expressing a measure of competitiveness with Dr P., a competitiveness that may have been stirred up not only by my need to be heard, but also by my unconsciously resonating, as it were, with competitiveness between Dr P. and her patient, an acupuncturist who had been seeing a patient of her own "like an analyst", as Dr P. had put it, several times a week.

Dr P. expressed gratitude for my candour about both of us. She had been puzzled about my extending the session; she was aware that I probably needed to stop (a light indicated the presence of someone in the waiting room) yet I did not, and was telling her about my patient.

In our further discussion, she told me that she really likes when I share anything with her – whether it be case material, theory, personal experience or my recent trip to Greece (a country that has particular family significance for her) – especially when she sees that I am enthusiastic and animated about it. She conveyed that she finds this most engaging: "So I guess I sort of enjoyed getting the extra time that day, even though I felt slightly guilty knowing your patient was waiting!" She added that all these feelings likely tied in with the complexity of her pleasure-cum-guilt about being a favoured sibling. And she did think it likely that these feelings reflected issues with which she and her patient were struggling, about which she would like to learn more. She also felt there were other aspects of our process that were relevant to her work with this patient.

Dr P. was aware that she "had done all the talking" in the last supervision session – in effect, she had alluded to it with a tad of guilt during the session itself – yet she was also aware that, since she hadn't seen me for several weeks, there was a whole lot to tell me in a short time, in order to catch me up. She allowed that she did tend to talk a good deal in her supervisions, as this helped her to clarify for herself what was happening in the analytic work with her patient. In other words, this was a cardinal way in which Dr P. learned. She was also aware that she could be "dominant"; and, as a result of discussing our experiences and thoughts about this, she had begun to consider that, in taking up so much of the talking time in her supervisions, she might, at times, have been interfering with her learning experience. She told me, "You did indeed pick up on something I have been unaware of. That [part of] it has been a blind spot." Dr P. conveyed that she did find value in my ideas and perspectives – which was evident to me in many discussions we had had – yet at this time, with this patient, she was especially grateful for her experience of me as an attentive and perceptive listener. With regard to my acknowledged "countertransference" reaction – which I believe is more accurately regarded as *a disruption that was specific to our process*[13] (see also Bacal, 2011a, p. 104) – she wondered whether her tendency to be "dominating" in her interactions might have triggered an experience in me that reflected problems with which I had struggled with my mother, which she had read about in a published paper (Bacal, 2006). I told Dr P. that my mother did listen to me, but that her reaction of "superior knowingness" that I had written about was not how I experienced Dr P. Rather, I thought my reaction to Dr P.'s monopolizing the talking time in that session likely reflected a residue of my feeling eclipsed, long ago, by the liveliness of a similarly bright younger sister.

Interestingly, in our supervisory process, disruptively matching specificities of connection were emerging across our dyads: Dr P. with her patient and me with Dr P. Dr P. responded by telling me that, in her interaction with important others, including her analyst, she greatly valued knowing about the other person.

As we were talking in this way, Dr P. told me that she was now thinking about further experience with her patient, N. She did recall that N was indeed doing a kind of "analysis" with one of her acupuncture patients, but had not been consciously aware that this may have evoked some competitiveness within her in relation to N. She had felt more like N was doing this as a way to feel close to her, even merge with her. Yet, Dr P. recognized that this also appeared to be suffused with conflict.

While N had felt seduced by her mother's attention, she struggled to free herself from her mother's need for her to serve as an accommodating archaic selfobject. I commented that N had apparently been making progress in respect of this conflict. During a recent European vacation with her parents, on which N's sister was not invited, she had been able to leave for a week and enjoy a holiday bicycling in Rome, on her own, about which Dr P. jokingly remarked to me that this was more than she would attempt! Dr P. was initially surprised, though, when N "cut me out completely" when N returned from her vacation. Dr P. sensed that N might be suffering from a guilt-laden depressiveness that was also likely overdetermined. She understood this as N's guilt about feeling that Dr P. was more important to her than her mother. Dr P. also interpreted that N may have been enjoying her time away not just from her parents, but from *her*, too, while she was bicycling and tango dancing her way through Rome. She understood this as N's "not wanting to have to worry about my missing her and having difficulty with the separation, like her mother does". N quite agreed with these interpretations.

I shared with Dr P. my recollection of how her awareness of struggling with her own guilt (which she had spontaneously shared with me earlier on) about her experience of being preferred by her parents in certain ways over her own sister, has also been helpful to Dr P. in resonating with analogous issues in the relationship with this patient. I further shared with Dr P. that I had also wondered whether my "enactment" at the end of our supervision session last week was derived in part from some mutually dissociated awareness (see Donnel Stern, 2004) from feelings variously operating within Dr P. and myself about being cut out and cutting out with regard to more than one sister-related dyad. Dr P.'s response was that our discussion about this felt "very useful and apt"; and that the themes of competitiveness (both "sibling" and "Oedipal") that were highlighted by my sharing of my reaction (to her earlier monopolization of the talking time) were valuable and useful, "since I may tend to deny and minimize due to guilt about various triumphs in my family (my mother/sister/siblings). It's also really interesting to hear about your mother/sister stuff and how that may have interfaced with my stuff in the process".

Our discussion of these experiences was illuminating and valuable for me as well as for Dr P. Its usefulness for the treatment of Dr P.'s patient became especially apparent when Dr P. and I looked closely at the particularities of our own process. I also learned more about how Dr P. learned, and how – and why – I, and Dr P., might at times find ourselves interfering with her learning.

My account of this work with Dr P. illustrates how supervision informed by specificity theory may enhance its effectiveness through focusing attention on the emergent process of that supervisor-supervisee dyad and on that analyst–analysand dyad, and how these systems may reciprocally affect one another.

The focus on the specificity of process between Dr P. and her patient and between Dr P. and myself also illuminates how understanding of what is traditionally regarded as separate occurrences of transference and countertransference or aspects of a mysterious "parallel process" can be enhanced by apprehending them as reflections of the specificity of interfacing processes.

The value of maintaining both personal therapy and supervised work as pillars for the training of psychoanalytic therapists continues to be widely recognized. Yet, the nature of the variegated, and particular, learning needs of each student in treating that patient optimally may emerge in either setting; and the extent to which they may – or may not – be effectively responded to, in either setting, will be discovered within the specificity of the unfolding process of its particular participants. Perhaps analytic training institutes may yet undertake a serious study of the Budapest model of supervision, which has not been officially practised since 1970, when Michael Balint was offering it at the Institute of Psychoanalysis in London.

Notes

1 This model, which evolved under the strong personal influence of Sándor Ferenczi, would appear to have been practiced as such by Hungarian analysts until World War II. According to Szőnyi Gábor (personal communication), it continued as an option within the Hungarian Psychoanalytic Society when it reintegrated with the International Psychoanalytical Association in 1975. Since then, the Budapest model underwent various transformations (see Gábor, 2014). Currently, the Hungarian regulation allows the first supervision with the personal analyst, but does not further specify the setting.
2 The research was published as the book *Six Minutes for the Patient: interactions in general practice consultation* (Balint and Norell, 1973).
3 For a comprehensive account of *specificity theory* and its application in psychoanalytic treatment and supervision, see Bacal (2011a).
4 Required at the Institute of Psychoanalysis in London.
5 Not everyone who worked with Balint in this kind of supervision found it so useful. Some years after completing my analytic training, I learned from a fellow student who had also undertaken supervision with Balint in this way, that he found it noxious – an interesting reflection of the specificity of pedagogic and personal experience.
6 For further elaboration, see Bacal (2011a, chapter 10).
7 Attendees at the "four countries conferences" (Austria, Hungary, Czechoslovakia and Italy) also included analysts from other European countries, such as Holland and Germany.
8 Fleming and Benedek (1966, p. 14) clarify that the word "control" has a stricter and more limiting connotation in English than in German. In German, the word "Kontrolle" translates as "*supervision* in the first place and *checking in the second*".
9 More recently, Rosbrow (1997) described the teach–treat split as a false dichotomy based on the spurious premise that only interpretive work is legitimate.
10 In a supervision course Kantrowitz gave recently, what emerged to affirm her research was discovering that the most important variable for supervisory work was the *match* among supervisee, patient and supervisor (Kantrowitz, personal communication).
11 The Budapest model, at least as Balint carried it out with me, focused on process between the supervisee and his patient. It did not address process occurring between the candidate and his training analyst.
12 From what I gather in reading Mészáros's descriptions of how Ferenczi worked (Mészáros, 2010, 2014), I think that the application of specificity theory to the supervisory process must very much reflect Ferenczi's way of applying the Budapest model of supervision.
13 Because specificity theory holds that psychoanalytic treatment reflects the operation of a *unique reciprocal process for each analyst-patient couple* – in effect, a system that may be complexly affected by other systems, both adjacent and distant – we would refer to what happened between Dr P. and myself as an example of

disruption that is specific to a particular relational process rather than only speaking in terms of transference and countertransference, terms we regard as too narrow, circumscribed and linear to account for such complexity (see also Bacal, 2011a, chapter 8, "How Specificity Theory Alters Our View of Psychoanalytic Concepts and Principles and How This Affects Therapeutic Action").

References

Aronson, S. (2000). Analytic supervision: All work and no play? *Contemporary Psychoanalysis*, 36: 121–132.

Bacal, H.A. (1972). Balint groups: Training or treatment? *International Journal of Psychiatry in Medicine*, 3: 373–377.

Bacal, H.A. (1975). The treatment aspect of Balint training. *Journal of the Balint Society*, 4: 10–13.

Bacal, H.A. (2006). Specificity theory: Conceptualizing a personal and professional quest for therapeutic possibility. *International Journal of Psychoanalytic Self Psychology*, 1(2): 133–155.

Bacal, H.A. (2011a). *The Power of Specificity in Psychotherapy: When therapy works – and when it doesn't*. Lanham, MD: Jason Aronson.

Bacal, H.A. (2011b). Specificity theory: The evolution of a process theory of psychoanalytic treatment. *American Imago*, 68: 267–283.

Bacal, H.A., & Newman, K.M. (1990). *Theories of Object Relations: Bridges to self psychology*. New York: Columbia University Press.

Balint, A. (1935). Communication reported by Glover, E., 1935, Four Countries Conference. *Bulletin of the International Psychoanalytic Association*, 16: 505–509.

Balint, M. (1935). Critical notes on the pre-genital organization of the libido. In *Primary Love and Psycho-Analytic Technique*, new and enlarged ed., London: Tavistock, 1965, pp. 37–58.

Balint, M. (1937). Early developmental states of the ego: Primary object-love. In *Primary Love and Psycho-Analytic Technique*, pp. 74–90.

Balint, M. (1948). On the psycho-analytic training system. *International Journal of Psychoanalysis*, 29: 163–173.

Balint, M. (1957). *The Doctor, His Patient, and the Illness*, 2nd ed. London: Tavistock.

Balint, M. (1968). *The Basic Fault*. London: Tavistock.

Balint, M. (1969a). The structure of the training-cum-research-seminars. *Journal of the Royal College of General Practitioners*, 17: 201–211.

Balint, M. (1969b). Trauma and object relationship. *International Journal of Psychoanalysis*, 50: 429–435.

Balint, M., & Balint, A. (1939). On transference and counter-transference. *International Journal of Psychoanalysis*, 20: 223–230.

Balint, E., & Norell, J.S. (1973). *Six Minutes for the Patient: Interactions in general practice consultation*. London: Tavistock.

Balint, E., Courtenay, M., Elder, A., Hull, S., & Julian, P. (1993). *The Doctor, the Patient, and the Group*. London: Routledge.

Bromberg, P. (2013). Hidden in plain sight: Thoughts on imagination and the lived unconscious. *Psychoanalytic Dialogues*, 23: 1–14.

Coburn, W.J. (1997). The vision in supervision: Transference-countertransference dynamics and disclosure in the supervision relationship. *Bulletin of the Menninger Clinic*, 61: 482–494.

Coburn, W.J. (2002). A world of systems: The role of systemic patterns of experience in the therapeutic process. *Psychoanalytic Inquiry*, 5: 655–677.

Coburn, W.J. (2014). *Psychoanalytic Complexity: Clinical attitudes for therapeutic change*. New York: Routledge.

Dewald, P. (1981). Aspects of the supervisory process. *Annual of Psychoanaysis*, 9: 75–89.

Ekstein, R., & Wallerstein, R. (1958). *The Teaching and Learning of Psychotherapy*. New York: International Universities Press.

Fleming, J., & Benedek, T. (1966). *Psychoanalytic Supervision*. New York: Grune & Stratton.

Gábor, S. (2014). The vicissitudes of the Budapest model of supervision: Can we learn from it today? *Psychoanalytic Inquiry*, 34(6): 606–618.

Kantrowitz, J. (2002a). The external observer and the lens of the patient-analyst match. *International Journal of Psychoanalysis*, 83: 339–350.

Kantrowitz, J. (2002b). The triadic match: The interactive effect of supervisor, candidate, and patient. *Journal of the American Psychoanalytic Association*, 50: 939–996.

Kindler, A. (1998). Optimal responsiveness and psychoanalytic supervision. In H.A. Bacal (ed.), *Optimal Responsiveness: How therapists heal their patients*. Northvale, NJ: Jason Aronson, pp. 357–382.

Kovacs, V. (1936). Training- and control-analysis. *International Journal of Psychoanalysis*, 1: 346–354.

Levy, J., & Parnell, Y. (2001). The benefits and hazards of working through the supervisee's counter- transference in psychoanalytic supervision. *Journal of Clinical Psychoanalysis*, 10(1): 91–116.

Mészáros, J. (2010). Sándor Ferenczi and the Budapest school of psychoanalysis. *Psychoanalytic Perspectives*, 7(1): 69–89.

Mészáros, J. (2014). *Ferenczi and Beyond: Exile of the Budapest School and solidarity in the psychoanalytic movement during the Nazi years*. London: Karnac Books.

Pulver, S. (1984). Psychoanalytic supervision: A method of clinical teaching: By Joan Fleming and Therese F. Benedek. Republished in *Classics in Psychoanalysis, Monograph 1*. New York: International Universities Press 1983, and *International Journal of Psychoanalysis*, 65: 489–492.

Rosbrow, T. (1997). From parallel process to developmental process: A developmental plan/formulation approach to supervision. In A. Goldberg (ed.), *Conversations in Self Psychology, Progress in Self Psychology*, vol. 13, Hillsdale, NJ: Analytic Press, pp. 149–164.

Solnit, A. (1970). Learning from psychoanalytic supervision. *International Journal of Psychoanalysis*, 51: 359–362.

Stern, D. (2004). The eye sees itself: Dissociation, enactment, and the achievement of conflict. *Contemporary Psychoanalysis*, 40: 197–237.

Wolf, E. (1995). How to supervise without doing harm: Comments on psychoanalytic supervision. *Psychoanalytic Inquiry*, 15: 252–267.

Chapter 9

Psychoanalysis' neglect of the incest trauma

The Confusion of Tongues between psychoanalysis and society[1]

Arnold Wm. Rachman

Sexual seduction as the cause of psychological disorder

At the beginning of Freud's career as a clinician, he made an important discovery, which he chronicled in his *Letters to Wilhelm Fliess* (Freud, 1954), which became known as his Seduction Hypothesis. Most of his patients were women, some of whom reported instances of sexual molestation. They were given the common Victorian-age diagnosis of hysteria. These hysterical patients reported sexual abuse, most often naming their fathers as the abusers. Freud drew a causal connection between sexual abuse and neurosis. This idea was the first statement about the psychological connection between child abuse and adult disorder. There have been a variety of comments about Freud's so-called abandonment of the Seduction Hypothesis, varying from seeing it as a theoretical tour de force (Jones, 1957) to a loss of courage in the face of professional opposition (Masson, 1984). Freud then adopted the Oedipal theory as the cornerstone of psychoanalysis.

Reevaluation of the psychoanalytic concept of infantile sexuality

Freud's Oedipal theory of infantile sexuality squarely placed the issue of sexuality on the child. The child's lust for the parent became the issue. In the traditional concept of the Oedipal conflict, the focus is on the intrapsychic mechanisms for resolving the lust for the mother and fear of the father. One can view the Oedipal theory as a factor in the psychoanalysis neglect of the incest trauma:

> *We believe the conceptionalization of child sexuality moved psychoanalysis away from the relevance of child abuse.*
>
> (Rachman & Mattick, 2012, p. 169, italics in original)

This cannot be overemphasized; the Oedipal theory placed the issue of childhood sexuality as the child's issue. Freud's change in focus from the actual seduction of children to the sexual fantasies of children had enormous meaning for the neglect of the incest trauma in psychoanalysis and in society. Instead of illuminating the prevalence of sexual abuse of children and its role in the development of psychological disorder, it actually diminished childhood sexual abuse as a concern of psychoanalysis. The legacy of the Budapest School can be used to contrast the Oedipal view with Ferenczi's Confusion of Tongues theory, which restored the focus on the adult abuser.

The Confusion of Tongues paradigm

Ferenczi's Confusion of Tongues paradigm returned the issue of child sexuality to the sexuality of the parental abuser. Focus is on the disturbed behavior of the adult. The child is not suffering from an Oedipal conflict. The child is suffering from the emotional trauma of having been molested by his/her parent. There is no longer a focus on interpretation of the Oedipal dynamics in order to develop insight into the child's unconsciousness striving for parental love. In the Ferenczian framework the focus became an empathic attitude toward helping the individual have a reparative therapeutic experience with a non-traumatic therapeutic agent. The most significant conclusion derived from the Confusion of Tongues concept is that childhood sexual seduction *is not a figment of a child's imagination, but an actual traumatic event in the child's life.* The focus switches to the sexuality of the adult (the abuser), not the sexuality of the child. In fact, even if a child is seductive and the adult responds with a sexual response, it is still the issue of the adult's sexuality. It is the adult's emotional responsibility to protect the child from unwanted and damaging sexual contact.

The paradigm

The Confusion of Tongues paradigm (Ferenczi, 1933) has been expanded into a theory of the Incest Trauma (Rachman, 1994, 1997a, 2000, 2003a; Rachman & Klett, 2015):

1. The child is sexually abused by an adult, usually a parent or parental surrogate, which is the narcissistic expression of the adult's sexuality.
2. The sexual seduction initiates the incest trauma whose psychodynamics are explained by the Confusion of Tongues paradigm.
3. The child, in a desperate attempt to maintain self-cohesion, employs a series of characteristics defense mechanisms:
   a. a profound sense of personal confusion
   b. development of denial and dissociation
   c. blunted affect
   d. a loss of a sense of reality
   e. a loss of a sense of power and agency
   f. robotic-like functioning; becoming stilted and emotionally inhibited
   g. profound feelings of shame
   h. feelings of self-blame

The continued use of these mechanisms constitutes an Incest Trauma.

4. The child's functioning is so altered that he/she is under the power of the abuser. The child loses his/her full conscious functioning and hold on reality. What is more, the child, in order to maintain the fantasy of being loved, and avoid feelings of abandonment and annihilation, as well as to maintain self-cohesion, becomes the emotional slave of the abuser. The child develops a state of emotional helplessness, emotionally surrenders to the abuser, losing the capacity to remember and speak of the trauma. The child becomes tongue-tied.
5. Unless the abused individual receives therapeutic help, he/she becomes emotionally vulnerable to developing Confusion of Tongues symptoms, which produced developmental arrest.

6. The establishment of the psychodynamics of childhood sexual abuse by Ferenczi was a significant contribution, because it attempted to establish the Incest Trauma as a disorder that could be treated by psychoanalysis. Ferenczi was also very concerned about the welfare of children, having been active in social causes since he became a psychiatrist (Rachman, 1997a, 2003a; Rachman & Klett, 2015).

The orthodox community objection to the Confusion of Tongues paradigm

The Confusion of Tongues paradigm was almost lost to psychoanalysis and psychotherapy because Freud and his orthodox followers attempted to suppress it. Freud, Jones, and others, felt that Ferenczi's idea that the Incest Trauma necessitated a new theory and method to understand and treat trauma disorders was labeled stupid, senile, regressive (Rachman, 1997a, 1997b). There is a dramatic history in the attempt to prevent Ferenczi from giving the Confusion of Tongues paper at the 12th International Psychoanalytic Congress in September of 1933 and the attempt not to publish the paper in the International Journal of Psychoanalysis (Rachman, 1997b). Psychoanalytic orthodoxy was not successful in preventing Ferenczi from giving his paper at Wiesbaden, even after Freud virtually condemned Ferenczi for writing it (Fromm, 1959). But, Freud's mean-spirited rejection of Ferenczi and the uniformly negative reaction at the Wiesbaden Congress to the Confusion of Tongues paper was a crushing personal and professional blow to Ferenczi (Fromm, 1959; Masson, 1984; Rachman, 1997b; Roazen, 1975). Psychoanalysis developed a method to silence dissidents like Ferenczi. The practice of *Todschweigen* ("Death by Silence") (Menaker, 1994a, 1994b; Rachman, 1999a) removed their work from publication and study in the approved analytic training institutes, thereby, *silencing them*. Ferenczi's work virtually disappeared from psychoanalysis after his death in 1933. Several generations of psychoanalysts, psychotherapists and mental health professionals were deprived of his ideas and pioneering clinical work on trauma (Rachman, 1997a, 1997b, 1999b). The Ferenczi lamp flickered in the period 1940 to 1960, kept alive by his students Michael Balint, Izette De Forest, Elizabeth

Severn and Clara Thompson (Rachman, 1997a, 2003a, 2015). In the late 1970s to 1990s, a Ferenczi renaissance developed, spurred on by the French analysts working with Judith Dupont (1984), with the Swiss analysts working with André Haynal (1989), the Hungarian group led by Georgy Hidas (1993) and Judit Mészáros (1993), the publication of his *Clinical Diary* (Ferenczi, 1988) in America, and analysts working in the Relational Perspective (Aron & Harris, 1993).

I have tried to contribute to the Ferenczi Renaissance by focusing on Ferenczi's ideas in the Confusion of Tongues paradigm. Eric Fromm believed that the Confusion of Tongues paper was one of the greatest papers in the history of psychoanalysts (Fromm, 1959). I have found the Confusion of Tongues paradigm to be very valuable in understanding the psychodynamics of trauma. Over the last twenty years or so, I have attempted to expand and apply the Confusion of Tongues paradigm to a Relational Theory of Trauma (Rachman, 1994, 2000, 2003a, 2010; Rachman & Klett, 2015; Rachman & Mattick, 2012). I have applied the Confusion of Tongues idea to understand a wide variety of historical and clinical situations, for example, parental child abuse in the publicized case of Joel Steinberg and Hedda Nussbaum (Rachman, 1992); the Confusion of Tongues in the relationships between adolescents and adults (Rachman, 1995); the emotional seduction of Anna Freud by Sigmund Freud (Rachman, 2003b); the trauma in clinical relationship between Sándor Ferenczi and Elizabeth Severn (Rachman, 2010, 2017) and the Confusion of Tongues in the psychoanalytic therapy relationship (Rachman & Mattick, 2012).

Neglect of the incest trauma

I am using my expansion of the Confusion of Tongues paradigm to understand psychoanalysis' neglect of the Incest Trauma, and society's, in the following way:

1. A psychosocial trauma occurred when psychoanalysis moved away from accepting childhood sexual incest as an actual emotional/interpersonal experience for a child.
2. The Oedipal theory established childhood sexuality as a fantasy issue. The Oedipal explanation for childhood sexuality places the issue under the control of the psychoanalytic establishment.

In order to treat the problem of childhood sexuality, psychoanalysts believed their task was to understand and treat the Oedipal complex.

3. A Confusion of Tongues developed when analysts and therapists did not help incest survivors with their actual childhood sexual experiences, because they were interpreted as symbolic not real events.
4. The incest/survivor analysand felt confused, alienated and misunderstood by psychoanalysis because their real trauma was not believed. The incest survivors felt they were not being helped because they were asked to analyze *their fantasized sexual feelings* towards their parents. The survivor really wanted to analyze their actual sexual trauma toward their abuser and the experience of being abused.
5. Psychoanalysis presented a double-bind message to survivors: "Let us help you with your emotional issues." But, when the survivor said: "Help me with the fact that someone sexually abused me," the analyst said: "I will help you if you analyze your unconscious sexual feelings toward your parents." Psychoanalysis gave the mixed message: "We will help you, but, if you do it our way." Or worse, "We are not interested in your report of actual sexual abuse, we are only interested in your fantasies about abuse." Or, still worse: "We will convince you, if you let us, that *your idea of being sexually abused is really a function of your imagination*," i.e., it is your internal struggle to solve your Oedipal complex. This kind of mind alteration is a powerful defense mechanism that Ferenczi first identified as a being part of the Confusion of Tongues paradigm; he called it Identification with the aggressor. The abused individual, in order to gain the approval and love from their abuser, is willing to do their bidding. Victims of abuse need to maintain the fiction that their abuser cares about them. Incest survivors need to believe that their abuser really loves them. When a child or vulnerable adult is being abused, they are particularly emotionally vulnerable. It is the time they need loving the most. Survivors identify with their aggressors, willing to barter emotionally for what they need. The child victim, developmentally speaking, needs and wants love, attention and acceptance, tolerating the abuse (which is false love) and does the adult's bidding.

The analysand who wishes to be a good analysand needs the love and attention of the analyst, who can use his/her superior status to intimidate the analysand. The analyst can give the impression that he/she has the analytic truth. If accepted, this truth the analyst implies, will produce a cure. The analysand complies, hoping for a cure.

The identification with the aggressor, an important component of the Confusion of Tongues leads to the individual relinquishing his/her own view of reality. The analysand/survivor may feel that Oedipal interpretations, which are given by the analyst, are incorrect, unhelpful or making things worse. But, the analysand can change his/her mind or, worse, loses his/her mind. The mind of the analysand incorporates the mind of the analyst. The analyst has contributed to an emotional merger with the analysand/survivor, creating a dissociative state whose emotional functioning is dictated by the other. Ferenczi called this being an "automaton," a robot-like person.

6. Interestingly enough, Freud did exactly what I have just described in his famous Case of Dora (Freud, 1905). Paul Mattick and I believe Dora left treatment prematurely because Freud did not address her sexual trauma with an older family friend because he insisted on interpreting her psychological symptoms as a function of her Oedipal issues with her father (Rachman & Mattick, 2012). Furthermore, Freud insisted that the Oedipal complex was the cornerstone of psychoanalysis, and needed to be protected (Masson, 1984). Protecting the Oedipal complex, unfortunately, became more important than helping incest survivors with the reality of the incest experiences.
7. Incest survivors who were treated traditionally could become confused, lose contact with their subjective reality, develop dissociative reactions, blamed themselves for their trauma, were overwhelmed by shame, experienced a sense of powerlessness and lost their voice. They became "tongue-tied".
8. Society suffered from the insistence of psychoanalysis' Oedipal interpretation of childhood sexuality because psychoanalysis was so influential in determining what is studied, treated and valued in our society. The Incest Trauma consequently, became neglected until forces in our society, like the women's movement and the incest survivors' movements shed a light on the neglect.

9. The neglect of the incest trauma constitutes a social tragedy. Incest has been cited as the most common form of child abuse. The first national survey of adults concerning the history of childhood sexual abuse reported that 27 percent of the women and 16 percent of the men indicated childhood sexual victimization (Finkelhor, Hotaling, Lewis, & Smith (1990). More than 90 percent of abusers are people children love, know and cherish. These statistics actually verify the original finding of Freud and Ferenczi that the sexual predators of children were not as had been thought, strangers who solicited children in dark alleys, but were the children's parents (Ferenczi, 1933; Freud, 1954). They reported that middle-class children are the victims of abuse. In other words, middle-class parents were molesting middle-class children. In fact, I believe the analytic community's negative reaction to Ferenczi's Confusion of Tongues paper was, at least in part, due to their perception that Ferenczi was accusing middle-class parents of molesting their children. Ferenczi's verification of Freud's finding at the Wiesbaden Congress in 1932, gathered to hear the Confusion of Tongues paper, was seen as calling the middle-class psychoanalysts child molesters. In return for Ferenczi's accusation that analysts were child abusers, the analytic community shunned him (Ferenczi, 1933; Rachman, 1997a, 1997b). Psychoanalysis consequently never developed another theory of psychological disorder where actual trauma was a significant dimension.
10. The statistics on the incidence of sexual child abuse indicate that the issue of the incest trauma is a very relevant issue for study by psychoanalysis. *The incest trauma should not be neglected any longer.*

A psychodynamic explanation for the neglect of the Incest Trauma: Freud's childhood sexual trauma

Since psychoanalysis is built upon a psychodynamic explanation for human behavior, society deserves a psychodynamic explanation for the neglect of the incest trauma. Freud, Jones and the orthodox circle which surrounded them, did not hesitate to use psychodynamic explanation to criticize dissidents (Rachman, 1999a, 1999b). However, one of the most taboo areas of scholarship has been any meaningful discussion of Freud's personal functioning. Freud's sexuality has been, perhaps, the most taboo. The most notable attempt to discuss Freud's adult sexuality has been Peter Swales, the maverick historian of psychoanalysis. Swales (1982a, 1982b) believed he had discovered that Freud had a sexual affair with his sister-in-law, Minna Bernays. Traditionalists, such as Jones (1957), Gay (1988), Eissler (1965) and Young-Bruehl (1988), dismissed Swales' assertions as if they were ridiculous. Bettelheim (1990), however, believed it was plausible that Freud had a sexual interest in his sister-in-law.

I have been interested in two other issues in Freud's personal sexual history which bear on his theory and technique. Roazen (1969,1975) was the first to verify Freud's analysis of his daughter, Anna, after years of silence and denial by the traditional analytic establishment. The analysis of Anna created a Confusion of Tongues between Anna and Sigmund (Rachman, 2003b). Anna had the dubious distinction of having *to disclose her sexual feelings about her father to her father*. It created an atmosphere of sexual anxiety, fear of disclosure, emotional seduction and inauthentic interaction. Freud's willingness to analyze his own daughter seems to put into question Freud's commitment to his beloved Oedipal theory. The symbolic love affair between parent and child needs to remain unconscious, and remain a developmental phase to be worked through. It should not become an actual event in the emotional/interpersonal experience of everyday life between parent and child. Such an experience created what Ferenczi would call a retraumatization (Ferenczi, 1933, 1988) in the psychoanalytic situation and in my terms, a Confusion of Tongues Trauma (Rachman, 2012).

Freud's childhood sexual trauma with nursemaid Resi Wittek

There is a second issue in Freud's sexuality that is very relevant to our topic of the incest trauma. It is the issue of Freud's own childhood sexual trauma. Freud's sexual abuse by his nursemaid was first chronicled in the *Freud/Fliess Letters* (Freud, 1954). To Freud's credit, he openly discussed his childhood abuse in their correspondence. These self-disclosures, as well as the ones in Freud's interpretation of his dreams, were the result of Freud's self-analysis. It is a remarkable accomplishment of great emotional courage and therapeutic skill that Freud was able to retrieve his childhood sexual abuse when, those of us who work with incest survivors, know how difficult it is for analysands to accomplish this feat. In fact, years into an analysis, some analysands cannot fully own that they have been sexually abused. Freud's exploration of his sexual abuse has implications for his idea about child sexuality. More specifically, what is the implication of Freud's personal experience with child sexual abuse for the abandonment of the Seduction Hypothesis and the development of the Oedipal complex?

There are two basic sources for discussing Freud's childhood sexual trauma. First, we have Freud's own words in his letters to Fliess, when he discussed his self-analysis (Freud, 1954). Second is the research done by Marianne Krüll, a German sociologist who did an extensive study of Freud's family and childhood which was first published in German in 1984, then in English in 1986 (Krüll, 1986). The following sequence elaborates the sequence of Freud's childhood sexual trauma:

1. In Freud's attempt to uncover the mystery of whether his parents were involved in the development of his neurosis he said this about his father:

   I can only say that in my case, my father played no active role, though I certainly projected on to him an analogy from myself.

   (Freud, 1954, p. 219 – Letter, Freud to Fliess, October 3, 1897)

2. But, on a note of optimism, Freud said that in four days of self-analysis he had been making progress in identifying the origins of his neurosis. At this point, he was still trying to verify his Seduction Hypothesis, looking for incidences of sexual seduction in his own childhood. In a remarkable moment in psychoanalytic history, Freud recovered his childhood sexual seduction and self-disclosed it to Fliess as if he had solved "the riddle of the Sphynx." Freud named his nursemaid as the primary source of sexual seduction:

   my "primary originator," was an ugly, elderly but clever woman; (between the ages of two and two-and-a-half) libido towards *matrem* [mother] was aroused; the occasion must have been the journey with her from Leipzig to Vienna, during which we spent a night together and I must have had the opportunity of seeing her *nudom* [naked]. (You have long since drawn the conclusions from this for your own son, as remark of yours revealed).

(Freud, 1954, p. 219 – Letter, Freud to Fliess, October 3, 1897)

3. Freud continued his self-analysis about his sexual seduction through the reporting and analysis of a dream he reported to Fleiss on the following day, after his first self-disclosure.

Last night's dream produced the following under the most remarkable disguises:

She was my instructioness in sexual matters, and chided me for being clumsy and not being able to do anything ... Also, she washed me in reddish water which she had previously washed herself (not difficult to interpret; I find it nothing of the kind in my chain of memories, and so I take it for a genuine rediscovery).

(Freud, 1954, p. 220 – Letter, Freud to Fliess, October 4, 1897)

4. Freud was not able to name his instructionness: in sexual matters. Besides Freud's selfdisclosure we can now also turn to research on his childhood trauma by Marianne Krüll, a German sociologist who investigated his childhood and family (Krüll, 1986). This material was first presented in a German edition in 1984, then in English in 1986. Krüll identified Freud's nursemaid:

Freud's nursemaid, ... played a role of extraordinary importance during his early life in Freiberg. J. Sajner and I have recently discovered an entry in the list of visitors taking the cure at Roznau ... Roznau Register of Spa visitors for 5 June 1857: 108, Amalie Freud wool merchant's wife with child Sigmund and maid Resi Wittek from Freiberg, "*which makes it most likely that she was in fact Resi Wittek*"

(Krüll, 1986, p. 119)

Krüll goes on to elucidate Resi Wittek as a person;

> She was a Czech and a Catholic, … and it is possible that she was solely responsible for little Sigmund at the time of Julius's death [Freud's brother] and Amalie's new pregnancy followed by the birth of Anna, from April to December 1858 [Amalie Freud born Amalie Nathanson was his father's second or third wife and Freud's mother]. It is not known if Resi Wittek was married and had children of her own, but she had obviously taken little Sigmund to her heart, and he supposed later that he must have loved her in turn.
>
> (Krüll, 1986, p. 120)

Both Freud and Krüll indicate that Resi Wittek took little Sigmund to church. He would come home and lecture his parents about God and Hell. His parents did not seem to realize how emotionally attached little Sigmund and Resi Wittek were.

5. Freud also disclosed his emotional struggles to establish whether his recovered memories of childhood sexual abuse with Resi Wittek were real or imagined. As we now know, this is a fundamental issue with which all incest survivors struggle (Rachman, 2000, 2003a, 2013). Freud asked his mother if his retrieved memories were real:

> I have succeeded in finding a number of real points of reference. I asked my mother whether she remembered my nurse. "Of course", she said, "an elderly woman, very shrewd indeed. She was always taking you to church when you came home you used to preach, and tell us all about God conducted his affairs."
>
> (Freud, 1954, p. 22 – Letter Freud to Fliess, October 15, 1897)

6. Freud's early childhood experience with Resi Wittek also produced an abandonment trauma. His mother also told him that his nursemaid was a thief and was sent to jail:

> all the shiny Kreuzers and Zehnrs and toys that had been given you were found among her things. Your brother Philipp went himself to fetch the policeman, and she got ten months.
>
> (Freud, 1954, pp. 221–222 – Letter Freud to Fliess, October 15, 1897)

Freud was able to verify that his nurse was taken away from him. Freud admitted that a screen memory of the cupboard haunted him:

> A scene occurred to me which for the last twenty-nine years has been turning up from time to time in my conscious memory without any understanding.
>
> (Freud, 1954, p. 222 – Letter Freud to Fliess, October 15, 1897)

He went on to describe the emotional remnants of the missing nursemaid, Resi Wittek, when she disappeared after she was sent to jail for ten months and never returned to the Freud family:

> I was crying my heart out, because my mother was nowhere to be found. My brother Phillip ... opened a cupboard ... and when I found that she was not there either I cried still more until she came through the door, looking slim and beautiful. What can that mean? ... I feared she must have vanished, like my nurse not long before. I must have heard that the old woman had been locked, or rather "boxed" ... up ... The fact that I turned to him [Freud's brother Phillip] shows that I was well aware of his part in my nurse's disappearance.
>
> (Freud, 1954, p. 223 – Letter Freud to Fliess, October 15, 1897 [the screen memory of the cupboard was used in Freud's *The Psychopathology of Everyday Life*])

7. To Freud's self-disclosure regarding the sexual experiences with his nursemaid, Resi Wittek, we can also add Krüll's interesting formulations – Krüll speculates about Wittek's additional sexual behavior of manipulating little Freud's genitals:

> Now why did she [Resi Wittek] think Freud clumsy and incompetent? Perhaps it was because of his toilet training, his inability to urinate without wetting the floor? ... Did Resi perhaps manipulate his penis, not simply when teaching him to urinate but on other occasions, too? Freud wrote: It is well known that unscrupulous nurses put crying children to sleep by stroking their genitals.
>
> (Freud, 1931)

"Did his nursemaid also send little Sigmund to sleep in this way?" (Krüll, 1986, p. 121).

8. Resi Wittek's disappearance from Freud's life was also an issue of speculation by Krüll:

> Sigmund aged two and a half, probably did not understood why Resi disappeared so suddenly ... She was simply gone, and he missed her very much. The picture of a screaming child who asked Phillip to open the box because he was afraid that his mother had been "boxed up" like the nursemaid who had just disappeared ... clearly reflects this feeling, that the episode was traumatic is also borne out by the fact that he kept recalling it year after year without really understanding what had happened.
>
> (Krüll, 1986, p. 122)

Freud's disclosure from his self-analysis in his letters to Fliess clearly indicated that Freud admitted he was the victim of childhood sexual abuse. Freud and Resi Wittek had an emotionally and interpersonally close relationship. It is likely they shared loving feelings and a physical closeness. Freud's parents may not have realized how important his nursemaid was in his life. They did not seem to know about their sexual relationship. What is more, they did not know about her being a thief. When Resi Wittek was sent to prison and never returned, it clearly created an abandonment trauma. Freud indicated that as an adult, he was preoccupied with the feeling of emotional abandonment in his screen memory of the cupboard. Was Freud allowed to mourn when Resi Wittek disappeared?

Integrating the data, from Freud and Krüll about Freud's childhood sexual seduction and abandonment trauma experiences, it is hypothesized that:

1. Freud's childhood sexual and abandonment experiences became a Confusion of Tongues Trauma (Rachman, 1994, 1997a, 2003a; Rachman & Klett, 2015). As a child, Freud was seduced and abandoned by an adult, his nursemaid, Resi Wittek.
2. His parents had no idea of the nature of the sexual relationship between their son and their nursemaid. What is more, Resi Wittek's sudden disappearance was a further shock that was perpetuated

upon him by his family. They took the nursemaid away from their son, with no idea of the emotional bond with the nursemaid. It is not known if any empathy or emotional support was provided to little Sigmund to deal with the loss of his nursemaid.

3. Little Sigmund could not turn to them for solace or help with his trauma. The family felt they were doing the proper thing in getting rid of a thief in their midst and protecting their child from a negative influence. Ironically, they were unknowingly helping him to break a sexual seduction experience.
4. Freud could also not speak of his trauma because he was told by his father to maintain the family prohibition on not revealing family secrets (Krüll, 1986).
5. Freud repressed his childhood traumas. He became tongue-tied, another element of the Confusion of Tongues trauma. He was unable to speak of his trauma. Elective mutism developed. Ferenczi suggested the child is alone in their trauma, fearing that the abuser will further injure them either physically or emotionally, if they give voice to the trauma (Ferenczi, 1933). We do not know if Resi Wittek threatened little Sigmund not to disclose their sexuality.
6. We know from the contemporary study and treatment of the Incest Trauma (Rachman, 2000, 2003a, 2013; Rachman & Klett, 2015) that the split-off portions of personality can produce disturbed feelings, thoughts and behavior unavailable to consciousness and rationality. I believe this is what happened to Freud. His childhood traumas were unavailable to him because he did not confront them in his self-analysis and would not allow anyone else to analyze him. He turned down Jung and Ferenczi, who had, at different times, offered him help with his neurotic issues. Freud would not relinquish his role as the Master and head of psychoanalysts (Rachman, 1997b, 2003a; Rachman & Klett, 2015).
7. His repressed sexual trauma emerged as moral outrage towards Ferenczi for focusing so dramatically on the role of childhood sexual trauma in the development of personality and psychological disorder (Rachman, 1997b; Rachman & Klett, 2015).
8. Freud and the orthodox analytic community were successful in suppressing Ferenczi's idea about the incest trauma. At least four generations of analysts and mental health professionals were taught to ignore the significance of the Incest Trauma in the

development of psychological disorder. It was not until the 1980s, when Ferenczi's *Clinical Diary* was finally published in French and English, that psychoanalysis became reacquainted with Ferenczi's pioneering work on the study and treatment of the Incest Trauma (Ferenczi, 1988).

9. The women's movement and incest survivors have led the way towards helping to lift the veil of denial regarding the prevalence of Incest Trauma.
10. Psychoanalysis, as well as the lay public, need to contribute to the awakening of the necessary for maintaining the study and treatment of children and adults who have been sexually molested. We need to connect to our pioneering past, when the importance of protecting and helping children was understood. It is possible that Freud first, then Ferenczi, got it right the first time, that the actual sexual abuse of children is a significant dimension in the development of psychological disorder.

Note

1 Revised and expanded version of a presentation at the International Psychohistorical Association, Kimmel Center New York University, 60 Washington Square Park South, June 8, 2012 (Rachman, 2012).

References

Aron, L., & Harris, A. (1993). *The Legacy of Sándor Ferenczi.* Hillsdale, NJ: Analytic Press.

Bettelheim, B. (1990). *Freud's Vienna.* New York: Alfred A. Knopf.

Dupont, J. (1984). Entre Freud et Ferenczi: Groddeck. *Confrontation* 12 (Autumn): 33–42.

Eissler, R.R. (1965). *Medical Orthodoxy and the Future of Psychoanalysis* New York: International Universities Press.

Ferenczi, S. (1933). The Confusion of Tongues between adults and children: The language of tenderness and passion. In M. Balint (ed.), *Final Contributions to the Problems and Methods of Psycho-analysis.* New York: Bruner/Mazel, vol. 3, pp. 156–167.

Ferenczi, S. (1988). *The Clinical Diary of Sándor Ferenczi*, ed. J. Dupont, trans. M. Balint & N.Z. Jackson. Cambridge, MA: Harvard University Press.

Finkelhor, D., Hotaling, G., Lewis, I.A., & Smith, C. (1990). Sexual abuse in a national survey of adult men and women. Prevalence, characteristics, and risk factors. *Child Abuse and Neglect* 14(1): 19–28.

Freud, S. (1905 [1907]). Fragment of an analysis in a case of hysteria. *SE*, 7: 263.

Freud, S. (1931). *Three Essays on the Theory of Sexuality. SE*, 7: 125,180.

Freud, S. (1954). *The Origins of Psychoanalysis: Letters to Wilhelm Fliess.* New York: Basic Books.

Fromm, E. (1959). *Sigmund Freud's Mission*. New York; Harper & Row.
Gay, P. (1988). *Freud: A life for our time*. New York: W.W. Norton.
Haynal, A. (1989). *Controversies in Psychoanalytic Method: From Freud and Ferenczi to Michael Balint*. New York: New York University Press.
Hidas, G. (1993). Flowing over transference, countertransference, telepathy: Subjective dimensions of the psychoanalytic relationship in Ferenczi's thinking. In L. Aron & A. Harris (eds.), *The Legacy of the Sándor Ferenczi*. Hillsdale, NJ: Analytic Press.
Jones, E. (1957). *The Life and Work of Sigmund Freud, vol. 3, The Last Phase: 1919–1939*. New York: Basic Books.
Krüll, M. (1986). *Freud and His Father*. New York: W.W. Norton & Co.
Masson, J.M. (1984). *The Assault on Truth: Freud's suppression of the seduction theory*. New York: Farrar, Straus & Giroux.
Menaker, E. (1994a). Personal communication. Wednesday, January 12.
Menaker, E. (1994b). Personal communication. Friday, March 11.
Mészáros, J. (1993). Ferenczi's preanalytic period embedded in the cultural streams of the fin de siècle. In L. Aron & A. Harris (eds.), *The Legacy of Sándor Ferenczi*. Hillsdale, NJ: Analytic Press.
Rachman, A.W. (1994). The Confusion of Tongues theory: Ferenczi's legacy to psychoanalysis. In A. Haynal and E. Falzeder (eds.), *100 Years of Psychoanalysis*. London: Karnac Books.
Rachman, A.W. (1995). The Confusion of Tongues between adolescents and adults: Communication and interaction in adolescent group psychotherapy. Presentation at Fourth Annual Conference Missouri Group Psychotherapy Society, St Louis, Missouri.
Rachman, A.W. (1997a). *Sándor Ferenczi: The psychotherapist of tenderness and passion*. Northvale, NJ: Jason Aronson.
Rachman, A.W. (1997b). The suppression and censorship of Ferenczi's Confusion of Tongues paper. *Psychoanalytic Inquiry* 17(4): 459–485.
Rachman, A.W. (1999a). Death by silence (*Todschweigen*): The traditional methods of dealing with dissidents in psychoanalysis. In R. Prince (ed.) *The Death of Psychoanalysis: Suicide, murder or rumor greatly exaggerated*. Northvale, NJ: Jason Aronson, pp. 154–164.
Rachman, A.W. (1999b). Ferenczi's rise and fall from "analytic grace": The Ferenczi renaissance. *Journal of Eastern Group Psychotherapy Association* 23(3–4): 103–119.
Rachman, A.W. (2000). Ferenczi's Confusion of Tongues theory and the analysis of the incest trauma. *Psychoanalytic Social Work* 7(1): 27–53.
Rachman, A.W. (2003a). *Psychotherapy of Difficult Cases: Flexibility and responsiveness in contemporary practice*. Madison, CT: Psychosocial Press.
Rachman, A.W. (2003b). Freud's analyses of his daughter Anna: A Confusion of Tongues. In A. Roland, B. Ulanov, & C. Babre (eds.), *Creative Dissent: Psychoanalysis in evolution*, Westport, CT: Praeger, pp. 59–71.
Rachman, A.W. (2010). An "invitro" study of intersubjectivity: Sándor Ferenczi's analyses of Mrs Elizabeth Severn. Presentation at 17th Conference of the International Forum of Psychoanalysis, Athens, Greece.
Rachman, A.W. (2012). The analysis of the incest trauma: From the Seduction Hypothesis to the Confusion of Tongues trauma. Presentation at the First Annual Sándor Ferenczi Seminars, the Hungarian House, New York City, Saturday, November 17.

Rachman, A.W. (2014). Sándor Ferenczi's analysis of Elizabeth Severn: "Wild Analysis" or pioneering attempt to analyze the incest trauma. In *Sándor Ferenczi and the evolution of psychoanalysis: Innovations in theory and technique. Psychoanalytic Inquiry*, 34(2): 145–168, February/March.

Rachman, A.W. (2017). *Elizabeth Severn, the Evil Genius of Psychoanalysis*. London: Routledge.

Rachman, A.W., & Klett, S. (2015). *The Analysis of the Incest Trauma: Retrieval, recovery, renewal*. London: Karnac Books.

Rachman, A.W., & Mattick, P. (2012). Confusion of tongues in a psychoanalytic relationship. *Psychoanalytic Social Work*, 19(1–2): 167–190.

Roazen, P. (1969). *Brother Animal: The story of Freud and Tausk*. New York: New York University Press.

Roazen, P. (1975). *Freud and His Followers*. New York: Alfred Knopf.

Swales, P.J. (1982a). *Freud, Johann Weier, and the Status of Seduction: The role of the witch in the conception of fantasy*. New York: Peter J. Swales.

Swales, P.J. (1982b). Freud, Minna Bernays and the conquest of Rome. *New American Review* 1: 1–23.

Young-Bruehl, E. (1998). *Anna Freud: A biography*. New York: Summit Books.

Chapter 10

Confusion of Tongues trauma in child abduction

Revising the Stockholm Syndrome

Arnold Wm. Rachman

Sexual abuse of children: the Budapest School's relevance to psychoanalysis and society

Freud first linked childhood sexual abuse by parental behavior to psychological disorder. Freud's decision to change this direction in his efforts on building a cornerstone for psychoanalysis to his concept of the Oedipal conflict (Freud 1954), solidified an intrapsychic focus for the child/parent drama. A refocus to the interpersonal sphere occurred when Ferenczi pioneered analysis of difficult cases. He tried to return psychoanalysis to the study of childhood sexual abuse believing it was the casual factor in psychological disorder (Ferenczi 1980a, 1988).

Ferenczi's work pioneered the study of the child as the victim of the adult's sexual abuse, which reversed the traditional idea that the child was the Oedipal seducer of the parent. His work changed the focus from the sexuality of the child to the sexuality of the adult. Ferenczi was interested in the welfare of the children (Rachman 1997). He is thought to have said: "There are no bad children, only bad parents."

Neglect of child sexual abuse

The longest-running issue in the history of psychoanalysis has been the controversy about childhood sexual seduction. The controversy concerns whether or not there is a belief in the actual occurrence of child abuse or the belief in the unconscious sexual feelings of the Oedipal complex (Mitchell 1996). The controversies which divide the Freudian and Relational perspectives, for example, overshadow a more fundamental issue, e.g., that psychoanalysis has neglected the study and treatment of childhood sexual trauma (Rachman 2012a, 2012b).

The switch from the Seduction to the Oedipal theories moved psychoanalysis away from the social concern of the sexual abuse of children. If one examines the major theoretical orientation in the history of psychoanalysis, from Freud to Mitchell, for example, only two analysts have conceptualized child sexual molestation as a central issue. Freud, in his original formulation of the etiology of neurosis, the Seduction Hypothesis (Freud 1954; Masson 1984) and Ferenczi, expanding on Freud's seduction hypothesis in his Confusion of Tongues paradigm (Ferenczi 1980b). It was Ferenczi who maintained his belief in the importance of the psychodynamic that when a child is sexually molested by a parent (or parental authority) this experience initiates a trauma, which has profound effects on child personality development, developmental arrest, and adult psychological disorder. In his research on Ferenczi's clinical work with child molestation, Masson (1984) felt that Ferenczi's focus on the incest trauma demonstrated that he was an outstanding advocate for abused children. This idea of Ferenczi's interest in social welfare has been lost in the controversies which surround Ferenczi's contributions (Rachman 1997).

If one examines the theoretical and clinical writings of major analytic scholars after Ferenczi, we find little mention of the issue of child molestation. Balint, Ferenczi's student and heir to the Budapest School of psychoanalysis, was definitely interested in both actual and unconscious trauma. In fact, Balint extended the issue of childhood trauma to include emotional trauma. Balint extended Ferenczi's Confusion of Tongues paradigm beyond the actual molestation of the child, to focus on the emotional trauma of the child when there is a disturbed object relations between mother and child (Balint 1965). This was an important step in analytic theorizing as it advanced Ferenczi's idea of *actual trauma* in the disturbed interpersonal relationship between parent and child as causative of psychological disorder. What is more Balint, who had left Hungary to escape the Nazi occupation of Europe, became an influential member of the British Middle Group at the London Psychoanalytic Institute. He contributed to the development of the British Object Relations perspective in the Middle Group. Yet, with all his focus on childhood trauma, Balint did not advance the issue of the study and treatment of child molestation. However, his trauma theory (Balint 1992) and the concept of primary object loss did extend

Ferenczi's Confusion of Tongues paradigm. Balint was attempting to remain in mainstream psychoanalysis and not suffer Ferenczi's negative fate. But, more importantly, Balint was interested in integrating Freud and Ferenczi's theories. He proposed a tripartite focus, e.g., the basic fault, the Oedipal Complex, and the zone of creativity (Balint 1992, pp. 28–29), extending psychoanalysis to a focus on the mother/child relationship and to an understanding of trauma disorder beyond the family of origin to the social network. The basic fault was used to understand trauma and psychological disorder beyond neurosis. The Oedipal complex was an integration of Freud's ideas about neurosis. Balint added the idea of a level of conflict-free functioning where creativity is the focus (Balint 1992).

In contemporary psychoanalysis, attention needs to be directed toward the neglected area of the incest trauma and child molestation. Within this issue, child abduction needs further study. The phenomenon is occurring with some regularity in contemporary society, highlighted in the recent past by the highly publicized case of Elizabeth Smart. The Budapest School can make a contribution to this social issue.

Abduction and trauma

In America there is a history, going back to Colonial times, of individuals who have been taken hostage and suffered trauma. One of the first such cases of abduction occurred during King Philip's War in the 1670s. Mary Rowlandson, a Puritan maiden, was the wife of a minister, and was kidnapped by Narragansett Wampanoag and Nashaway Indians on February 10, 1675 in Lancaster, Massachusetts (Rowlandson 2009). For eleven weeks, she and her three children were forced to travel through the wilderness while the Indians carried out raids and avoided the English militia. Rowlandson was ransomed for £20, raised by the women of Boston (Perlstein 2008). In Rowlandson's captivity narrative, the severe conditions of her captivity are described in visceral detail. The text is considered a seminal American work in the literary genre of captivity narratives. It is not clear if sexual abuse was part of her captive experience, but what is clear is that she felt her captors were barbarians and wild animals. Her Puritanical beliefs separated her spiritually and emotionally from her captives.

In a contemporary abduction case, Elizabeth Smart's religious beliefs helped her to maintain an emotional, interpersonal, and intellectual separation from her captives. But, in Smart's case, sexual abuse was a significant event in what became her Confusion of Tongues trauma.

Abduction of white women and children by Indians was part of life in the Western frontier in the 1800s. One of the most famous abductions, which included a very dramatic trauma bonding with the captors, is the case of Cynthia Ann Parker, whose narrative is a seminal American work in the literary genre of captivity narratives (Gwynne 2010). She was kidnapped by the Comanche Indians at the age of 9 on May 19, 1836. Her family was massacred and their settlement burned down. She was adopted by the Comanches and lived with them for 24 years, completely assimilating as an Indian. She was given the Indian name of Naduah, meaning "someone who is found," and handed over to a Tenowish Comanche couple, who adopted her and raised her like their own daughter. She was emotionally and interpersonally separated from her American way of life; in essence, she became a Comanche. She married the Comanche chieftain, Peta Nocona, and they enjoyed what has been described as a happy marriage. Nocona never took another wife, although it was traditional for chieftains to do so. They had three children, including the great Comanche Chieftain Quanna Parker.

The Parker family did not give up trying to rescue Cynthia Ann. In December 1860, after years of searching, on the request of her father, Texas Rangers found a band of Comanches at Pease River. Among the fleeing band of Comanches were Chief Nocona and a woman. When the Rangers began questioning the woman, they noticed she had blue eyes. When Ranger Lawrence Sullivan Ross told her no Comanche children were killed, so her sons were safe, she identified herself as "Me Cincee Ann." Realizing that Cynthia Ann Parker has lost her capacity to speak English, and could be unhappy if she were separated from her Indian life, some Rangers advised that she be returned to the Comanches. However, Ross, the Texas Ranger leader, decided to return her to her uncle.

Her rescue was celebrated in the United States because it gave hope to so many of the Western settlers who had lost children to abductions and were killed. She was given a grant by Texas, which included land

and a stipend. However, she remained unhappy. There was a discrepancy between the abductee's emotional reaction to being rescued and her original family's and the public view. The American public, her family, and the Texas Ranger were appalled that a white child/woman was living with savages. There was no doubt in their minds she needed to be rescued. However, Cynthia Ann Parker became a white squaw, totally assimilated as a Comanche. *In actuality, she did not want to be rescued.* She did not want to adjust to American life. She attempted to escape. She wanted to be returned to the Comanches. What people could not accept was that she did not want to be redeemed. It was very difficult for the public to believe that Cynthia Ann Parker was happier as a Comanche than as a white woman. It was well-known, however, that abducted children who lived among the Indians for many years did not readapt to their original life. Cynthia Ann missed her two sons she had left behind. She never stopped worrying about her children. When her daughter, Prairie Flower, died of pneumonia, she was so distraught about having no more contact with her children, she virtually committed suicide by refusing food and water. She died shortly after (Exley 2001; Frankel 2013; Gwynne 2010).

The abduction and so-called rescue of Cynthia Ann Parker raises some important issues about the trauma caused by abduction. Another case of child abduction by the Comanches is that of Bianca Biff – abducted and then adopted by the Comanches, and treated with kindness. In fact, a family member called this "*bonds of affection* almost as sacred as family ties" (Gwynne 2010, p. 107). On the one hand the Comanches were capable of empathy, but on the other they usually abducted prepubescent children. There is also the fact that these captives were treated brutally: "were terribly abused, sexual and otherwise" (Gwynne 2010, p. 104). Certainly, kindness and brutality experienced by an abducted child leads to confusion and vulnerability. Ferenczi (1980a) was well aware of this mixed kind of emotional experience which leads to subjection and domination of the captive by the aggressor.

The role of sexual abuse in the abduction experience

Abduction of youth usually involves sexual abuse, a factor often overlooked in attempts to understand the psychodynamics of captivity.

The present Relational Orientation informed by the Budapest School of psychoanalysis integrates the importance of actual trauma in the relationships between children and adults (Ferenczi 1980a, 1988). In the Confusion of Tongues theory of trauma (Rachman & Klett 2015), childhood sexual abuse of children is a powerful psychodynamic which can so alter the child's functioning that he/she can become an emotional slave to the abuser. Ferenczi described the process in his Confusion of Tongues paradigm (Ferenczi 1980a, 1988), which will be discussed later in more detail. For now, mention should be made of the process – occurring between an abuser and victim – where the sexual abuse can lead to a severe dissociative reaction. The individual can become dissociated, which can cause an emotional and interpersonal process that Ferenczi called becoming an automaton (Ferenczi 1980a). The victim becomes robot-like in his/her functioning. In the psychodynamics of abduction it would refer to the child becoming the emotional slave of his/her captor. The captor through sexual abuse of the child would be able to keep the child captive, not only by physical means but, more importantly, by emotional attachment through a form of perverse love. It is this form of perverse love that needs our attention.

Why are children abducted? Many are abducted to be used as "sex slaves" by adults who have serious emotional problems. These are adults who need to have children and youth as sexual objects because of emotional difficulties, which can range from impotence to impulse control issues, to the need for domination, control, and manipulation, and, of course, a sexual perversion for children.

Sexual abuse is rarely mentioned in reports of abduction. For example, in the case of Elizabeth Smart, which will be discussed in detail, media reports of sexual abuse were missing. As we shall see, sexual abuse was actually the major dimension of the abduction experience, a basic motivation of child abduction of children and in the psychodynamics of understanding the trauma suffered by the child.

Stockholm Syndrome

The most cited explanation for *trauma bonding* or *capture-bonding* that can develop between the captive and abuser is referred to as the Stockhom Syndrome (Bejerot 1974; Ochberg 2005). Basically, this phenomenon is characterized as a psychological experience where a captive develops either sympathy or empathy with their captor, sometimes to the point of identifying with them. These feelings, on the surface, do not make sense in the light of danger, risk, and abuse endured by the victim. The understanding of this seeming irrational event, however, comes from an explanation of the Confusion of Tongues trauma which occurs during captivity.

The Stockholm Syndrome was named after a famous robbery in Sweden, in which several Stockholm bank employees were held hostage in a bank vault from August 23 to 28, 1973. As the captors negotiated with the police, the hostages became emotionally attached to their captors. What is more, some hostages defended their captors and rejected assistance from governmental officials (Bejerot 1974; MacKenzie 2004; Ochberg 2005).

Case of Patty Hearst

One of the most famous examples of the Stockholm Syndrome was that of Patty Hearst, newspaper heiress and granddaughter of publishing magnate William Randolph Hearst (Boulton 1975; Hearst 1988; Pascal & Pascal 1974). On February 4, 1974, the 19-year-old Hearst was kidnapped from her Berkeley, California apartment by a left-wing urban guerrilla group called the Symbionese Liberation Army (SLA), who initially failed in their attempt to exchange Hearst for jailed members of their group (Rumband 2014). A second plan involved forcing the Hearst family to donate money for needy Californians.

When Hearst's father distributed food to the poor of the Bay Area, the SLA continued to refuse to release Patty. By this time, a Confusion of Tongues bonding with her captors had developed. In a tape recording by Patty released to the press, she criticized the quality of the food her father gave to the poor. The most dramatic indication of the Confusion of Tongues bonding occurred when she announced on audiotape that she had joined the SLA and assumed the name Tania. Then on April 15, 1974, wielding a M1 carbine, Patty Hearst helped robbed the Sunset District branch of the Hibernia Bank in San Francisco. A warrant for her arrest was issued by the FBI and San Francisco Police Department (Graebner 2008; Weed 1976).

While captive, Hearst was blindfolded, locked in a closet, and physically and sexually abused (Hearst 1988), and her behavior while captive aroused controversy (Benedict 2008; Conway & Seigelman 1995). One expert, Afton, believed Hearst was a victim of brainwashing, caused by trauma. But, another expert, Harry L. Kozol (Benedict 2008) – who was well-known for his work with neurological disorders, sex offenders, and high-profile mentally ill criminals – dramatically stated that Hearst was a rebellious person looking for a cause. Furthermore, Hearst's participation in the robbery had been an act of free will, not a result of trauma.

In the trial, F. Lee Bailey, Hearst's defense attorney, used psychiatric experts, most notably Robert Jay Lifton, to demonstrate that her emotional bond to her captors, referred to as *the Stockholm Syndrome*, was a result of brainwashing. Lifton's understanding of the personality alteration during captivity is a social psychological explanation that emphasizes the environment, which impinges on the individual's sense of self (Lifton 1989, 1993).

These formulations are inadequate, because they do not provide a comprehensive psychodynamic formulation for the emotional and interpersonal changes that occur with captivity during trauma bonding. It must be understood that the abductor's behavior is geared toward fulfilling a specific purpose. Although what I am about to say may sound exaggerated, there is an unfortunate analogy between training an animal's behavior and training a child/captive to be a sex slave. Ferenczi, in his paper "Taming of a Wild Horse" (1980b), observed that a wild animal could be "broken" by using a method which alternates between affection and punishment. In this way the animal becomes *confused, loses its own will, and needs the trainer's will in order to function.* Ferenczi's astute observation of a wild horse being broken was an early dimension of the Confusion of Tongues paradigm. He later used this observation to explain the effects of childhood sexual abuse on the child's personality.

To the Stockholm Syndrome, the trauma abuse concept (Dutton & Painter 1981), the brainwashing concept (Lifton 1989, 1993), and the evolutionary concept (Cosmides & Tooby 2013), we need to add the Confusion of Tongues paradigm (Ferenczi 1980a; Rachman 1994), which can explain psychodynamically what occurs to a child or youth in abduction. The captor uses sexual abuse to manipulate, control, and dominate the child. In particular, sexual abuse is used to break the will of the child and separate him/her from the previous belief system. The captor becomes a substitute parental figure to whom the child becomes beholden for their physical and emotional welfare. Abducted children especially need love and affection, since they are separated from their family, feel abandoned, and fear for their lives.

The Confusion of Tongues theory of trauma

Ferenczi attempted to inform psychoanalysis as well as society of the importance of sexual abuse in childhood as a significant factor in psychological disorder and personality development (Rachman 1994, 1997, 2003; Rachman & Klett 2015). He explained that when children are molested by their parents or other adults, profound psychological effects are produced that need to be treated by psychoanalytic means. What is important to consider is that Ferenczi's formulation highlighted that *the adult's sexuality is at question when a child is molested.* Freud's Oedipal theory focused on *the sexuality of the child* (Rachman & Mattick 2012). *The most significant change derived from the Confusion of Tongues concept is that sexual molestation is not a fantasy. It is not a figment of a child's imagination, but an actual traumatic event in a child's life that has profound psychological implications.*

The Confusion of Tongues paradigm (Ferenczi 1980a) has been expanded into a theory of the incest trauma (Rachman 1997, 2003; Rachman & Klett 2015), which can be outlined as follows:

1. The child is sexually abused by an adult, usually a parent or parental surrogate, which is the narcissistic expression of the adult's sexuality toward the child. This is an exploitation of a child by an adult.
2. The sexual seduction sets off the incest trauma.
3. The child, in a desperate attempt to maintain self-cohesion, employs a series of characteristic defense mechanisms:
   a. a profound sense of personal confusion
   b. development of denial and dissociation
   c. blunted affect
   d. a loss of a sense of reality
   e. a loss of a sense of power and agency
   f. robotic-like functioning, becoming intellectually, emotionally, and interpersonally stilted and inhibited

g. profound feelings of shame
h. feelings of self-blame

The continued and intense use of these mechanisms in the years after the sexual trauma experience constitutes an Incest Trauma Disorder (Rachman 2014; Rachman & Klett 2015).

4. The child's functioning is so altered that he/she feels under the power of the abuser. The child loses his/her full conscious functioning as well as their hold on reality. What is more, the child, in order to maintain the fantasy of being loved to avoid feelings of abandonment and annihilation, as well as to maintain self-cohesion, becomes the emotional slave of the abuser. The child in a state of emotional helplessness, emotionally surrenders to the abuser, losing the capacity to remember and speak of the trauma. *The child becomes tongue-tied.*
5. Unless the abused individual receives therapeutic help, he/she becomes emotionally vulnerable to developing a Confusion of Tongues trauma disorder.
6. The elicitation of the psychodynamics of childhood sexual abuse by Ferenczi was a significant contribution because it attempted to establish the incest trauma as a disorder, and one that could be treated by psychoanalysis.

The Confusion of Tongues theory can aid our understanding of the psychodynamics of child abduction. The adult abuser manipulates the child by molestation, which encourages a perverse false love bond. The child is told the sexual experience is an expression of love from the adult abuser. In order to fulfill the need for love and attention that every child needs, especially when he/she is separated from their real parents, the child succumbs to the will of the abuser.

The case of Elizabeth Smart: Confusion of Tongues trauma in abduction

In June 2002, the abduction of a Mormon youth in Utah became a human interest story in the United States and the world. It was a shocking disappearance of a child, taken from her own bedroom in a tightly knit, religious family living in a Utah suburb. This was not a disadvantaged child from a broken family looking for love and attention. This was not an abused child easily lured into a relationship where there is an unconscious enactment of an earlier trauma. What is more, this was not an emotionally disturbed child whose psychopathology was easily exploited by her captors.

The data for the description of the abduction, captivity, and recovery comes from three primary sources: Elizabeth Smart's testimony in the federal trial of her captors (Hicken-Brown 2009); the book written by her parents, Ed and Lois Smart, entitled *Bringing Elizabeth Home* (Smart & Smart 2003); and Elizabeth Smart's book, *My Story* (Smart & Stewart 2013). These primary sources contain Elizabeth Smart's and her parents' own words about the abduction. Secondary sources provided the practical details of the events and the aftermath.

The abduction

On June 5, 2002, between 2 a.m. and 3 a.m., a man broke into the house of Elizabeth Smart in a suburb of Salt Lake City, Utah, and abducted her. This 14-year-old was taken from her own bed, as her younger sister Katherine made believe she was asleep. However, she saw the abductor, remaining silent to protect her sister when she saw that the abductor had a knife to her throat. The man, later identified as Brian David Mitchell, threatened to kill Elizabeth and her family if she resisted. The abductor was looking for a sexual partner. He made sure he had the teenage, Elizabeth, not her younger sister, Katherine, because he touched Elizabeth's chest to make sure she had breasts (Hicken-Brown 2009, pp. 5–6).

At the initial period of abduction, Elizabeth reported that her captor said "he was taking me hostage and holding me for ransom" (Hicken-Brown 2009, p. 7). That turned out to be a lie, one of many that he was to tell Elizabeth. Brian David Mitchell was accompanied by Wanda Ileen Barzee. Immediately after the abduction, Elizabeth said: "he took me up into the mountains" (Hicken-Brown 2009, p. 8). For a period, Elizabeth was living in close proximity to her home with Mitchell and Barzee in a makeshift campsite, [about] "three miles up close to the top of the mountain ridge – there were lots of trees surrounding it, where he had a camp he had been at for a while"

(Hicken-Brown 2009, p. 9). In order to insure Elizabeth would not escape, he chained her between two trees. He had the key to the chains around his neck the entire time (Hicken-Brown 2009, p. 10). In other words, Elizabeth was chained to a tree like a wild animal, with her captor as her keeper.

Sexual abuse of Elizabeth Smart

As I have already mentioned, it is my belief that one of the primary motivations for child abduction is to have a victim that the abductor can sexually abuse at will. The adult abuser is searching for someone they can dominate, control as a sex slave. The abductor/abuser may have a variety of emotional disturbances which fuel the need to have a child for sexual contact. Sexual abuse was a central dimension of Elizabeth Smart's experience with Brian David Mitchell. In her testimony at Mitchell's federal trial, Elizabeth made it very clear that sexual exploitation was the primary motivation of her captor, as she answered questions by her lawyer about her molestation:

Q: Now, you indicated that the first thing he did was to rape you when you were in this camp. Without going into any of the details, how often did he rape you, Elizabeth?
A: On a daily basis up to three or four times.

The lawyer asked her to specify:

Q: And during your nine months with the defendant, Elizabeth, what was the predominant focus?

Elizabeth's answer was very revealing:

A: Sex.

(Hicken-Brown 2009, p. 11)

Mitchell tried to give Elizabeth the impression that he was a religious person of the same faith as Elizabeth, the Church of the Latter Day Saints, known as the Mormons. He used religious phrases, references to God, and talked about himself as a prophet, Jesus's mouthpiece, and a follower of Emanuel. This was actually pseudo-religious speech used to manipulate and control her. From the beginning of their interaction, Elizabeth was not taken in by Mitchells' attempts to use religion to manipulate her into having sex. She succumbed to his sexual desires, not because she felt she was fulfilling God's desires, but because she didn't want to die at her captor's hands. Nor did she ever report she enjoyed the sex, or became accustomed to it. In other words, Elizabeth Smart was never a willing participant in the sexual experiences. Rather, she was basically raped on a regular basis. Her normal assertive personality was altered by her captor by his giving her alcohol, drugs, and showing her pornography. Elizabeth was forced to give her body to her captor, but never gave him her spirit.

Hidden in plain sight

Although Elizabeth Smart was moved around by her captors, eventually they settled about 18 miles (30 kilometers) from her home. Under the influence of the Confusion of Tongues trauma, Elizabeth Smart took on a new persona. The usually perky, happy, outgoing Elizabeth became quiet, reserved, detached, and withdrawn. The reachable and responsive child became reticent and removed. Elizabeth's natural appearance of a clean-cut, all-American beauty with blonde hair was completely obliterated by her new persona. Her face and figure was covered from head to toe in a pseudo-hippie outfit made of gauze. She was forced to wear a veil over her face, and a hood covering over her head. Her captives were dressed in a similar fashion. Together, they appeared to be a New Age hippie trio, who were seen around town, being the object of curiosity. They were tolerated, but were not approached, by town's people. It is interesting to note that the captors and Elizabeth Smart were perceived as a unit, a family. At no time, when they visited town where people and authorities were visible or easily accessible, did Elizabeth Smart ever try to make contact with anyone or did she try to escape. This is the most puzzling aspect to abduction. *Why doesn't the abductee try to escape?*

The sexual abuse of Elizabeth Smart was a key factor in the transformation that was visible in her appearance and behavior. She was transformed from a beautiful, happy, and responsive teenager into a bizarre-looking, reticent, zombie-like pseudo-adult. When the media reports of Elizabeth Smart's abduction began to reach television, newspapers, and magazines, I searched for any mention of her sexual abuse by her captors. I don't remember hearing about any such report of abuse. In the book her parents wrote about her abduction and return (Smart & Smart 2003), no mention was made of their daughter's sexual abuse. Actually, some reports on the internet said her parents only found out about the molestation at the trial.

The return

When the abductors and Elizabeth Smart were found, it was as shocking an announcement as was the announcement of the kidnapping. Elizabeth Smart was found alive, in the company of her kidnappers in the town of Sandy, Utah, about 18 miles from her home in Salt Lake City. It was nine months after her abduction on March 12, 2003. According to the police report, a female policewoman spotted Elizabeth Smart in the company of her captors and became suspicious. The policewoman had remembered the police reports and media publicity about Elizabeth's kidnapping. She approached Elizabeth, who was dressed in aforementioned pseudo-hippie outfit. She asked the youngest of the trio if she was Elizabeth Smart. Elizabeth did not answer. The policewoman then watched Elizabeth walk around. She asked her again if she was Elizabeth Smart. This time, Elizabeth hesitantly said, "Yes." The policewoman then acted psychologically appropriately for the situation, and separated Elizabeth from Brian David Mitchell and Wanda Ileen Barzee. She called over other police personnel to deal with the situation. By correctly isolating Elizabeth from Mitchell, she began the process of therapeutically dealing with the Confusion of Tongues trauma. Elizabeth was under the influence of a Confusion of Tongues experience when approached and the policewoman's forced separation initiated Elizabeth's separation from her abusers.

Elizabeth Smart's recovery

What are the factors that allow a youth to recover from intense and sustained sexual abuse during a period of abduction? Strength must be garnered from inner resources, since there is no direct affirmation, empathy, or emotional support emanating from her captors. Being able to call upon inner resources means having developed significant inner resources before being abducted, and Elizabeth Smart had such inner resources in three basic ways. She had a fully developed religious and spirited faith that contributed to a belief system that gave her hope. She believed that her faith as a Mormon provided her with a *reservoir of strength* that she could call upon in a time of need. She and her family used the writing of Mormon minister Spencer Kimball, specifically hs book *Faith Precedes the Miracle* (Kimball 1972), to develop this idea. Her parents expressed it this way:

> Though our experience was terribly painful, through our faith and trust in God's power we gained tremendous strength, which became the cornerstone of how we survived ... you need reservoirs of faith ... that can carry us over the terrifying moments.
>
> (Smart & Smart 2003, pp. 7–8)

Faith and hope can come from religious and spiritual belief, but it can also come from any meaningful belief system that includes a set of principles that allow an individual to deal with and recover from trauma, such as psychoanalysis.

Elizabeth Smart demonstrated meaningful personality strength during her captivity. Although she was in the midst of a personality alteration through a Confusion of Tongues trauma, it was a temporary alteration. In her own words from her testimony at the federal trial of her captor, Brian David Mitchell, Elizabeth never became a fully dissociative, automaton, or robot-like captive who had suspended her own thinking and feeling. Here are several examples of Elizabeth's maintaining her sense of self during her trauma:

> The night I was kidnapped, I turned to him and I said, you know you're going to go to jail for this if you get caught. And he said, yes and *I said that, if you would let me go right now, you know, I would speak in his behalf*. However, he did not.
>
> (Hicken-Brown, 2009, p. 11, lines 12–16, italics added)

A: He turned to me and he said *how much he needed to have sex with me right then and there* and that Wanda would never know and she would understand ... nobody would find out.
Q: And did you say no to him?
A: Yes.

(Hicken-Brown, 2009, p. 15, lines 20–25, italics added)

Q: And how did that *make you feel to say no to him* on that occasion?
A: Wonderful.

(Hicken-Brown, 2009, p. 16, lines 1–3, italics added)

Q: Did the defendant ever try to convince you that it would be bad if he stopped having sex with you?
A: Yes.
Q: What happened?
A: He said that – one time he was trying to, and *I bit him*: And he said that if I ever did that again, he would never have sex with me again and I would be the most miserable woman in the world. However, I mean, it didn't make a difference that he said that.

(Hicken-Brown, 2009, p. 16, lines 4–13, italics added)

Confusion of Tongues: psychodynamics in the abducted child

The legacy of the Budapest School of Psychoanalysis is Ferenczi's Confusion of Tongues paradigm (Ferenczi 1980a, 1988) and the expansion of it in the early object relations perspective of Balint (Balint 1992). This frame of reference can provide a meaningful set of assumptions which has been used to develop a Confusion of Tongues theory of trauma (Rachman 1994, 1997, 2003; Rachman & Klett 2015). This theory can aid in the understanding of the psychodynamics of an abducted child's trauma experience, and expands previous formulations to understand the trauma bonding that occurs between the hostage and captor. Attention needs to be paired to the developmental issues of children, their characteristic defense mechanisms, and their capacity to negotiate trauma.

The Confusion of Tongues theory of trauma incorporates Ferenczi's original formulation of the child-in-the-adult who was abused by a parent or a parental surrogate. What is more, the missing psychodynamic of sexual abuse is necessary to understand why an individual child in particular would become a partner of their captive, an unusual and often misunderstood phenomenon. The public is dumbfounded by such an occurrence and psychoanalysis has not contributed enough to our understanding (Rachman 2012a).

The psychodynamics in the trauma experience of an abducted child (such as Elizabeth Smart), which leads to a disturbed bond between her and her captor (Brian David Mitchell) is considered a Confusion of Tongues trauma in the following way:

1. The child is psychologically disoriented when they are abducted and their captor takes them away from their home and parents. Physically, and psychologically, they become so disorientated that they do not know where in the world they are. Their surroundings are not only unfamiliar, but can be a version of a prison. Their freedom is limited. Elizabeth Smart was chained to a tree. They are held in restricted, unsanitary conditions, where they cannot attend to their cleanliness. If there is no mirror to maintain grooming, they can lose interest in their appearance. The child develops body odor, which causes a negative self-evaluation. They lose a sense of a positive body image. Self-esteem is diminished. They become dependent on the evaluation of their captor for self-esteem. Such vulnerability strengthens a trauma bond with the abductor.
2. Abduction, by its very nature, is a violent experience for the child. A child is not usually trained to fight off or run away from adults. Even if they fight, they are easily overpowered. If they are seduced into going away, the trip away is filled with terror. The child can suffer guilt and shame for succumbing to the captor. Very shortly, the child realizes they no longer have their parents or home. A profound sense of abandonment develops as the captivity endures. The

child loses hope that they will ever again see their parents. Even more profoundly, the child can come to believe their parents no longer care about or love them. The feeling of loss is often encouraged by the captor. The captor uses a lack of parental contact as proof of the child's abandonment. A loss of a belief in parental care and love is devastating. The child is unhinged from their sense of security, safety, object consistency, and belief in their parents as protectors and nurturers. A belief system – whether religious, spiritual, cultural, or communal – helps the child to sustain hope. Elizabeth Smart had her Mormon faith in her darkest moments. But the trauma also encourages dependency on the captor. Elizabeth Smart, even with her constant belief in her parents' and sister's love, and a belief that God was looking after her, became under the psychological domination of Brian David Mitchell.

3. The abuser isolates the child from interpersonal and communal contact. Emotional and interpersonal contact occurs exclusively with the abuser. The captor has every desire to replace the child's parent. He/she wants to become a parental surrogate. To survive, the child must depend upon their captor to satisfy their developmental needs. As Ferenczi first suggested, the child, in the throes of sexual seduction with an adult, identifies with the aggressor (the abuser) (Ferenczi 1980). The child's developmental needs and trauma experiences are interwoven. They become agents to discern and satisfy the needs of the seducer. The child-captive attempts to insure positive response from their surrogate parent. Such emotional need to please the abuser creates a diabolic dynamic, which the abuser (aggressor) can use to manipulate, control, and overpower the child.
4. By the *terrorism of suffering* (Ferenczi 1988), the captor creates a vacuum of affection, love, empathy, and safety, which makes the child susceptible to the abuser, so that they can lose their own capacity to test reality. *The child loses their capacity to discern their own reality from the reality of the captor.* In the most extreme cases, their realities mesh. The abducted child is an *emotional slave of the abuser*, entering into an emotional bargain with the devil: "I will give what you want if you will fulfill my needs."

5. Sexual abuse of the child is a power dynamic that is generally overlooked in understanding the disturbed emotional bond that develops between the child and aggressor. In the case of Elizabeth Smart, Brian David Mitchell sexually abused her on a regular basis. This creates a Confusion of Tongues trauma where this child's desperate need for the missing and necessary parental love creates the trauma experience. Sexual contact, to which the child succumbs, by a combination of force and emotional need, becomes the perverse bargain the child must make to gain what passes for affection and love. But the sex is not love. It is aggression against the child, fueled by the abuser's own narcissistic needs. Such needs involve the desire to dominate and overpower a child, the inability to have satisfactory sexual contact with a adult peer and sexual impotence. The child's experience is one of intense confusion. Two languages are spoken in the sexual abuse of the child. The child speaks the language of tenderness and affection; the abuser speaks the language of aggression. Using the child to satisfy his own sexual desires is rape. It has nothing to do with affection and love. The child has to accept sex as love; it is a Confusion of Tongues. Intuitively, the child senses the contradiction but cannot reconcile the discrepancy. The child is left with confusion as to whether the sexual contact is love or a forbidden and destructive experience.

The actual events of the Confusion of Tongues trauma, and the psychodynamics which ensue in the individual's behavior, do not constitute an indication of weakness of character in the traumatized captive. Exactly the opposite is true. The trauma experience can encourage a Confusion of Tongues trauma in any individual when placed in similar trauma conditions. An excellent example of this issue is the aforementioned abduction of the Puritan woman Mary Rowlandson. In her narrative of her captivity by Indians, she changed her functioning from a strict Puritan woman, making a very negative distinction between herself as a civilized God-fearing Englishwoman and her captors as beasts of the wilderness. Yet the Confusion of Tongues trauma produced a dramatic change in her behavior and values in the strictly religious woman who carried and read her Bible daily for comfort and sustenance. A potent entry from her narrative illustrates her change in functioning:

> [King] Philip spoke to me to make a shirt for his boy, which I did, for which he gave me a shilling. I offered the money to my master, but he bade me to keep it, and with it I bought a piece of horse flesh ... he asked me to make a cap for his boy, which he invited me to dinner, I went and he gave me a pancake, about as big as two fingers. It was made of parsed wheat, beaten and fried in bear's grease, but I thought I never tasted pleasanter meat in my life ... but the thought it was bear made me tremble. But now that was savory to me that one would think was enough to turn the stomach of a brute creature.
>
> (Rowlandson 2009, pp. 11, 13)

Recovery and psychotherapy

Elizabeth Smart's emotional recovery from abduction, sexual, emotional, and physical abuse, and a Confusion of Tongues trauma, is very important for psychoanalysis to understand. When psychologists were asked, after her return, whether or not psychotherapy would be crucial for Elizabeth Smart's recovery, they all agreed (Allen 2003). All psychoanalysts would say that recovery from severe trauma necessitates not just counseling or psychotherapy, but some form of psychoanalytic treatment. As I followed this case, I also believed that Elizabeth Smart needed such treatment (Rachman 2012b). But Smart's recovery may become a historically significant insight-provoking case.

In the early days of 2003, when Smart returned to her family, there was no evidence from any sources that she received any formal therapeutic help. At that time, my searching the Internet, popular media outlets, television and radio programs transcripts, etc. did not produce any data that Smart received therapeutic help. However, two early sources suggested that Smart did receive professional help. The first came from a posting on a Recovery from Mormonism (RM) discussion forum – Recovery Board.

> I can't discuss the source. But I know a friend of the family and professionally indirectly involved. *She did get very good therapy for what happened to her.*
>
> (Cristina 2010)

A second aspect to whether or not Elizabeth Smart received therapy is to examine her testimony. Cristina (2010) believed that Elizabeth's testimony revealed a young lady whose words and demeanor could indicate an individual who has undergone therapy. Her memory for the events that occurred during her captivity, her strong sense of self, her capacity not to be intimidated by the defendant's lawyer's cross-examination, and her desire to fully self-disclose her sexually abusive experience, may indicate that Elizabeth Smart underwent some form of successful therapeutic experience.

More than a decade after the abduction, we can now better answer this question, by consulting Elizabeth Smart's own book on her abduction, and up-to-date interviews with her, a spokesperson for children who have been abducted. First, we have the reports of her parents:

> Although her parents offered counseling, Smart has put her life back together without the help of a therapist, preferring instead to speak with her parents and grandparents when issues came up. "I don't feel the need to talk about what happened to me, but if I do, I know my family is there", she says. Ed Smart insists his daughter won't just keeping everything bottled up inside. "We haven't gone through what happened to her blow by blow, but Lois and I have heard different things from her," he says. "It's a part of her life she can never forget, but it's nothing she wants to dwell on. So we try not to dwell on it either."
>
> (Free & Tresniowski 2008)

Her parents – based on their own means of dealing with feelings, as well as respecting Elizabeth's way of dealing with her feelings – offered therapy to their daughter.

Now that we have Elizabeth's story, in her own words (Smart & Stewart 2013), two important questions can be answered. Did Elizabeth Smart receive therapy? What were the mechanisms that helped her survive the abduction and recover successfully from her Confusion of Tongues trauma? She answered these questions as follows:

> I always get asked the same questions, "How did you survive?" and "How did you overcome what happened to you?" The answer to the first question is pretty simple. The main reason I was able to

> survive is because of my God, my family, and my community … Some [people] … might think, *given the fact that I haven't received any professional counseling*, that something must still be wrong with me, that I'm hiding my wounds or putting on a happy face … that there are certain things that I'm not ready yet to face.
>
> (Smart & Stewart 2013, p. 297)

Her parents offered Elizabeth counseling, but she made it clear she had her own means of recovery, and that every survivor should be allowed to use or create their own method of recovery from abduction and abuse.

Elizabeth's path of recovery involved: her Mormon faith and belief in God; contemplation and self-reflection; conversations with her immediate family; and the regular participation in the activities of horseback riding and playing the harp. Elizabeth came from a tight-knit religious Mormon family who found great hope, nurturance, and direction in their religious faith. Psychoanalysts as well as mental health professionals can neglect the positive importance that religious faith can have for an individual. When I was getting my doctorate at the University of Chicago, this importance was brought home to me by the late psychoanalyst Bruno Bettelheim. One day in supervision Bettelheim illustrated the practice of empathic understanding in his clinical interaction with a practicing Christian analysand. The individual, at one intensive emotional moment in an analytical session, fell to his knees and asked Bettelheim to pray with him for his recovery from his emotional illness. Bettelheim told me he then dropped to his knees and joined his analysand in prayer. At the time he told me this, about thirty years ago, I was astonished at his clinical behavior. I was very impressed with his being so responsive and flexible in his clinical approach, demonstrating the therapeutic value of empathy. More particularly, Bettelheim was not antagonistic to an individual's religious or spiritual belief. Elizabeth Smart successfully used her religious and spiritual beliefs in her recovery. But why was she not more responsive to using counseling in her recovery?

It does not seem that Elizabeth rejected therapy as much as she had developed, as a child and adolescent, a different attitude and activity to dealing with feelings and emotional disturbance. There were two relationships and two activities, which formed her therapeutic approach. The relationships (which Elizabeth cited as therapeutic) were with her her grandfather and mother.

Elizabeth's grandfather was a medical doctor by profession, but "a true cowboy" (Smart & Stewart 2013, p. 300) by vocation. Horseback riding with her grandfather provided Elizabeth with two very important therapeutic tools: the value of silent contemplation, and communing with animals and nature.

> There was something simply wonderful about horseback riding with him and we did a lot of it after I got back.
>
> Grandpa never pushed me or pried. He used to say that some people talked too much. *Ride more, talk less*. That was his approach to life. Going with him, ... you knew you would be left alone to your thoughts.
>
> (Smart & Stewart 2013, p. 300)

In addition to horseback riding, Elizabeth found playing the harp therapeutic:

> When I came home, nothing could speak my feelings better than the harp. Music is the unspoken language that can convey feelings more accurately than talking ever could. So playing the harp became extremely therapeutic for me. If I ever felt sad or angry or frustrated, I would sit down and start playing. Once I submerged my heart into my music, my feelings evaporated and I go out and face the world again.
>
> (Smart & Stewart 2013, p. 301)

The importance of Elizabeth's mother in her life and recovery is further illustrated in her words about how Elizabeth should put her trauma to rest:

> At the end of the day, God is our ultimate judge. He will make up to you every pain and loss that you have suffered. And if it turns out that these wicked people are not punished here on Earth, it doesn't matter. His punishment are just ... If you go and feel sorry

for yourself, or if you dwell on what has happened, if you hold on to your pain, that is allowing him to steal more of your life away ... Don't you let him! Not one more second of your life. You keep every second for yourself ... It's been ten years since my mother said those words. The years have proven she was right.
(Smart & Stewart 2013, p. 286)

Smart as an activist on behalf of abducted children

After a period of return in which she was reunited with her family and enjoyed being free of abduction, Elizabeth went back to her high school and graduated. She then attended and graduated from Brigham Young University in Provo, Utah. After announcing a January 2011 engagement, Elizabeth Smart and Matthew Gilmour were married in a Mormon ceremony in Hawaii. She agreed to help the United States Department of Justice put together a sixty-three-page guide for survivors of kidnapping (Free & Tresniowski 2008). On July 7, 2011, Elizabeth Smart was hired as an ABC news correspondent (Carter 2011). The same year, she founded the Elizabeth Smart Foundation, which supports the Internet Crimes Against Children Task Force, and educates children about violent and sexual crime. In 2013, she wrote a book about her abduction experience (Smart & Stewart 2013). She testified in February 2014, before the Utah State House of Representative in favor of a bill that would create a non-mandated curriculum for use in Utah schools to provide training on child abuse prevention.

Children who have been abducted usually have undergone sexual abuse by their captor, whether or not the child, captor child's parents, or the media report the sexual abuse. Such molestation is actually a key component in the abduction. Adult abusers need children to fulfill their distorted need for domination, power, and perverse sexual desire. We need to have meaningful ideas to understand the prevalence of sexual abuse in child abduction, and the need to have children undergo psychotherapy or psychoanalysis when they are returned.

Elizabeth Smart's Confusion of Tongues trauma during captivity

There were encounters with the outside world which indicated the negative effects of the Confusion of Tongues trauma with which

Elizabeth had to struggle. After her abduction, the police, her family, and hundreds of volunteers searched for her, and her picture was prominently displayed in her hometown and Salt Lake City. Her captors took trips to Salt Lake City with her, on occasion. The trio walked the streets, went to restaurants and grocery stores, took the bus, and were approached by people (Smart & Stewart 2013). Apparently, this strange trio usually repelled people by their pseudo-hippie and disheveled look. In addition, a self-styled prophet with two women in tow was not that out of place (Talbot 2013). However, the issue to discuss is not that people did not approach *her*, but that she never approached *people*.

There were instances when Elizabeth was approached:

> Once or twice, someone would come up and ask what religion we belong to, Mitchell always did the talking. A few of these people would look at me much longer than they looked at Mitchell or Barzee, when they did, I would stare back into their eyes, trying to communicate with them. *Yes! You are right, I am Elizabeth Smart!* But that is as far as it would ever go. Stares. Brief conversations. Nothing more.
>
> (Smart & Stewart 2013, p. 181, italics added)

Elizabeth, however, does not connect her inability as a captive to approach anyone, or speak to someone who approached her, as an indication of trauma. She believed the basic issue was fear; that she was afraid for her life and for family (Talbot 2013). Of course, fear is a meaningful concern, but the additional and specific psychodynamics of sexual abuse produce a dissociative reaction which puts the abductee in an emotional vulnerable position. This sexual abuse produces a Confusion of Tongues, which places the child in a distorted love experience about which the child cannot verbally express, yet to which he/she is emotionally bound. I do not think Elizabeth Smart was aware of the psychodynamic of her inability to respond or approach people when she was in captivity. Although she has made a remarkable recovery, she would have developed a greater emotional understanding of her Confusion of Tongues trauma had she received therapeutic help. Perhaps, now, she would also be an advocate for therapeutic help for survivors of sexual abuse.

References

Allen, C. (2003). Therapists react to Elizabeth Smart case. *Psychology Today*, March 1.

Balint, M. (1965). *Primary Love and Psychoanalystic Technique*. London: Tavistock.

Balint, M. (1992). *The Basic Fault: Therapeutic aspects of regression*. London: Tavistock. [Originally published 1968. Evanston, IL: Northwestern University Press, paperback edition.]

Bejerot, N. (1974). The six day war in Stockholm, *New Scientist* 61(886): 486–487.

Benedict, C. (2008). Harry L. Lozol, expert in Patty Hearst trial, is dead at 102. *New York Times*, September 1.

Boulton, D. (1975). *The Making of Tania Hearst*. London: New English Library.

Carter, N. (2011). Elizabeth Smart hired as ABC's news correspondent. *New York Daily News*.

Conway, F., & Siegelman, J. (1995). *Snapping America's Epidemic of Sudden Personality Change*. New York: Stillpoint Press. [Original edition published 1970.]

Cosmides, L., & Tooby, J. (2013). Evolutionary psychology. *Annual Review of Psychology* 64: 201–229.

Cristina (2010). Recovery from Mormonism. Discussion forum (RfM). Retrieved from the internet.

Dutton, D.G., & Pointer, S.L. (1981). Traumatic bonding: The development of emotional attachments in battered women and other relationships of intermittent abuse. *Victimology: An International Journal* 1(4): 139–155.

Exley, J.E.P. (2001). *Frontier Saga: Saga of the Parker family*. College Station: Texas A&M University Press.

Ferenczi, S. (1980a). The Confusion of Tongues between adults and children: The language of tenderness and of passion. In M. Balint (ed.), *Final Contributions to the Problems and Methods of Psycho-analysis*. New York: Bruner/Mazel, vol. 3, pp. 156–167. [Original work published 1933.]

Ferenczi, S. (1980b). Taming of a wild horse. In M. Balint (ed.), *Final Contributions to the Problems and Methods of Psycho-analysis*. New York: Bruner/Mazel, Vol. 3, pp. 331–340. [Original edition published 1913.)

Ferenczi, S. (1988). *The Clinical Diary of Sándor Ferenczi*, ed. J. Dupont, trans. M. Balint and N.Z. Jackson. Cambridge, MA: Harvard University Press.

Frankel, G. (2013). *The Searchers: The making of an American legend*. New York: Bloomsbury.

Free, C., & Tresniowski, A. (2008). Heroes of the year: A second chance. *People Magazine* 69: 24.

Freud, S. (1954) *The Origins of Psychoanalysis, Letters to Wilhelm Fliess; drafts and notes: 1887–1902*, ed. M. Bonaparte, A. Freud, & E. Kris, trans. E. Mosbacher & J. Strachey. New York: Basic Books.

Graebner, W. (2008). *Patty's Got a Gun: Patricia Hearst in 1970s America*. Chicago: University of Chicago Press.

Gwynne, S.C. (2010). *Empire of the Moon: Quanah Parker and the rise and fall of the Comanches, the most powerful Indian tribe in American history*. New York: Scribner.

Hearst, P.C. (1988). *Patty Hearst: Her own story*. New York: Aron.

Hicken-Brown, K. (2009). Transcript of proceedings. Testimony of Elizabeth Ann Smart. Case 2: 08CR125. October 1.

Kimball, S. (1972). *Faith Precedes the Miracle*. Salt Lake City, UT: Desert Book Company.

Lifton, R. (1989). *Thought Reform and the Psychology of Totalism: Brainwashing in China*. Raleigh: University of North Carolina Press. [Originally published in 1961 by Norton.]

Lifton, R.J. (1993). *The Protean Self: Human resilience in an age of fragementation*. New York: Basic Books.

Mackenzie, I.K. (2004). The Stockholm Syndrome revisited: Hostages, realtionships, prediction, control and psychological science. *Journal of Police Crisis Negotiations*, 4(1): 5–21.

Masson, J.M. (1984). *The Assault on Truth: Freud's suppression of the Seduction Theory*. New York: Farrar, Straus & Giroux.

Mitchell, S.A. (1996) Introduction. Symposium on the "False Memory" controversy. *Psychoanalytic Dialogues*, 6(1): 151–153.

Ochberg, F. (2005). The ties that bind captive to captor. *Los Angeles Times*, April 8.

Pascal, J., & Pascal, F. (1974). *The Strange Case of Patty Hearst*. New York: American Library.

Perlstein, R. (2008). That girl: The captivity and restoration of Patty Hearst. *The Nation*. December 29.

Rachman, A.W. (1994). The Confusion of Tongues theory: Ferenczi's legacy to psychoanalysis. In Haynal, A. and Falzeder, E. (eds.), *100 Years of Psychoanalysis*. London: Karnac Books.

Rachman, A.W. (1997). *Sándor Ferenczi: The psychotherapist of tenderness and passion*. Northvale, NJ: Jason Aronson.

Rachman, A.W. (2003). *Psychotherapy of Difficult Cases: Flexibility and responsiveness in clinical practice*. Madison, CT: Psychosocial Press.

Rachman, A.W. (2012a). Psychoanalysis' neglect of the incest trauma. Presentation at the Psychohistorical Association, Kimmel Center. New York University, New York City, Friday, June 8.

Rachman, A.W. (2012b). The psychodynamics of abduction: The Confusion of Tongues trauma. Presentation at the International Forum of Psychoanalytic Societies "Working with Conflict and Alienation: 50 years of IFPS", Mexico City, Mexico, October 10–12.

Rachman, A.W. (2014). Sándor Ferenczi's analysis with Elizabeth Severn: "Wild analysis" or pioneering treatment of the incest trauma. *Psychoanalytic Inquiry*, 34 (2): 145–168, February.

Rachman, A.W., & Klett, S.A. (2015). *Analysis of the Incest Trauma: Retrieval, recovery, renewal*. London: Karnac Books.

Rachman, A.W. & Mattick. P. (2012). The Confusion of Tongues in the psychoanalytic relationship. *Psychoanalytic Social Work* 19(1–2): 167–190.

Rowlandson, M. (2009). *Narrative of the Captivity and Restoration of Mrs Mary Rowlandson*, D. Widger and Anonymous, eBook #851. [Originally published in 1682 in the United States and England.]

Rumband, K. (2014). Hearst, Soliah and the SLA. *Criminal Library: Criminal Minds and Methods*. Retrieved October 2, 2014.

Smart, E., & Smart, L. (2003) *Bringing Elizabeth Home: A journey of faith and hope*. New York: Doubleday.

Smart, E., & Stewart, C. (2013). *My Story*. New York: St Martin's Press.

Talbot, M. (2013). Gone girl: The extraordinary resilience of Elizabeth Smart. *The New Yorker*, October 21, 1–56.

Weed, S.S.S. (1976). *My Search for Patty Hearst*. New York: Crown.

Epilogue

Arnold Wm. Rachman

In recent years, I have been very fortunate to have established a working relationship and friendship with Joseph Lichtenberg, editor-in-chief of the journal *Psychoanalytical Inquiry*. His editorship changed the intellectual climate of psychoanalysis by helping it move away from orthodoxy towards a plurality of ideas and perspectives. He has sponsored two previous issues on Ferenczi (Rachman 1997, 2014). Recently he suggested an issue on the Budapest School of Psychoanalysis. I was delighted to be invited to edit the issue. Several years ago, I had submitted an article about Ferenczi to a prominent analytic journal when a reviewer questioned my use of the term the Budapest School of Psychoanalysis. This reviewer said no one knew about this school of psychoanalysis, so I should eliminate this notation. I was hopeful I could gather together a group of Ferenczi and Budapest School scholars who would help establish the reality of the Budapest School's influence on the evolution of psychoanalysis.

When the invited papers were collected together and evaluated by Mel Bornstein, the editor of *Psychoanalytic Inquiry*, he concluded the contributions should be published as a book rather than an issue of the journal. Joseph Lichtenberg agreed with these recommendations. These editors, consequently, have made a significant contribution to raising the awareness in the psychoanalytic community regarding the contributions of the Budapest School of Psychoanalysis.

The contributors to *The Budapest School of Psychoanalysis: The Origins of a Two-Person Psychology and Empathic Perspective* have demonstrated, as Joseph Lichtenberg discussed in his Introduction, that it is meaningful to consider that there has arisen out of the work of the pioneering Hungarian analysts who were influenced by Sándor

Ferenczi a distinct and significant perspective that has evolved into an alternative to the Freudian tradition. This alternative perspective has, by now, become a tradition in its own right, which needs to be recognized and respected.

The contributions to this volume demonstrate that there is a group of contemporary analysts in the United States and Europe who are working and writing in the tradition of Ferenczi, Balint, and the Budapest School. All of the contributions clearly demonstrate an historical connection to the Budapest School while indicating the contemporary relevance of these ideas and methods. Judit Mészáros, Ph.D., one of the present leaders of the Budapest School, is a founding member and currently the president of the Sándor Ferenczi Society, in Budapest. She has written a paper, "The Ferenczi House as a Space for Identity Formation." Mészáros (along with Carlo Bonomi, Ph.D.) spearheaded a movement which purchased the Ferenczi villa in the Buda section of Budapest. It was here that Ferenczi practiced psychoanalysis and wrote his famous *Clinical Diary*.

The Ferenczi House is not only "a site of memory" for Ferenczi's ideas and works, but also about the analysands who were treated there. It is a missing link in psychoanalytic history, as well as the family site of the Budapest School, where the "Hungarian children" of Ferenczi's Budapest School came together. The importance of the Ferenczi villa evolved from a site of memory and testimony to Ferenczi's pioneering work on clinical experimentation, the analysis of the groundbreaking cases of Izette De Forest, Elizabeth Severn, and Clara Thompson, to the development of the Confusion of Tongues paradigm and the study and treatment of trauma. It is also a memory bank for Ferenczi's colleagues, such as Balint, who helped shape the Budapest School. From 2011, when the Ferenczi House originated, and continuing on into the future, it will become a factor in helping students, scholars, and psychoanalysts contribute to an identity formation which integrates a consciousness of Ferenczi and the Budapest School.

Judith Dupont, M.D., is the senior member of the contemporary Budapest School. Hungarian by birth, she was a childhood visitor to the Ferenczi household. Her mother, Olga Dormandi (Olga Székely-Kovács), was a well-known artist, and painted pictures of Ferenczi and Margaret Severn. She was the literary executor of the

Sándor Ferenczi estate. In the role she was instrumental in saving Ferenczi's *Clinical Diary* for prosperity, having received the diary from Michael Balint who was given it by Ferenczi's wife, Gizella Pálos. Dupont was the editor of the *Clinical Diary* first in French in 1985, then in English in 1988. The diary was crucial in returning Ferenczi ideas and clinical work to relevance and prominence in psychoanalysis. Dupont's contribution to the volume is "A Multifaceted Legacy: Sándor Ferenczi's Clinical Diary" (translated from the French by Michael Larivière). The Ferenczi community and psychoanalysis owes a great debt to Judit Dupont, and her journal and translation group, Le Coq-Héron, for the translation and publication of Ferenczi's *Clinical Diary*.

Dupont showed us how the *Clinical Diary* is a unique text, like no other in psychoanalysis (or, perhaps, in any other field of study). Ferenczi described his feelings as an psychoanalyst and how these feelings affect the treatment of individuals. The diary is a phenomenological roadmap of one analyst's step-by-step journey into the world of commingling subjectivities and the origins of a two-person democratic therapeutic encounter. Ferenczi had the courage to show the world his failures and mistakes, along with his triumphs.

Dupont has also contributed another focus of this volume, namely Lacan's interest in Ferenczi. When Michael Larivière and I discussed this volume, he mentioned that he believed Jacques Lacan, M.D., founder of the Freudian School of Psychoanalysis in Paris (France), was interested in Ferenczi and Balint's ideas and taught them to his students. I had never heard of Lacan's interest in Ferenczi within the Budapest School community. Dupont recommended Yves Lugrin to represent the Lacanians' interest in the Budapest School. Larivière and Lugrin's contributions to this volume discuss the little-known fact of Lacan's connection to Ferenczi.

Yves Lugrin, Ph.D., Associate Member of the Society of Freudian Psychoanalysis in Paris, contributes "Ferenczi: Lacan's Missed Rendez-Vous?" (translated by Michael Larivière) to this volume, in which he outlines the history of Lacan's intellectual and emotional struggle to appreciate and integrate Ferenczi's ideas and career as a psychoanalyst. This history aids our understanding of Lacan's struggle with the French Psychoanalytic Society, as well as with the Budapest School.

Lacan's relationship with the Budapest School was confusing and ambivalent. He lectured about Ferenczi's work at his Institute, but used Michael Balint's work as the conduit for conveying Ferenczi's framework. Also, when he first introduced Ferenczi to his Institute, he did so in a negative way. Lacan identified with Ferenczi as a marginalized figure in psychoanalysis on the one hand, feeling like a pioneering figure; but fighting the analytic establishment on the other hand, he didn't want to be identified as a dissident or suffer Ferenczi's condemnation by the analytic community.

Michael Larivière, Ph.D. is in private practice in Strasbourg, France, and contributes "From Lacan to Ferenczi." This chapter is a personal and poetic description of a journey to find an analyst's authentic self. In his first attempts at personal analysis, Larivière was faced with a Lacanian analyst, whom he experienced as negative, silent, withholding, and distant. This experience may have been an enactment of a fundamental childhood experience.

His devotion to finding himself and have an analytic career moved him towards Joyce McDougall, referred by Wladimir Granoff, a French analyst who knew Lacan and was a Ferenczian. Larivière believed that McDougall became one of the main legatees of Ferenczi in France and, with McDougall, Larivière gave voice to this authentic self.

André Haynal, M.D., one of the leaders of the contemporary Budapest School, is Professor of Psychiatry at the University of Geneva (Switzerland) and scientific editor of *The Freud/Ferenczi Correspondence*. He contributed "A Wise Baby?: Ferenczi's Presence" to this volume, in which he pays tribute to Ferenczi's special qualities as a person and psychoanalysts, namely his authenticity. Ferenczi was a "Wise Baby" before and after he became a psychoanalyst. He had the capacity to understand and respond to human behavior with honesty, clarity, and empathy.

Ferenczi, as Haynal discerned, had the psychological acuity of an innocent child. Children are "wise" in their perception, ideation, and expression of feelings. Ferenczi pioneered authenticity in the analytic encounter and in the analyst. He was the "Wise Baby" who anticipated many of our contemporary discoveries and was able to find his own authentic voice in writing his *Clinical Diary*.

Lewis Aron, Ph.D., ABPP, is the director of the New York University Postdoctoral Program in Psychotherapy and Psychoanalysis and co-founder and co-chair of the Sándor Ferenczi Center at the New School for Social Research. Karen Starr, Psy.D., is a clinical supervisor at the Graduate Center, City University of New York and Long Island University/C.W. Post. Together they contribute "Freud, Ferenczi and the Case of Schreber: A Mutual Enactment of Homoerotic Longings, Homophobia, and Internalized Anti-Semitism." Their chapter is an analysis of the difficulties Freud and Ferenczi experienced at the beginning of their relationship, which characterized their emotional, interpersonal, and intellectual struggles for the twenty-five years of their friendship, and contributes to an understanding of how the Freud/Ferenczi relationship affected the evolution of psychoanalysis. In this instance, the authors contribute an understanding of how anti-semitism, Jewish enlightenment, and homoerotic feelings created a mutual enactment when Freud and Ferenczi tried to cooperate in writing the Schreber case.

Peter T. Hoffer, Ph.D., Professor Emeritus of German, University of the Sciences in Philadelphia (Pennsylvania), and translator of the *Freud/Ferenczi Correspondence*, contributed "The Dimensions of the Freud/Ferenczi Correspondence." He indicates that the *Freud/Ferenczi Correspondence* is the richest source of data about the relationship between Freud and Ferenczi, the history of psychoanalysis, and the issues in the development of the field in its formative years. He outlines the intellectual and personal relationship between the two pioneers of psychoanalysis, from their first difficulty about the Schreber case in 1910 to their final crisis over the controversial Confusion of Tongues paper of 1933. Hoffer traces Ferenczi's emotional need for honesty and mutuality and Freud's criticism of Ferenczi, as if he were an underdeveloped child searching for the love of a parent. This emotional scenario was played out throughout their relationship and influenced the development of psychoanalysis.

Howard A. Bacall, M.D., Training and Supervising Analyst at the Institute of Contemporary Psychoanalysis and the New Center for Psychoanalysis, Los Angeles, contributes "The Budapest School's Concept of Supervision: Michael Balint's Legacy to the Development of Specificity Theory." Bacal is in a unique position to speak about the Budapest School, since he was in supervision with Michael Balint, an analysand, intimate, and student of Ferenczi. Bacal also led "The Balint Groups" at the Tavistock Clinic and at University College Hospital,

London. Bacal traces the influence of the Budapest School model on the development of psychoanalytic supervision. The Budapest model was characterized by the analysand's training analyst supervising his first control case. The candidate shares his experience of his patient in the course of his associations in his control analysis. No separate session is set aside for this supervision. The British Psychoanalytic Institute allowed Balint to offer the Budapest model as long as it was voluntary by the candidate and another control case was supervised in the traditional way.

Bacal has applied the countertransference, relational, and co-created interaction pioneered by the Budapest model to the development of his Specificity Theory. "This is a contemporary psychoanalytic system theory that regards therapeutic effect as being a function of the therapeutic capacities of each analyst-patient as they interact within a unique reciprocal relational process in the moment and over time.

Arnold William Rachman, Ph.D., FAGPA, is a Faculty Member of the Trauma Studies Program, New York University Postdoctoral Program in Psychotherapy and Psychoanalysis, and Honorary Member of the Sándor Ferenczi Society, Budapest, Hungary. His contributions are "Psychoanalysis' Neglect of the Incest Trauma: The Confusion of Tongues Between Psychoanalysis and Society" and "Confusion of Tongues in Child Abduction: Revising the Stockholm Syndrome." Rachman has been a historian of Ferenczi's Confusion of Tongues idea and believes this paradigm is a landmark contribution to psychoanalysis. In previous publications, he has focused on attempts to suppress Ferenczi's Confusion of Tongues idea and to develop a Confusion of Tongues theory of trauma. However, the present contributions focus on understanding why the Confusion of Tongues paradigm has been neglected when it has the potential to provide understanding for what many social scientists consider a major social problem – that is, the incidence of childhood sexual abuse. It also examines the incidence of sexual abuse and its psychological consequences in the neglected area of child abduction, and offers a more comprehensive theory than the Stockholm Syndrome for understanding victim bonding with the abuser.

The contributors to this volume are among the contemporary leaders of Budapest School scholarship in the United States and Europe, as well as three Hungarian contemporary members of the Budapest

School. Their contributions demonstrate the breadth and depth of the Budapest School's potential for influencing contemporary psychoanalysis.

Arnold William Rachman
Guest editor

References

Rachman, A.W. (ed.) (1997). Psychoanalysis' favorite son: The legacy of Sándor Ferenczi *Psychoanalytic Inquiry* 17(November): 4.
Rachman, A.W. (ed.) (2014). Sándor Ferenczi's contributions to the evolution of theory and technique in psychoanalysis. *Psychoanalytic Inquiry* 34(March): 2.

Index